DREAMERS

ENTERTAINERS FROM
SMALL TOWN TO BIG TIME

Best Wishes,

Jerry Ford

DREAMERS

ENTERTAINERS FROM SMALL TOWN TO BIG TIME

by

Jerry Ford

Southeast Missouri State University Press • 2012

Dreamers: Entertainers from Small Town to Big Time
Copyright 2012 by Jerry Ford

ISBN: 978-09830504-2-1

First published in the United States of America, 2012

Southeast Missouri State University Press
One University Plaza, MS 2650
Cape Girardeau, MO 63701
http://www6.semo.edu/universitypress

Cover design by Scott Lorenz, The Wright Group
Cover photographs by Tom Neumeyer

also by Jerry Ford:

The Gordonville Grove:
Stories of Tombstones, Tambourines, & Tammany Hall
Southeast Missouri State University Press

Honor to St. Vincent's:
A History of St. Vincent's College and the River Campus, 1838-2003
Missouri Catholic Conference

Acknowledgments

Once again, Dr. Susan Swartwout and Donna Essner of Southeast Missouri State University Press did an amazing job keeping this superfluous writer on course. I will be forever indebted to them for their professionalism in assembling the myriad of components to guide this book to its glorious conclusion. They are my new best friends! Scott Lorenz gave of his creative talents in designing the wonderful cover; he's the best. Thanks, Scott. My wife Margaret is relieved (I think), having endured four years of my hours sitting at the word processor. She has the patience of Job. Thanks, Mac. This book has been a blast to write because of the time spent with the unique, artistic personalities chronicled here. Thanks to all of you for sharing your lives, your hearts, and your *dreams* with all of us.

Contents

Inaugural Ball for Governor Jay Nixon, Jerry Ford Orchestra. State Capitol. Jefferson City, Missouri, 2009.

Foreword

I went to hear Harry James and his orchestra at the Colony Club in East Cape Girardeau, Illinois, on a Saturday night in 1959 between my junior and senior year in high school. It was thrilling to hear James's beautiful trumpet on the ballad "You Made Me Love You" and his classic rendition of "Ciribiriben," but he literally blew me away with his amazing technique on "Flight of the Bumblebee."

Around 11:00 P.M., as the large crowd was enjoying the amazing sounds of his 18-piece orchestra, a man came up to me, introduced himself as James's band manager, and inquired, "Do you play trumpet?" I responded with a simple, "Yes." "Follow me," he commanded. He led me out the back door to the edge of the cornfield that surrounded the club, handed me a trumpet, and ordered me to play for him. After I played a few bars of "Tenderly," he asked if I could play a high "C." I responded in the affirmative and proceeded to run the scale up to the high "C." Next, he asked if I could read. I responded that for a high school kid, I thought I was "a pretty good sight reader."

He then spoke the words I'll never forget, "Don't tell Harry, but the fourth trumpet player is quitting after tonight. We open in Dayton, Ohio, on Tuesday. If you want the job, it's yours. The bus leaves the Marquette Hotel tomorrow at noon; *be on it!*"

It was around 1:00 A.M. when I got home and woke Dad (the mayor of Cape Girardeau). "Dad, Dad, wake up; I'm going on the road with Harry James!" "What did you say?" he responded, as he rubbed his eyes. "I said, I'm going on the road with Harry James. *We* open Tuesday in Dayton, Ohio, and I have to be on the bus over at the Marquette by noon tomorrow." (We lived on Themis Street, one block from the Marquette Hotel.) He looked up at me and sternly commanded, "Get your ass back there and go to bed. You're not going anywhere until you finish high school *and* college!"

Well, that was the end of that. We never really talked about it much, other than we later agreed it was probably too big a step for me at the time, especially at age 16. And I've never really thought about it all that much until I started writing this book. I don't harbor any deep-seated regrets, but my life would certainly have been different had I been allowed to take the plunge at that early age, even if only for the remainder of the summer of 1959.

This book is primarily about musicians and entertainers I've admired, from in and around Cape Girardeau, who dared to dream. Cape Girardeau has been, and continues to be, blessed with a plethora of outstanding talented people. They are what this book is about. I've known and performed with many over the years. One of the challenges in writing this book was where to start and stop, who to include or not include. So I stayed primarily with people I knew or with whom I had close family ties, and others I've known who have achieved extraordinary accomplishments in the entertainment industry. My apologies to those not included.

Dreamers matter. They are the doers, the creators, the explorers. Their stories enrich our lives in many ways; they touch our hearts and lift our spirits. My friends in this book are those special people.

Salute!

Background

My hometown of Cape Girardeau, Missouri, has had a love affair with music and the arts from its earliest days. Founded by the French in the 1800s, and later settled by the Germans, Cape has maintained cultural diversity for over 200 years.

One way to trace music history is through religion. The Vincentians came to Cape in the early 1800s, holding church services at various places. A male academy was formed in 1838, where Gregorian chants would have been part of the liturgy. They established St. Vincent's College in 1843 on a hill overlooking the mighty Mississippi River. When they built their church on Main Street in 1853, adjacent to the river, full organ accompaniment followed.

In October of 2007, four years since my history of the River Campus was published,* two hundred years of history and support of the arts culminated in the opening of Southeast Missouri State University's $55 million Earl and Margie Holland School of the Visual and Performing Arts (the River Campus) on the seminary site. The 150-year-old buildings have been renovated. New performance venues for art, theatre, music, dance, classrooms, offices, practice rooms, and a Regional History museum have also been constructed.

Philanthropic Dreamers or Art Patrons

The $55 million was raised by our local, state, and federal governments, and patrons. Gifts large and small, from individual donors, totaling over $12 million played an integral part in the completion of the project. While more than eighty families gave substantial initial gifts, several patrons stand out.

Earl and Margie Holland provided the lead gift to spur the project. A native of Caruthersville and Hayti, Missouri, Mr. Holland recently retired as Vice Chairman and Chief Operating Officer of Health Management Associates, which operates more than fifty hospitals in fifteen states. The Hollands reside in Fort Myers, Florida.

Don Bedell is a successful business entrepreneur in the nursing home and banking industries. He owns and operates a chain of 35 nursing homes, with 3,334 beds, from his headquarters in Sikeston, Missouri. At the time of this writing (2010), his son Brad is President of the University's Board of Regents. The centerpiece of the River

---

* In my role as a representative of the City Countil on the River Campus Board of Managers, I've chronicled the history of St. Vincent's College from 1838 to the River Campus ground-breaking in 2003 in a booklet entitled *Honor to St. Vincent's* published by the Missouri Catholic Conference.

Campus is the 960-seat Donald C. Bedell Performance Hall, named in honor of Don for his major gift to ensure its completion.

Gary and Wendy Rust have been lifelong patrons of the arts. Although Gary built a multimillion dollar media group, Wendy is the creative one! The Rusts and Fords go way back to our school days when my brother Walter Joe and Gary spent several years together on Cape's American Legion Baseball team in the quest for a national championship. We almost made it. Gary has built a multi-state dynasty with 17 radio stations and over 50 newspapers in 8 states. Wendy and Gary provided money for the 200-seat "black box" Wendy Kurka Rust Flexible Theatre.

Bob and Gertrude Shuck were close friends of my mom and dad, and their sons, Bob and Jerry, are friends of mine. Bob has had a successful career in finance in Chicago, Illinois, and St. Petersburg, Florida. He was Vice-Chairman of Raymond James Financial. He provided the money for what I consider the "Crown Jewel" of the renovation portion of the project—the beautiful chapel in the Seminary, now known as the Robert and Gertrude Shuck Music Recital Hall. Some of the greatest basketball shootouts took place in the backyard of the Shuck home on Whitener Street! Bob and I continue our friendship in the brotherhood of the Sigma Chi Fraternity.

Harry and Rosemary Berkel Crisp provided the funds for the Rosemary and Harry Crisp Regional History Museum. As co-owners of their MidAmerica Pepsi-Cola conglomerate, they have been major patrons to many worthwhile causes, including area colleges and universities. Rosemary and my younger brother, Don, were kindred spirits. They were diagnosed with cancer the same year. At the time, they were working closely together, Don as Vice-President of Development for the University and Director of the University Foundation, and Rosemary as President of the Foundation and its President's Council. I always admired Rosemary for the grace and dignity she showed during the years of her recovery. Unfortunately, she passed away after her 12-year battle in December of 2007, as I was completing the first draft of this book.

John and Betty Glenn have been, like the other major donors, supporters of the University for many years. Their recent gift provided the John and Betty Glenn Convocation Center for programs and receptions at the River Campus. Mr. Glenn is a native of Puxico, and Mrs. Glenn, St. Louis. They met while attending Southeast Missouri State University. Mr. Glenn owned John Glenn Adjustors and Administrators Corporation, providing claims work for many major transportation companies. He passed away in 2008. Betty resides in Pebble Beach, California.

And then there was B.W. Harrison, who lived across the street from the seminary for almost sixty years. After the Vincentians closed the Seminary campus in the 1970s, it lay in disrepair. Several attempts to revive it failed. Mr. Harrison bought the property and donated it to the University.

Organizational Dreamers or Major Musical Groups

Further evidence in support of the arts can be found in community organizations who actively perform. Cape has many, but four unique ones deserve recognition.

The Cape Choraliers. COURTESY OF PAT BLACKWELL.

The Cape Choraliers was a community choir of about 50 voices that performed in our region for over 30 years. Jack and Susie Palsgrove were the driving force: Jack as director and Susie as accompanist on piano. They traditionally presented spring and Christmas concerts each year, and even represented the State of Missouri at the Seattle World's Fair in 1962. Their tradition continues with the Choral Union at the University composed of 150 voices from townspeople and university students.

The Cape Municipal Band.

The Cape Girardeau Municipal Band is one of a handful of the longest continual performing community bands in the country. First established in 1880 as the Eutonia Silver Cornet Band, it has continued with its Wednesday night summer concerts in Capaha Park for almost 130 years. During WWI, the entire band enlisted in the army at Fort Chaffee, Missouri. They formed the nucleus of the 140th Infantry Band. Most returned home, but one, Elwood Mills, died in battle.

In the 1930s, Karl L. King composed a march entitled *140th Infantry March* to honor the group and dedicated it to director Oscar Honey and the band. Since that time, the band proudly performs their march each season. The high quality, 50-member band is composed of high school and university students, teachers and professors, and community and regional professional and semi-professional musicians. Each of the 12 concerts (sponsored by the Cape Girardeau Parks & Recreation Department) highlights area performers as special guests. Crowds range from 200 to 500.

The Golden Troopers Drum & Bugle Corps was an outcropping of World Wars I and II. Returning veterans kept their camaraderie alive through their American Legion Posts by forming drum corps throughout the United States and participating in major competitions. Our Golden Troopers were a beautiful sight to behold march-

The Golden Troopers. Courtesy of Cape River Heritage Museum.

ing down the street in their cream-colored uniforms with gold sashes and plumes. In national competitions, they placed in the top ten for several years, and once in the top five. They won the Missouri American Legion Championship eight times.

The Jaycee Follies, an annual community show produced by Cape Girardeau Junior Chamber of Commerce, ran for 20 years. The Cape Girardeau Junior Chamber of Commerce was a vibrant service club in the '40s, '50s, '60s, and '70s, with consistently over 200 members. Their numbers have dwindled in recent years, but back then they were an army of progress for our city. An outcropping of Cape State's Benton-Clio Follies, the Jaycee Follies featured many of Cape's most talented entertainers. Members of the civic club, housewives, doctors, lawyers, corporate executives, plumbers, electricians, carpenters, teachers, etc., all participated. It was truly a cross-section of our community.

1967 Jaycee Follies Playbill. COURTESY OF CAPE JAYCEES.

A New York City director was hired for each year's show. He brought costumes, music, story-line, props, everything for a first-class production. He then spent two weeks choreographing dances, rehearsing musical numbers, helping construct scenery, advising the technical crew, and on and on. The Follies generally ran for two nights and always played to standing-room-only crowds. It was the highlight of the entertainment season in those days.

Jazz

Jazz began in the late 1800s to early 1900s in the deep South around New Orleans. It was a melding of gospel, blues, folk, African rhythms, and European classical music. In addition, it had an informal, spontaneous, creative element of movement, like the Mississippi River itself. The helmsman was Louis Armstrong. "Satchmo" was the pied piper of the pack who exemplified this new art form that America gave the world. There would be Dixieland, Ragtime, Blues, Swing, Bebop, Cool, Latin, and others, all emanating from the cradle of jazz, New Orleans.

Cape Girardeau musicians were beneficiaries of this new music as it spread up and down the Mississippi River on the great paddlewheel boats at the beginning of the twentieth century. We have some pioneers of jazz of our own.

R.F. "Peg" Meyer. Courtesy of Shivelbine Music.

R.F. "Peg" Meyer

Peg Meyer was the first entrepreneur musician on our local commercial music scene. His Melody Kings Orchestra played throughout Southeast Missouri and Southern Illinois from its beginnings around 1918. It was a staple on the regional excursion steamers on the Mississippi River starting with the *Majestic* in 1921–1923, and other paddlewheelers for Eagle Packet Company out of St. Louis in 1924 and beyond.

Peg nurtured many outstanding musicians who went on to great fame. Among them: Jess Stacy, piano: Benny Goodman Orchestra; Martell Lovell, trumpet: many name bands in California; Lynn Brumback, trombone: Meyer/Davis Orchestra, Mayflower Hotel, Washington D.C.; Earl Center, bass: Ted Weems Orchestra; Bruce Goodwin, piano: Steamer *Cape Girardeau* to Mardi Gras in New Orleans three years; Orin Sepp, saxophone: St. Louis Symphony, New York orchestras, and VIP in music supplies, manufacturing, and marketing.

Peg owned a music store in Cape Girardeau where he taught many youngsters to play musical instruments. He started school bands throughout Southeast Missouri and Southern Illinois. In later years, he sold the store to the Shivelbine family and became their instrument repair technician, gaining a regional reputation for his skill, especially with woodwind instruments.

Also a great storyteller, Peg is the author of *Backwoods Jazz in the Twenties*.

Peg Meyer's Original Melody Kings. L to r: Berg Snider, Peg Meyer, Jess Stacy, Martell Lovell. Courtesy of Shivelbine Music.

COURTESY OF DR. WALTER KEMPE.

Jess Stacy

Cape Girardeau pianist Jess Stacy rose from living in a railroad boxcar as a small boy to become a legendary figure in jazz. He's the only musician to perform in the three seminal events in jazz history.

The first was as pianist with the Benny Goodman Orchestra. The orchestra had been broadcasting back to the West Coast on NBC's radio program *Let's Dance,* which aired there late at night. When the orchestra opened in L.A. at the Palomar Ballroom August 21, 1935, over 4,000 screaming teenagers greeted them. It took the band completely by surprise because their appearances on the long drive west had been so minimal; they even talked about disbanding. It was the first music mob scene, similar to the later Frank Sinatra, Elvis Presley, and Beatles phenomenons. That appearance symbolically kicked off the "Swing Era."

Second was the 1938 Benny Goodman Orchestra performance in Carnegie Hall. Music historians hail that concert as the most important in jazz history. It was the point in which jazz was legitimized in the mainstream of America. Stacy's piano solo in "Sing, Sing, Sing" is universally regarded as the highlight of the evening.

Jess described the solo to Dr. Frank Nickell, Director of the Center for Regional History at Southeast Missouri State University: "It was never supposed to happen," Jess told Nickell.

> Drummer Gene Krupa and Benny did a duet, and then Benny looked at me, and I surprised him and everyone in the band. I just took off! My solo lasted over two minutes, when most piano solos of the day lasted only a few seconds. The orchestra arrangement was to last about six minutes, and ended up taking almost twelve. I had been listening and studying the great music of impressionistic composers, Maurice Ravel and Claude Debussy. If you listen closely to my solo, you will hear Debussy's influence.

The third occurred the very next day. Still feeling the effects of the historic night before, Stacy joined musicians he had performed with earlier in Chicago for the initial recording session of Commodore Records. It is generally regarded as the definitive session for small, improvising ensembles.

Milt Gabler operated Commodore Music Shop on East 42nd Street in New York City. It was a mecca for record collectors even though it was only *nine* feet wide! It was a hangout for musicians and jazz fans from all over the world. Gabler preferred the loose, lively, vibrant format of small ensembles.

For his new record company, Commodore Records, he assembled the finest players of the day for the session at 1780 Broadway in Manhattan. Although in their mid-twenties, they were seasoned professionals. The group went under the name "Eddy Condon's Windy City Seven" for the historic session. They were: Jess Stacy, piano; Eddie Condon, guitar; Artie Shapiro, bass; George Wettling, drums; Bud Freeman, saxophone; George Brunies, trombone; Pee Wee Russell, clarinet; and the great cornet of Bobby Hackett.

They had been among the greats that included Louis Armstrong, Jelly Roll Morton, and Earl Hines, who assembled in Chicago years earlier and were credited with establishing "Chicago Style" jazz. Jess was an integral part of that Chicago enclave of visionary musicians for a decade. So, one can make the claim that Chicago Jazz was Jess's fourth gift to jazz.

Jess Stacy was named best dance band pianist by *DownBeat* and *Metronome* magazines for many years. We need to go back to his beginnings. Jess Stacy was born in 1904 at Bird's Point, Missouri, on the Mississippi River near Charleston, just a few miles south of Cape Girardeau. His father was an engineer for the railroad, and the family lived, for a time, in a railroad boxcar. They moved around some before finally settling in Cape Girardeau in 1918. Jess was 14 at the time.

Jess studied piano with local college professor Clyde Brandt and hooked up with R.F. "Peg" Meyer in high school to form The Agony Four, the forerunner of Peg's Melody Kings. They performed in Southern Illinois, Southeast Missouri, and on the riverboats for three years. Jess first met and heard Fate Marable's great orchestra on the *S.S. Capitol* riverboat on its stop in Cape Girardeau.

The Melody Kings Orchestra got a job performing on the *Majestic* riverboat. On a stop in Davenport, Iowa, he heard the legendary Bix Biederbecke for the first time. Jess was stunned by the cool sounds of Biederbecke's trumpet. "That man plays like I think," Jess remarked many times.

In several interviews over the years, he recalled his riverboat days, and how those years traveling and performing on the boats honed his craft. He especially liked to talk about his versatility as the boat's calliope player.

"I got five bucks extra to play the calliope named 'The Whooper'," Stacy reminisced. "From time to time, I'd get a full face of cinders from the smokestacks. I had to wear gloves due to the heat on the copper keys from the steam. Calliope players were the original hot keyboard players."

Jess continued playing on the river, and he made it to Chicago in 1925. He stayed there for ten years, helping develop the growth of jazz in Chicago. He finally got to New York in 1935 when Benny Goodman called. He was a member of the famous Goodman Orchestra for many years, and also did stints with the Bob Crosby,* Horace Heidt, and Tommy Dorsey orchestras.

---

* One night after a gig with Bob Crosby in the late '80s, I conversed with him until the wee hours of the morning in the lobby of the Mark Hopkins Hotel atop Knob Hill in San Francisco, California. Bob was in a melancholy mood and wanted to talk. We relaxed in an overstuffed couch as he reminisced about his career: about always being in the shadow of his brother, Bing. He talked about great players

Radio, television, vocalists, and changes in styles of music dealt a blow to big band musicians. Jess moved to California in the late '40s where he continued to play smaller clubs and lounges. He even took a job with Max Factor Cosmetics to earn enough money to raise his family and pay the bills. He was sensitive, and sometimes bitter, about those days. He had a short battle with alcohol, and when called "An old has-been," he would reply, "It's better than never having been one."

The Carnegie Hall concert was re-released in 1950, and he again gained national notoriety. Author Whitney Balliett, in his book *American Musicians II*, included a detailed account of Jess's rebirth entitled *Back From Valhalla*. It chronicles Jess's schedule at jazz festivals, concerts, and time split between New York and California, performing and recording, as he once again enjoyed the national spotlight. The Valhalla article also appeared in *The New Yorker* magazine, August 18, 1975.

Jess came back to Cape Girardeau on several occasions to visit doctors, family, and his old friend Peg Meyer. On occasion, he would play for the locals. Musicians "Freck" Shivelbine and Dr. Fred Goodwin remember Jess's gorgeous chords, partly attributed to his enormous thirteen-note reach on the keyboard.

It was on one of those trips that Stacy visited the home of Sue Vogelsanger in Morley, about 20 miles south of Cape. Sue's mother, Ruth Finney, was a friend and contemporary of Stacy's, and an accomplished pianist in her own right. Vogelsanger, a teenager at the time, describes her excitement at Stacy's visit this way:

> When you are a young teenager from Morley, Missouri, in the 1940s, you don't expect world-renowned pianist Jess Stacy to come to your home and entertain you. But one summer afternoon, he did. He was visiting my mother with whom he had been friends for years. Earlier, they were part of a collection of musicians who entertained in and around Cape Girardeau. When Mother told me Stacy was coming, I was floating on air at the thought that the man who played piano with Benny Goodman's band was actually going to be in our living room. I remembered meeting him a few times at his parent's home on Park Street in Cape when I was younger, but this was special. As he played mother's piano, I noticed his fingers were long and thin, seeming to take on a life of their own, as they moved effortlessly over the keyboard. I was spellbound as I saw firsthand how he could span thirteen keys with no effort, five keys above an octave. (Mother had forewarned me.) I especially remembered how his open-collared white shirt

---

in his Bobcats Orchestra, like drummer Ray Daudac and bassist Bob Haggart. If I had known then that Stacy had been a member of his orchestra for a time, we would have had an intimate conversation about him. My ignorance cost me that rare opportunity.

complemented his black hair. He was fairly tall and thin, handsome, easy going, with a charming smile that spread to his eyes, giving them a twinkle.

Another contemporary of Jess's was Pete Propst. Pete was an old barroom piano player. I played with his combo on occasion as a young boy. He would stop at our family's funeral home on his mail route and play the piano for a few minutes. He told us of the time he went to Los Angeles to visit Jess:

> Jess took me to a jam session early one morning after all the "cats" had finished their gigs. Jess introduced me as "Paddle Fingers Propst," because the tips of my fingers were so wide. They asked me how I got my fingers up between the black keys, and I replied—I don't!

Jess continued periodic recording, performing at festivals and small lounges through the '60s and '70s, and can be heard on over 400 recordings. He played background music in a short scene in the movie *The Great Gatsby* in 1973. He appeared at the Newport Jazz Festival several times in the '70s. In 1981, jazz pianist Marian McPartland featured Jess on her weekly National Public Radio Series on great pianists.

Jess's widow, Pat, is alive and well at the age of 87 as of this 2011 writing. She lives in an assisted living apartment in Rancho Palos Verdes, California. Pat recalls:

> I met Jess many times when some of my girlfriends and I went to the Goodman performances. I guess you would say today, we were groupies. Jess would work the room during intermissions, so we got to know him fairly well. He was humble; not caught up in self-importance. He was a wonderful, sweet, affectionate man. While he was initially disinterested in animals, he learned to love our series of cats. He had a great, silly sense of humor, and in later years, loved to work in our garden. He loved to grow plants and flowers at our quiet little house on Lookout Mountain Avenue in West Hollywood, with the mountains as a backdrop. While we lived there in relative peace and obscurity, the small log cabin next door was used as a set in several movies because it was owned by Carrie Fisher. Fisher would come over in her pajamas in early mornings to play Jess's piano. Her friend Teri Garr also lived there for a time.

Looking back on the Goodman years, Pat said Benny Goodman was rather cold, and many of the musicians didn't particularly like him. "Jess had his differences with Benny, mainly over money. But in later years, Benny would call Jess from New York, and they would talk for long periods."

Dr. Walter "Dub" Kempe, of Tulsa, Oklahoma, reflecting on his lifetime friendship with Jess and Pat, said:

> Jess used to hold me when I was a baby. My father was a partner in the old Clark Music Store in Cape where Jess worked, and Dad and I followed his career over the years. Jess told me they would lock the doors at 5:00 P.M. and go to the back room, turn on the RCA Victrola, and listen to recordings of Louis Armstrong's "Hot 5" and "Hot 7," and drink "medicinal" alcohol! Louis Armstrong influenced many pianists' "right hand."
>
> At home, we would turn to the front room radio at 8:00 P.M. to listen to Jess and the Goodman Orchestra on the Camel Caravan. As an adult, I talked to Jess frequently on the phone and visited him and his wife Pat out in Hollywood from time to time. An auspicious event took place at Sullens College in Bristol, Tennessee, where my Aunt Mary was the librarian in the early '30s. She was a Goodman fan and introduced Pat to Jess when the band performed a concert on the campus.

In describing Stacy's piano style, Kempe observed, "Nobody played like Jess. He was a great, rhythmic, big-band pianist, and a master of counter melodies, producing solid chords and solo lines."

"The last time I saw Jess," Kempe remembered, "was in 1988 when he was honored during the 50th anniversary of the acclaimed Carnegie Hall Concert by the International Association of Jazz Record Collectors in Los Angeles. Jess was a featured speaker along with Martha Tilton, Art Lund, Jack Sheldon, and other living alumni of the Goodman Orchestra. Afterward, we had dinner, and as we parted, Jess, a private man, who generally kept his distance from people, asked me to bend down— and he kissed me on the cheek. I just melted."

The Quiet Man of Jazz by Derek Coller* is the definitive book on Stacy. The title derives from Jess's laid-back personality and descriptions of his piano style by his contemporaries such as "the ultimate supporter," "his light pensive touch," "his rhythmic grace," "the sensitive soul of a poet."

Jess was inducted into the American Jazz Hall of Fame at Rutgers University

---

* I was lucky to purchase one of two known available copies of Mr. Coller's book through Barnes & Noble. I donated my copy of Coller's book, Peg Meyer's definitive book of Jess's riverboat days, *Backwoods Jazz in the Twenties*, along with a copy of Marian McPartland's NPR Radio Show, and several other cassette tapes of Jess's performances I've been able to acquire, to the Southeast Missouri State University Special Collections. For additional information about Jess Stacy, contact the Special Collections & Archives Department in Kent Library on the Southeast Missouri State University Campus in Cape Girardeau, Missouri.

in 1986, and *Jazz Beat*'s All Time Hall of Fame in 1993. Jess Stacy died quietly of congestive heart failure on January 1, 1995, at the age of 90 in his home on Lookout Mountain Avenue in West Hollywood, California. His contribution as a founder of America's greatest art-form gift to the world (Jazz) lives through his many recordings.

Jess Stacy. COURTESY OF DR. WALTER KEMPE.

Sue Vogelsanger. COURTESY OF FRED LYNCH, *SOUTHEAST MISSOURIAN*.

Sue Vogelsanger

Never was there a stranger circumstance in researching material for this book than stumbling upon Sue Finney Vogelsanger's amazing career. I remembered some of her family, especially the Finneys, when briefly reunited with her and her husband Sonny, at a Christmas house-party in Cape, hosted by opera diva Judith Farris in 2007. (Farris's career is chronicled in a later chapter.) As I was writing the first chapter for this book *Dreamers*, I was searching for a contemporary of Benny Goodman's great jazz pianist, Jess Stacy, who grew up in Cape many years ago. Most of Stacy's contemporaries in Cape had long passed away.

In September of 2008, my wife Margaret and I drove down below Benton to the Morley Café to eat lunch with the proprietor, Virginia Pobst Grant, Margaret's former sister-in-law. After chitchatting, Margaret discovered Ginny was selling cookbooks by a former Morley resident, Sue Finney Vogelsanger, entitled *Cookin' & Talkin'*. The book looked interesting, so Margaret bought the last copy available at the time. Upon returning home, Margaret discovered Vogelsanger had included various stories about growing up in her little town of Morley, Missouri. Margaret was especially interested because she was raised just a few miles south and west of Morley in Vanduser, Missouri.

As Margaret read, she occasionally laughed out loud. (I knew it must be good.) Then she yelled, "You won't believe this; Sue has a story in her book about Jess Stacy coming to visit her home in Morley." "You've got to be kidding," I answered. "Let me see it." Sure enough, Vogelsanger had related the events in her cookbook of the day Jess Stacy, pianist for the great Benny Goodman band, visited Morley, Missouri. I had been looking for someone who knew Stacy (without much luck), and there she was. I called her, and we met shortly thereafter. As we talked about Jess Stacy over several days, her eclectic background and amazing exploits were revealed.

Sue Finney was born July 22, 1929, in Cape Girardeau. She graduated from Morley High School in 1946 and Lindenwood College in St. Charles, Missouri, four years later, with a B.A. degree in Speech and Drama, and minors in Psychology and Education. Later, she completed graduate studies in Narration, Education, and Psychology of Exceptional Children. She was also certified by the Library of Congress as a literary Braille transcriber. She's been married to her husband Sonny for 60 years, has two sons, four grandsons, and one granddaughter. The Vogelsangers retired and live in Cape Girardeau.

Vogelsanger possesses a rare, mischievous twinkle in her eye. From the moment you meet her, you know there are fascinating stories stirring. She's a housewife, mother, grandmother, newspaper reporter, columnist, reviewer, feature writer, author, songwriter, award-winning cook, and world traveler. Her travels with her husband, Elbert

"Sonny" Vogelsanger, a retired thirty-five-year manager with McDonnell-Douglas, have taken her all over the world, quite a feat for a little girl from Morley, Missouri, population 522!

Wherever Sue's husband's profession took them, she often worked outside the home. She wrote columns for *The Vegas Voice*, Las Vegas, Nevada; *The Placer Herald*, Rocklin, California; was reporter, columnist, and feature writer for *The Valley Times*, Pleasanton, California. She was executive secretary to the vice-president of McDonnell-Douglas Services Peace Sun Program, Riyadh, Saudi Arabia, for two years. She placed in the finals of the Gilroy Garlic Festival Great Garlic Cook-off in Gilroy, California, winning second place in 1997 for her Tipsy Brisket recipe, and was one of eight finalists for her Garlito Porkito recipe in 2001.

These and many more activities and experiences are unique to this eclectic woman; such as feeling the shock of horror at their farewell party in Florida in 1967, when a woman burst in the room shouting, "They're all dead, they're all dead," reporting the fire that caused the death of astronauts Gus Grissom, Roger Chaffee, and Ed White, as they sat in the 100% oxygen environment atop a Saturn rocket in the first Apollo Spacecraft; or writing a review of a Frank Sinatra concert at the Circle Star Theater near San Francisco, California, in 1977; or attending Saudi Arabia's annual King's Cup Camel Race in 1981. Her most cherished memories, however, are from watching blind children learn to read from printed materials she transcribed into braille in the late '60s, in Santa Maria, California.

Yet those exploits aren't why she is included in this book. No, she's in this book because of a spur-of-the-moment trip she took to Carol Burnett's television show in 1969, while living in Santa Maria, California, and what she did during the show. This began one of the unique episodes in my life developed among TV star Carol Burnett, Sue Vogelsanger, and Bob Sisco. I took over Sisco's orchestra when he left Cape to find his fame and fortune in Los Angeles in 1960. After being musical director for organist Earl Garner, accordionist Dick Contina, and Rusty Warren of "Knocker's Up" fame, he landed a job as a young music arranger for the Gary Moore TV variety show and, later on, for Carol Burnett's hit show. I attended several rehearsals of *The Carol Burnett Show* during Bob's tenure there.

Sue's son, John, called and told her to get ready. "The tickets to *The Carol Burnett Show* have finally arrived in the mail." She really didn't want to go, but prodded by John, she acquiesced. Knowing his mother's penchant for the unusual, he appealed to her with these prophetic words, "And Mom, don't do anything stupid!"

One of the staples of Burnett's show was always a Question & Answer session where she talked to the audience. When she inquired of the audience on this evening, Sue got her attention by standing and waving a piece of sheet music in the air, announcing that she had written a song especially for Carol entitled, "Just Talkin'." The song was about a housewife bored with her mundane, repetitious life, dreaming of adventure and travel to exotic places. Sue thought it would be perfect for Burnett's classic mop-and-bucket routines. Carol invited her on stage, carefully looked over the song sheet and lyrics, and announced she would perform it on her show in a few weeks. Vogelsanger was shocked. She had tried to get some of her songs published, to no avail. She didn't dream her strategy would work, but it did. Sue describes it this way:

> It was surreal. I was nervous and apprehensive. As Carol moved toward me, flashing her famous smile, I began to feel at ease and was able to ignore the hundreds of audience eyes honed in on me. After I explained the music, Burnett quipped—"It's a dirty song!" By this time, she had made me feel so comfortable, I was able to laugh along with the audience. Carol continued her banter, announcing the formation of the new Broadway musical team, "Rodger's, Vogelsanger, and Hammerstein." When I left the show, I wondered if her staff would let her perform my song. I really didn't think she would pull it off, but she did.

To Vogelsanger's surprise, Carol Burnett personally called her several weeks later and asked her to come to the taping the following week. Sue and Sonny flew to Los Angeles (they had been transferred back to St. Louis in the meantime) for the show. Here's her account of the momentous event:

> I never could find out how they were going to do my song. They were very secretive. As we arrived at the artist's entrance, the doorkeeper laughed as he said, "Oh good, you're here; we've been waiting for you." We met Lucille Ball's mother as we entered back stage. (Lucille Ball and George Carlin were special guests on the show.) Sonny and I were escorted down to our special seats, and I was then taken backstage to sign some papers. On the way, I had to step through some huge obstacles. When my number was announced, I was electrified. I couldn't believe my eyes and ears, as it unfolded. I was totally stunned by the spectacle: glorious music, men in tuxes and tails, show girls and Burnett in formal evening gowns. And Carol was so on the mark. She sang the song perfectly. It would have made the great showman, Florenz Ziegfeld proud. I then realized the huge obstacle I stepped through was a G, one of fourteen, 6-foot-tall letters the dancers moved about the stage, which finally spelled my name at the end of the magnificent production, VOGELSANGER! Afterward, we were invited backstage. Carol told me she wanted to do this grand interpretation for me, "Because you were so sweet and shy." (She really didn't know me, but I was starstruck, and on my best behavior.) "We almost had a heart attack when you walked through the G. We wanted our production to be a complete

The Carol Burnett Show, featuring Carol Burnett performing a song written by Sue Vogelsanger on November 7, 1969. COURTESY OF LANDOV MEDIA.

surprise to you." (It was.) We left through the artist's entrance with Carol's entourage. She immediately signed autographs for her many fans who had assembled, and I even had several kids come up and ask for mine!

The show aired nationally on CBS, November 24, 1969. As the picture shows, it was not the mop-and-bucket routine Burnett was famous for, but a full-blown song and dance production. Vogelsanger has a copy of the full, six-minute, *one in a million*, production on video tape.

Several years later in 1975, she and Sonny went to see Burnett perform with Rock Hudson in *I Do, I Do* at St. Louis's famous outdoor theatre, The Municipal Opera. Here's Sue's account:

> The evening Sonny and I went to the show at the "Muny," I took along a copy of *St. Louis Fan*. I was writing columns and features for that magazine. I tucked a personal note to Carol inside the pages, stating I worked for the publication and Sonny and I were in the audience. Before show time, I went downstage and asked a stage guard if he would please deliver the magazine and my note to Carol. He asked me to come back during intermission in case there was a message. I did, and there was. The guard said, "I don't know who the hell you are lady, but after the show, Miss Burnett wants you personally escorted backstage. Do you know her?" "Sort of," I answered. After going backstage, we waited a bit in a small room. Some guy asked several times if we were there to see Rock Hudson, and each time we answered, "No, Carol Burnett." Shortly, we heard her asking loudly, "Sue, where's Sue?" Carol gave Sonny and me a big hug, and said how good it was to see us again. She made us feel so welcome and special. As we hugged, I noticed she was a lot thinner than I remembered. I mentioned that, and she laughed and said, "I've lost about 10 pounds prancing around this big stage in this heat and humidity." Her producer, Robert Wright, whom we had met in 1969 back in Hollywood, came out to greet us. He shook Sonny's hand, hugged me, smiled, and said, "Sue, all we needed tonight in the play was one of your songs!"

In October of 2010, I read in the *St. Louis Post-Dispatch* that Carol would be performing at The Fox Theatre in St. Louis on Friday, November 5, and asked Sue if she and Sonny would like to go. They said yes, and we worked out the details. In the meantime, Sue contacted Ms. Burnett, told her about my forthcoming book, and out of the blue, Carol called me. We had a great conversation, and she reminisced about Sue and the show:

She was so small and so sweet. I was immediately smitten with her and had a feeling her song would be neat. As I uttered the prophetic words, "I'm going to perform your song on one of our shows," I could see my manager and producers up behind the glass in the control booth in the back of the studio vehemently waving handkerchiefs and moving their heads side to side mouthing, "No, no, no!" We had so much fun with her name, Vogelsanger. At one point we kicked around phrases made out of the letters like, "Sue's Song Saves Lovers;" Artie Melvin finally came up with the idea of arranging the song as a "jazz waltz." We took it from there, constructing the letters six feet high, placing them on wheels, and moving them around the stage in grand style as we sang and danced Sue's song, all in formal attire. The show was an immediate hit. People loved it as much as we did performing it. We got many fan letters. At our post-show wrap-up, my producers implored me, *Don't ever do that again. Next time, we may not be as lucky!*"

As we concluded the call, Carol invited us to come backstage after the show. Margaret and I picked Sue and Sonny up and drove to the Fox Theater in St. Louis. There was a large crowd in attendance to participate in Carol's talk with her audience, interspersed with film clips from her TV shows of days gone by. At the conclusion, we made our way to the stage door where a mob of young college students had assembled. When our name was called, Margaret and I, Sue and Sonny, and Bill and Frankie Schott managed to squeeze through.

Sue talked to Carol among the rush of people, and we were able to spend a few minutes with her, take pictures, and wish her well. Ms. Burnett was remarkably calm amid the storm of admirers. Mission accomplished, we headed to Cape. All of this because Sue wrote a cookbook and Margaret purchased it at the Morley Café!

Sue and Sonny maintain an active social life in their retirement here in Cape Girardeau. Sue writes a weekly column for the *Marble Hill Banner-Press*, a subsidiary of the *Southeast Missourian* newspaper. When asked to comment on her life, Sue responded, "Fantastic; it's been quite a ride." One can look to the horizon to discover her next escapade.

Tommy Chambers and Frank Sinatra. COURTESY OF *SOUTHEAST MISSOURIAN.*

Tommy Chambers

"Little Tommy Chambers went from being a whiz on the piano in Cape Girardeau to a whiz on the piano in Hollywood," says a Thursday, November 11, 1947, article in our *Southeast Missourian* newspaper. During his career he accompanied Bing Crosby, Bob Hope, Pearl Bailey, The Andrews Sisters, and Tony Martin. He accompanied and recorded with Rudy Vallee and Frank Sinatra, and made a motion picture with the Catherine Dunham dancers.

Tommy spent a great deal of time with Fred Astaire. He collaborated with Astaire and composer Mason Van Cleave to write the song "Piano Dance" that was used in the 1950 Paramount movie *Let's Dance*, starring Astaire and Ginger Rogers. A *Life* magazine article of the day quoted Mr. Astaire: "Tommy Chambers is my favorite accompanist!" Chambers was also music director for Warner Brothers Movie Studios for twenty years!

Chambers was born and raised in Cape, graduated from Central High School, and attended Southeast Missouri State College, now Southeast Missouri State University, for a time, before moving with his family to Hollywood in 1932. He studied under Professor Clyde Brandt at the college and considered members of the old Glee club—Richard Wagner, Walter Aslin, and Earl Black—to be his best friends.

He lived on Themis Street with his parents, Mr. and Mrs. L.B. Chambers, and his older brother, Jimmy. The family operated a feed store on Good Hope Street. They pooled their money, moved to Hollywood, and purchased a ranch that turned out to be a great investment as the area flourished and grew. A Cape Girardeau resident and friend, Vivan Trovillion, visited Tommy at his home and described it as "a pretentious mansion on Ivarene Avenue in East Hollywood, the exclusive residential section. It had a sunken living room and other appointments that made it exceedingly impressive."

In later years, Tommy freelanced rather than being connected with any particular singer or movie company. His services were always in demand as he concentrated on arranging, scoring, and of course, accompanying the stars.

The Shivelbine Family. COURTESY OF *SOUTHEAST MISSOURIAN*.

Shivelbine Music Store

Shivelbine Music Store has been the hub for musicians in Southeast Missouri and Southern Illinois for more than sixty years. It was established even earlier in the 1930s, then known as the St. Louis Band & Instrument Company. When the company wanted to sell their Cape Girardeau branch to their manager, R.F. "Peg" Meyer, Peg enlisted the help of the local band director, William Shivelbine. They formed a partnership on January 1, 1947, and continued Peg's work building school bands throughout the area.

William August Shivelbine. COURTESY OF SHIVELBINE MUSIC.

Mr. Shivelbine had been a silent-movie theatre organist in Little Rock, Arkansas, before moving to Cape in the 1920s. He continued at the Broadway Theatre until movies added sound in 1929. Mr. Shivelbine got a job teaching music at the local high school from his sister's brother-in-law, Louis J. Schultz, Superintendent of the Cape Girardeau Public Schools.

On July 1, 1949, Mr. Shivelbine bought Peg Meyer's interest and then died unexpectedly in September. That left his son, Leland "Freck" Shivelbine, in charge. Freck had returned to work in the store after college and a stint in the U.S. Navy. Freck retained Meyer as an instrument repair technician. Two years later, in 1951, he convinced his brother Bill, who had a Masters Degree in Chemical Engineering, to leave his oil job in Texas and join the family enterprise.

Their business flouished.

As more college students graduated with music education degrees, the area public school instrumental programs thrived. The Shivelbines were the catalyst. They enhanced the personal and business relationships that Peg Meyer had established with Conn Instrument Company at Elkhart, Indiana; Selmer Woodwind Company of France; Leblanc Woodwinds at Kenosha, Wisconsin; and Ludwig Drum Company at Chicago, Illinois.

Freck became a good friend of Bill Ludwig, owner of the Ludwig Drum Company. Ludwig would pilot his large yacht each fall from Chicago to the Gulf of Mexico. He would generally stop in Cape to invite Freck and his friends on the yacht for relaxation. Those were the days of the great Canadian goose hunts, which brought hunters from all over the country to Cape and Southern Illinois, the Capital of goose hunting. The hotels, motels, and restaurants would fill to capacity during the hunting season. So each year, Freck would go to the end of the yacht and perform his famous goose call. "For years, Ludwig would always tell the story to people when I would run into him at national conventions," Freck laughed.

Freck also remembers Vito Pascucci, the repairman for the Glenn Miller Orchestra: "The Miller Orchestra performed for a time in Paris, France, right after its liberation. Vito met and married the daughter of the owner of LeBlanc Company while there, and subsequently moved the production of the student-line woodwind instruments to Kenosha."

As musical styles of Elvis Presley changed the music world in the late '50s and '60s, the store also changed. The product lines expanded to include guitars, keyboards, and amplifiers. Shivelbines was the first Peavey Amplifier dealer in the region. The store's location moved from 628-630 Broadway to 535 Broadway to accommodate the increased business of the new phenomenon, rock 'n' roll. In the 1970s, the third generation of Shivelbines emerged. Freck's sons Mike, Scott, and Greg joined the business, and Bill's son, Billy, came on board in 1982.

When Freck's brother Bill died in 1991, the firm reorganized into two companies under the same roof. Freck and his sons maintained Shivelbine Music Store, and Bill's son formed Shivelbine Music & Sound. Between them, they began selling TVs with the Magnavox brand. They added a store in Marion, Illinois, in 2001, and continue to dominate the school-band business in our region.

They sell all varieties of instruments, guitars, amplifiers, pianos, TVs, recorders, DVD players, and band and sheet music. In addition, they design and sell full home audio and video systems and complete concert audio systems. They also provide a full-service instrument repair shop, and even operate a school for beginner and intermediate music students.

Freck says, "It's a fun place to work. We meet all kinds of people, from great musicians to the not-so-great! Parents, students, business men and women, doctors, lawyers, teachers, professors, and curiosity seekers all walk through our doors. And, over the years, all the 'cats' still congregate here; the 'jazzers,' the 'rockers,' the 'punkers,' the 'hillbillies,' all of them." He also sees every day "the benefits and pleasure of what music can do for people, from young kids, to adults, to old fogies like me."

As in any business, it takes good employees and teamwork to be a success. The two companies employ twenty people. Freck mentions Betty Points, Sue Gleason,

Rick Parish, Kenny Martin, and Brad Lyle as employees who were there almost from the very beginning.

"Betty had this propensity to faint," Freck laughed. "One day when she had a fainting spell, we laid her out behind the counter, as we generally did. She usually recovered quickly. As this was happening, a customer walked in and about fainted when I stepped over Betty and inquired, 'May I help you?'"

Freck and Bill Shivelbine. Courtesy of *Southeast Missourian*.

When I asked Scott Bierschwal, a longtime employee and outstanding keyboard man, to describe the working environment at the store, he immediately responded, "Family, we're a family."

Another long-time employee, Sue Gleason, says, "I've been here many years. Bill and Freck were always good to me. It was an adjustment when the boys changed from employees to become my bosses. But it all worked out fine. Through it all, Freck is one of my best friends. He's a very good man."

The same sentiment resounds through Freck's boys. Scott Shivelbine talks about the fun times at the store. Scott remembers one cold, blustery day as Christmas approached:

> Dad and I were atop the store's front awning (about 18 feet high) trying, in vain, to install a large, heavy aluminum Christmas tree for everyone to see as they traveled down Broadway. A pleasant-looking woman approached us, looked up, and shouted through the wind with a heavy German accent, "Excuse me, Mister, would you like to buy a book about Cheesus?" Dad, exasper-

ated with the tree by this time, yelled, "What did you say, lady?" She replied emphatically, "I said, would you like to buy a book about Cheesus?" Dad answered, "Lady, I don't care for cheeses." She shot back, "Why you heathen, how can you be putting up a Christmas tree and not like Cheesus?" As she stormed off down the street, I had to explain to Dad her book was about Jesus!

Greg and Billy formed a hot rock band, Acme Blues, that was popular around the region for years. Acme members were Greg, drums; Billy, sax; Al McFerron, keyboards; Brad Springmeyer, guitar; and Tom Bloodworth, bass.

Greg and Mike both say, "Dad instilled a strong work ethic in all of us. Calling on schools requires 75 to 80 hour weeks at times." Mike believes parents who participated in band programs in school "know the value of music in their lives and encourage their kids to participate."

Freck tells a few of his most dramatic stories:

When we travel to schools, we usually fix instruments on the spot. Years ago down at Senath, they were having trouble with the sound of a baritone saxophone. When I ran a swab through it, out popped a dead mouse!

In the early '60s, Louis Schultz's twin brother, the Superintendent of the Cairo Public Schools, came to the door of the band room and told us, "Pack up and leave immediately, because a race riot has broken out just down the street."

And as recently as two weeks ago (September 2, 2009), while we were giving a display of instruments to beginners at Scott City, police cars from Scott City, Scott County, and Cape Girardeau forced us into a forty-five minute lockdown as they chased a fugitive.

One can imagine the close relationships the Shivelbines developed over the years with music educators and especially band directors in the Southeast Missouri Band Directors Association. Freck reminisced about some of the great ones: Keith Collins of Sikeston, W.L. Giddens of Gideon, LeRoy Mason of Jackson; and later, at Southeast Missouri State University where he formed the nationally acclaimed Golden Eagles, Nick Leist of Jackson, Hubey Moore of Festus, Ed Carson of Jackson, Bill Sayler of Poplar Bluff, and Tony Carosello and Bill Ewing of Cape Girardeau.

A fourth generation of Shivelbines is active in music. Mike's son, Matt, has a popular bluegrass group called Nomads, which has toured Europe. Billy's sister Donna Grantham has a daughter, Shelley Nierenberg, who received a degree from Barat Dance Conservatory in Lake Forest, Illinois. Children, music, and dance are her passions. She is currently Director of Children's Programs with Peridance, one of the largest dance schools in New York City.

The story of the Shivelbines is still being written. They continue to brighten our region with their support of the arts. Southeast Missourians and Southern Illinoisans are enjoying better qualities of life because of them. The twinkle in the eyes of children making their first sound on a musical instrument still brings smiles to parents young and old. And the band plays on. . . .

COURTESY OF KFVS-TV.

Don McNeely

Don said it would. When people hear that phrase in our area, they immediately think of Don McNeely, with his trusty umbrella, forecasting rain. Don was news anchor, and later meteorologist, on our local CBS television station for over forty years, and is still easily the most recognized personality in our town.

The founder-owner of the KFVS television station in Cape Girardeau was Oscar Hirsch, a pioneer in the broadcast industry. Before the advent of cable TV, KFVS had a monopoly on the CBS signal throughout parts of five states. The tower, constructed for their broadcast signal in 1960, was for a time the tallest man-made structure in the world.

Mr. Hirsch also owned six radio stations. Don McNeely began his fifty-year career in broadcasting with Mr. Hirsch as an announcer for KFVS radio in 1943 at the age of 16. Virginia "Jac" Bahn had been Don's teacher in the fourth grade at Franklin School. Being a cousin of Mr. Hirsch's, she also worked at KFVS radio. She knew Don wanted to work in radio, and when WWII broke out, their stable of announcers was depleted. She remembered, called Don, and offered him a job.

At the time, Don was a "printer's devil," an apprentice at Mississippi Valley Printing Company on North Sprigg Street. The job was hot and dirty, and he jumped at the chance to work at the radio station. Don recalled, "It's got to be better than this."

The war was raging. Everyone knew there would be an Allied invasion of Europe. The day was June 6, 1944. Don was 17, working fulltime at KFVS radio. At 4:00 A.M., the ringing of the phone cut through the darkness. It was Jac Bahn on the other end, "Don, get right over here; the *invasion* has begun!" He arrived before 5:00 A.M. and began broadcasting the teletype dispatches as they were received. Mr. Hirsch hooked up a large Philco radio out on the street in front of the station on Broadway, and turned the signal up as loud as he could so everyone could keep up with the action. Don broadcast the invasion for 14 straight hours that day.

Don was drafted into the army in 1945. One day during basic training, all soldiers with any college under their belts were told to step forward. Not knowing what he was getting himself into, he slowly stepped forward. As it turned out, the army was looking for potential Japanese interpreters. Don was tested and passed. He laughs when he recalls the event. He was to leave immediately for the University of Pennsylvania in Philadelphia, and would miss the last three weeks of basic training. The first sergeant, perturbed at the affair but thinking for some reason Don was going to prison, announced sternly, "McNeely, you're going to a Penn State!"

Late in 1945, after Glenn Miller's sudden death, the Miller family reorganized the band, featuring vocalist/tenor saxophonist Tex Beneke. The first appearance was to be at the Capital Theatre in New York City. Don, in Philly at the time, saw the ad in the newspaper, convinced a buddy to accompany him, and attended the historic event. Here's Don's description of the opening: "As the curtain slowly opened to Miller's classic theme song, 'Moonlight Serenade,' there they were: all the greats, and even a string section. I'll never forget it. . . . What a thrill!"

Six years later, back at KFVS in Cape Girardeau, Don saw another newspaper ad for Tex Beneke and the Glenn Miller Orchestra. This time they would be performing the following night just across the river in East Cape Girardeau, Illinois, at the renowned Colony Club.

The Marquette Hotel was next door to the radio station. All the big bands stayed there in those days when performing across the river. (This was before interstate highways and the motel chains that followed.) As luck would have it, Don ran into Beneke on the street walking up Broadway. Don stopped him, introduced himself, and told him he was at the premiere concert in New York City six years earlier. Don was surprised at Beneke's response: "Did you see my knees shaking?" Tex inquired. "I was never so scared in my life!" Tex invited Don over to the Colony Club to hear his new singer, Eydie Gorme. Being the dance band musician he was, Don asked, "You mean the gal from the Tommy Tucker Band?" "Why, yes," was Beneke's startled response.

Don studied Japanese at the University of Pennsylvania for one year. The war was winding down, so he was sent to Japan in May of 1946 as an announcer with the Armed Services Radio Network. He returned to Cape after earning an M.A. degree in broadcasting from Northwestern University in 1949 on the G.I. Bill. In those days, Northwestern had the reputation of having the best speech and drama school. He resumed his duties at KFVS radio, and then anchored the inaugural television broadcast in 1954. I remember it well.

Don enlightened me on a bit of interesting technology history: "Video tape had not been invented yet, so the first broadcast was filmed on 16mm movie film and sent to Memphis for processing several days before so it could be broadcast on the show."

Don was multi-talented. Besides his good looks and great voice, he was an outstanding alto saxophone player. He was a member of Champ Gilliland's and Martin Johnston's bands. When Johnston left for Florida, Don formed his own band. He led his popular dance orchestra for several years before disbanding in 1955 due to his increased responsibilities at the television station.

In the early days of TV, Don was a one-man band. He was program director, anchored the news at 6:00 P.M. and 10:00 P.M., forecast the "Watching the Weather" segment, and occasionally hosted the "Sports Final" for many of the broadcasts between 1954–1970. Things slacked off in front of the camera somewhat for him from 1970 to 1982 when Mike Shain arrived to give him some relief.

One evening years ago after a local Jaycee meeting, a traveling salesman in the Holiday Inn lounge asked several of us after viewing *The Ten O'clock News* with

Don McNeely, "Watching the Weather" with Don McNeely, and "The Sports Final" with Don McNeely, "Have I just been introduced to this guy *three* times in the past thirty minutes?"

Don's most important role all those years, however, was behind the scenes as program director. "Someone had to see that there were fresh programs on the air at all times," Don explained. *The Breakfast Show* was live five mornings a week. Hundreds of entertainers and performers were on the show over the years. Slim and Dusty Rhodes, and Porter Wagoner and Dolly Parton were especially popular, along with local personalities like the Mamanettes—Pat Blackwell, Virginia Boren, and Virginia Hill (who fashioned their style after the McGuire Sisters)— and country singers, Tom & Lee.

Bob Hope and Don McNeely. COURTESY OF KFVS-TV.

The original Cerebral Palsy Telethons were on the air live 24 hours a day. They raised several million dollars over the more than twenty years. Don produced all of them. Don interviewed James Arness, who played Matt Dillon on CBS's hit western *Gunsmoke*. Mr. Arness was appearing at the Sikeston Jaycee Rodeo. He was shy and usually didn't grant interviews. Mr. Hirsch threw his weight around up at CBS in New York, and the interview was granted.

"He was very laconic, so the interview was short," Don remembered. Upon returning to California, Mr. Arness's publicist released a statement to the affiliate stations announcing his client would no longer grant interviews to anyone, anytime! Don said, "From that time forward, my cohorts kidded me exclaiming, 'You're the guy who made Matt Dillon shut up!'"

An unexpected treat came when Gloria DeHaven appeared as a telethon headliner one year. Don had admired her back in the '40s, watching all those old MGM movie musicals she starred in. "She was in her fifties and still very attractive at that time," Don remembered. Bill Ewing was leading the live band. He and Don had performed together for years. Bill knew of Don's singing talents and put Don on the spot in front of the live camera.

"Hey Don, why don't you and Gloria sing one together?" Bill requested. Don was embarrassed and glared at Bill as if to say, *Are you absolutely out of your mind?* But Ms. DeHaven agreed. "Do you have one in mind?" she politely queried. "Well, how 'bout 'Embraceable You'?" Don responded. It was a done deal. Of course, everything went fine. They both enjoyed it so much, they did an encore later in the evening. "If someone had predicted 25 years before that I would be singing with Gloria DeHaven on live television, I'd have told them they were crazy," said Don, "but it happened!"

Then there was the *Muscular Dystrophy Labor Day Telethon*, which has lasted another twenty years through 2009. Much of the feed came from Jerry Lewis's base in Las Vegas, but Don was still on camera and still producing the show locally. After Bill Ewing's death, my combo replaced his as the live music background group. Don understood that live music added warmth, immediacy, and excitement to any show or broadcast.

One day Charles Kurault unexpectedly walked in the front door of the television station. He was following a carnival on his *On the Road* CBS TV Show. He needed to do some video editing. When finished, Don asked if he would consent to a short interview. Mr. Kurault obliged. Don said, "Mr. Kurault was a great storyteller, and the 12 to 15 minute interview was fascinating." At the conclusion, an engineer came out and said the equipment wasn't working properly, and the entire interview was lost. Don was devastated. Recognizing Don's disappointment, Charles Kurault said, "Let's do it again," and they did. Don remembered that story with fondness when, visiting the University of North Carolina at Chapel Hill, he saw Kurault's simple tombstone in the little cemetery nestled in the middle of the campus.

An interesting sideline of Don's was his role as announcer for Southeast Missouri State University's Golden Eagles Marching Band for over twenty years. The band was nationally known, having amassed more minutes for the National Football League's halftime shows than any other collegiate band in the country. CBS producers in New York loved the band's director, LeRoy Mason, for his inventive moving marquee formations mimicking the marquees on 42nd Street and Times Square. When the New York Giants came to St. Louis each year to play the football Cardinals, the producers insisted the Golden Eagles be the halftime band, so they could broadcast them back to the New York market.

Don was their announcer wherever they performed: local halftime football games, special performances, the NFL Runner-Up Game in 1970, and the 1971 Super Bowl featuring Anita Bryant in the Orange Bowl in Miami, Florida. Don announced the Super Bowl halftime show down on the field. An NBC executive told him it was being televised live to over 65 million people worldwide; Don responded tongue-in-cheek, "It was one of my larger audiences."

Don and his wife Sue have two talented, creative daughters. Donna McNeely, a former TV news anchor, lives in Los Angeles and recently released her first book,

50

Stuck in the Box: A Life in Local TV News. The paperback is available on Amazon.com and the audio book is on iTunes. In 2008, Donna was hired by the DNC to produce the first ever high definition daily webcast for the 2008 Democratic National Convention in Denver. Their daughter, Laura Montocchio, is a nationally recognized corporate trainer based in Raleigh, North Carolina. She is the creator and developer of the innovative online sales training program, "You Make the Call," which can be found at www.youmakethecall.us.

As the years rolled by, Don slowed down a bit. He became a certified meteorologist with the American Meteorological Society in 1982, and continued his passion for weather until retirement in 1993. In looking back over his career Don says:

> I had a great ride. It's hard to believe I spent all those long days and nights producing all those shows, interviewing all those senators, governors, congressmen, and celebrities from various walks of life. For over half a century, I've witnessed and reported about wars, including the Cold War, assassinations of our leaders, the hippie generation, the music revolution from big band to rock 'n' roll to country to hip-hop; all of it. It's all a *big blur* when I think back on it.

The McNeelys have traveled all over the world. He still marvels at the number of people who recognize him wherever they go. Some celebrities see these moments as unpleasant interruptions in their lives. Not Don. He's always been gracious. He explains, "Most times they're fun and add spice to my day. Like the time in church, when a little boy shouted out, 'Hey look, Mom, there's Walter Cronkite!'"

Don McNeely is still one of the most recognized personalities in our region, even though he and Sue recently retired to South Carolina to be with their daughters.

Dr. Jerry McNeely. COURTESY OF *SOUTHEAST MISSOURIAN*.

Dr. Jerry McNeely

Don McNeely's brother, Dr. Jerry McNeely is "The Natural." Not *The Natural* played by Robert Redford in the baseball movie, but a naturally gifted writer and producer of over 200 television scripts and plays like *Owen Marshall: Counselor at Law*, *Dr. Kildare*, *Marcus Welby, M.D.*, *The Man From U.N.C.L.E.*, *The Twilight Zone*, and *Hallmark Hall of Fame*. Don remarked, "Jerry had a love of literature at a very young age, and everybody was amazed he could be so good so young."

The McNeely brothers were hams in their youth. They were always putting on skits and play-acting around the house. They both had lead roles in high school plays. "We went to a lot of movies at the old Broadway Theatre in those days," Don reminisced. "Jerry was nuts about the movies."

Jerry attended Westminster College in Fulton, Missouri, for two years and returned to Southeast Missouri State College in his hometown for two years where he received his B.S. degree. There he met Arthur Dorlag, professor of Speech and Drama, one of many mentors who helped him in his career. Jerry starred in several plays during 1947, 1948, and 1949 under Dorlag's tutelage.

Upon graduation from Southeast, he enrolled in the University of Wisconsin and received his Masters degree in 1950. He returned to Southeast and taught for one year, wherein he met and married Priscilla Grant of Webster Groves, Missouri. He collaborated with Professor Dorlag, this time as a colleague. (Dorlag later finished his distinguished career at Florida State University.[*])

McNeely spent two years in the Army producing shows, playing in the band at Fort Riley, Kansas, and then returning to Wisconsin where he earned his Ph.D. He became the youngest person to earn a full professorship at the University of Wisconsin. It was, of course, in Theatre. He taught dramatic writing, directed the school plays, and wrote scripts for television, simultaneously for eight years. He described himself as "a professor who writes, not a writer who also does a little teaching."

It was during those years, a script Jerry wrote entitled *The Joke and the Valley* was read by the secretary of famed literary agent, Flora Roberts. She had been pouring over *unsolicited* stacks of scripts for Ms. Roberts for years. Upon reading Dr. McNeely's script, she ran into Ms. Robert's office and declared, "I've finally found one!" CBS bought it, and Jerry described his first major break as "a fluke."

Breaking into the business was tough enough, but living in Madison, Wisconsin, made it even tougher. Jerry credits producer Norman Felton, executive producer of

---

* Dr. McNeely had many mentors throughout his career. He hesitated to single them out because he didn't want to offend anyone. Professor Dorlag was obviously special since he's the only one McNeely alluded to.

Dr. Kildare, for his entrée, because Felton attended the University of Iowa and understood that the vast territory between coastlines was "more than just a list of places on a Nielsen Rating Report. He refused to be frightened by my postmark."

Jerry juggled the two careers until the late 1960s when he finally left the University of Wisconsin for Southern California, becoming one of television's most prolific writers and producers. In TV's early years, he wrote for live performances on CBS's *Playhouse 90* and *Climax*. His first two plays were *The Staring Match* on *Studio One* and *Two Tests on Tuesday* on *Climax* in 1956. He created *Three for the Road*, the NBC series *Our House* starring Wilfred Brimley, and *Lucas Tanner* starring David Hartman. He created several movies made for TV, including *Sin of Innocence* and the precursor to *ER*, *Trauma Center*.

McNeely knew strong central characters were essential for a long lasting series. "For centuries, the Greek and Shakespearean plays were about life and death situations," he explained. His script *The Staring Match* won the Writers Guild of America award for the best one-hour television play of 1958, and is included in the anthology of best TV plays. McNeely explains, "Plays work well when the playwright has something to say. If what I write is meaningful to others—that's marvelous. If it is entertaining to others, that's just as wonderful. If both, well, I've had a pretty good day!"

In those productive years, Jerry befriended many colleagues as they collaborated on the final products. Robert Young (Marcus Welby), Richard Chamberlain (Dr. Kildare), and Ed Asner (Lou Grant) were among the many he called friends.

Jerry received a Golden Globe Award and Emmy nomination for his *Something for Joey* script: the story of Penn State running back John Cappelletti's Heisman Trophy award as the outstanding collegiate football player in 1973. At the awards dinner in the downtown New York City Athletic Club, Cappelletti paid tribute in his acceptance speech for the great strength and courage his little brother showed in his battle with leukemia.

When asked if he had any favorites among the more than 200 television projects, McNeely responded, "The one I was working on at the time!" When asked his most fulfilling project, McNeely responded:

> That's tough. On dozens of occasions, I came close to doing what I wanted, given the constraints of the commercial-advertising television medium. If I had to choose one, I guess it would be the *Hallmark Hall of Fame* production, *The Joke and the Valley*. I was fond of the idea but there wasn't a market at the time. Two or three years after I wrote it, George Schaefer read it, liked it, and produced it for *Hallmark*.

Looking back on his storied career, Dr. McNeely has no regrets.

I would have done everything about the same. Like any person, it's all relative. I enjoyed my work. It was part of my plan for living—hopefully excelling at some kind of art. Me and my childhood buddies always wanted to be in the movies. Little did I know I would be only behind the camera with a typewriter.

Dr. McNeely currently resides at the Motion Picture and Television Fund Retirement Center in Woodland Hills, California. I asked if he had any advice or encouragement for young writers. He responded:

I know it seems hopeless looking from the outside from Cape Girardeau (or anywhere else) to Beverly Hills, but it's easier than most aspiring writers think. For much of my career, I was the right person at the right time. Go for it. Good luck. It's great fun!

McNeely's son Joel is an Emmy award-winning composer and conductor with over one hundred film and television credits. He's toured the world with Tony Bennett, Peggy Lee, Al Green, Melissa Manchester, Chuck Mangione, Bobby Caldwell, and others. As conductor, he's worked with the London Symphony Orchestra, Seattle Symphony, Munich Philharmonic, London Philharmonic, Western Australia Symphony Orchestra, and more. For more information on Joel, go to his website: joelmcneely.com.

Gustav B. Margraf. COURTESY OF SOUTHEAST MISSOURIAN.

Gustav B. Margraf

As I was talking on the phone with Dr. Jerry McNeely, who lives in Los Angeles, California, the conversation jogged my memory of Gustav Margraf, another Cape Girardeau-n, like McNeely, who played a unique role in early television, signing many celebrities of the day to contracts in his capacity as vice president, general counsel, and head of the talent and program administration of the National Broadcasting Company in New York City.

Margraf was born into a Cape Girardeau family of seven brothers and sisters in 1915. His father worked for the Frisco Railroad. He learned at an early age that most of his success in life would be strictly on his own power. He graduated from Central High School where he was active in music, drama, and debate; played trumpet in local dance bands; was elected Student Body President; and barely missed being valedictorian of his class.

He earned his way through Southeast Missouri State College doing various jobs, including selling vacuum cleaners and working in the mailroom of the local *Southeast Missourian* newspaper, answering the after-hours phone to relay the baseball scores received through Western Union. He even crossed the Atlantic Ocean several times, playing trumpet in a dance band aboard a Cunard ocean liner. He continued his interest in drama, debate, and music in college, and was business manager and editor of the school yearbook, the *Sagamore*. With all that, he still managed to graduate in 1936 as valedictorian of his class.

At Southeast, he also met and married the former Grace Houck of Shelbina, Missouri, great niece of Louis Houck, the railroad tycoon and historian generally credited for opening up the swamps of Southeast Missouri to development. Together they raised three children: John, Jim, and Patsy.

Margraf earned his law degree with special distinction—first in his class—from Duke University in 1939, while serving as editor of the *Duke Bar Journal*, attaining Order of the Coif, and serving as a research assistant for two law professors to help pay for his tuition. He also earned scholarships all three years. His class included former President Richard Nixon.

After graduation, his law career started with the New York City law firm Cahill, Gordon, Zackry, and Reindel, who represented NBC and its parent company RCA. He rose through their ranks swiftly and was appointed head of the firm's Washington, D.C., office in 1942, where he stayed for six years. It was a busy time, with television in its infancy requiring changes in AM and FM radio applications and new affiliate agreements. He represented RCA and NBC in numerous filings and legal proceedings before Congress, the U.S. Supreme Court, Court of Appeals, Court of Claims, Tax Court, FCC, and Treasury. He was then sent back to New York, where at age 33, he became vice-president and head of the legal department of NBC, the youngest man to ever head a network legal department up to that time.

In his role as head of talent and program administration, he signed Milton Berle to the longest running contract in television history. He signed the world-renowned conductor Arturo Toscanini and Jack Benny to RCA. Among his closest friends were Bob Hope, Gary Moore, Steve Allen, Jane Meadows, Skitch Henderson, and Fay Emerson.

He left NBC to go with Reynolds Metals Company in 1955 as general solicitor. He was elected to the board in 1959, a vice president in charge of the company's mining and shipping subsidiaries in 1960, and head of the marine, geological, and power departments Wyoming and Jamaica divisions. He was elevated to general counsel in 1963. As a practicing attorney for Reynolds, he again tried cases before the U.S. Supreme Court. In1964, he was top policy director and supervisor of British Aluminum's overseas operations, and in 1965, the managing director in London. He was president and chairman of Manicouagan Power Company in Quebec, Canada, and chairman of the Aluminum Wire and Cable Company of Wales. His office was in Norfolk House, St. James Square, where General Dwight David Eisenhower planned the D-Day invasion of Europe in WWII.

An article appearing in the London Telegraph in 1965 described Gus's management style as "an iron fist with a velvet glove." On a 1967 visit to Cape Girardeau, Margraf's executive assistant, Mary Christy, described her hectic schedule this way: "There are so many companies and operations, I long ago despaired of trying to compute my relationship with each one of them. I tell people, I simply work for Mr. Margraf."

My connection with Mr. Margraf was through his brother Henry. Henry owned a jewelry and watch repair store in Cape. Our families were close, and Henry and I played golf during the summers in the Tuesday Round Robin League at the Cape Girardeau Country Club. We were partners several years, and during those hours on the golf course, we talked about a variety of subjects, including family activity.

My first wife and I took a trip to England in 1980. Henry and Gus were contemporaries of Dad, and when Henry found that I was going to London, he arranged for Mary Christy and his chauffer Eddie to pick us up at our hotel early on Palm Sunday in a Silver Phaeton Rolls Royce. We spent the entire glorious day driving up through the Shakespeare, Stratford-upon-Avon countryside. It was like a fairytale adventure with the lush green countryside, people out enjoying the spring weather, geese swimming in the ponds and streams, and lunch in a thatched roof roadside inn. Later in the afternoon, college kids were hanging out every window and balcony of the Dirty Duck Pub on the outskirts of Cambridge University.

As we approached our hotel at dusk, we felt we had been on Cloud Nine the entire day. I've thought many times of the obvious love Ms. Christy had for the entire

Margraf family to have extended that kind of courtesy to me and my wife, whom she had met only briefly on one of her trips to Cape, even though Gus had passed away ten years earlier. Throughout his extensive career, Gus never lost his love of family, Missouri, or Blue Hole Barbeque Sauce.* He was a great cook, especially Sunday brunch. His niece, Kay Ancell, remembers him as a man who "always had a twinkle in his eye, a quick wit, an infectious laugh, and was a great bridge player." Margraf died in Charlottesville, Virginia, in July of 1969, after a brief illness at the early age of 54.

---

* The Blue Hole Barbeque was a famous local restaurant that made a sauce recipe that was touted as a deep family secret. Many tried to duplicate, but never quite got it right.

The Korean War

The Korean War spawned a virtual colony of outstanding jazz and big band musicians throughout the country. Men born in the '20s got caught up in the conflict that interrupted their plans for the future, whether school, family, or work. Unlike today, everyone shared in the sacrifice. There were very few "free rides." The draft was in place, and young men had to make tough decisions about their futures. Many enlisted rather than being drafted into military service in order to have some choices as to how they would serve.

WWII spawned popularity of big band and jazz music. Still in vogue, musicians flocked to the service bands of the Korean War. There they were able to hone their craft fulltime for two to four years and come out experienced, seasoned professionals. They returned to college and on to teaching and performing. The great rise and quality of popular music and jazz in the schools of our country in the '50s, '60s, and '70s can be attributed to them.

Cape Girardeau, with its college, was no stranger to this phenomenon. Local and regional musicians enrolled to finish their education in order to get jobs and raise their families. Most received the money for their education through the G.I. Bill.

L to r: Jack Schultz (accordian), Jerry Proffer (bass), Jim Wedeking (drums), Bill Ewing (woodwinds), Jerry Abernathy (piano). COURTESY OF JACK SCHULZ.

Jack Schultz

Jack Schultz crawled into his mother's Estey parlor grand piano at age four to see how it functioned, and after 10 years of lessons from Louise Eckhardt, began playing with local bands at age 14! That began more than a decade performing with a literal colony of outstanding musicians out of Cape Girardeau in the '40s and early '50s, as both WWII and the Korean War ended.

Many area musicians amassed impressive lineages with nationally acclaimed orchestras of the big-band era, such as Bob Kelly (sax, lead scientist Los Alamos, monitored Korean nuclear development), Sonny Stevens (sax/arranger), Bill Ewing (woodwinds, Billy Butterfield), Alan Baker (drums), Jerry Abernathy (piano, Tommy Dorsey), Jerry Proffer (bass), Jim Wedeking (drums), Bob Swink (trumpet), Tony Carosello (trumpet), Julian Porritt (bass, "Mr. Music Man," Hawaii), Martin Johnston (trumpet, Glenn Miller), Fred Goodwin (trombone), Butch Eggimann (piano), Oz Ramsey (drums, "Mr. Music Man," San Francisco), Charley Pendleton (trombone/arranger, Bell Telephone Orchestra, NYC), Bill Brandt (trumpet, Les Brown), Elwood Fisher, (sax), and Bill Crass (trumpet).

As acting Dean of Cornell College in Iowa, both Schultz and Cornell President Dr. Winston Ehrmann were featured in a 1966 *Look* Magazine article entitled "The Case for the Small College," where they promoted the fact that schools like Southeast had an abundance of truly talented, musically gifted sophisticates who could hold their own with anyone in the country.

Jack's older brother Bob entered college at the age of 15. Jack said, "He taught me the basics of boogie-woogie when I was 10. Jess Stacy even gave me a couple of lessons when he was back for medical treatment. By the way, Jess's son, Fred, earned a doctoral degree from Washington University and was principal trumpeter for the St. Louis Symphony."

Bob's first band included boys who would do remarkable things: Earl Johnson (piano, radiologist), Brandon Mehrle (drummer, Music Director of the UCLA Graduate School), Dan Cotner (trombone, dentist), LaVell Bess (reed player, D.D.S.), Bill Shivelbine (sax, chemical engineer), Charles McKinnis (trombone, engineer/lawyer), Bill Brandt (trumpet, Les Brown Band), Sonny Slinkard (sax, TV executive), and Jimmy Thompson (vocalist, Dick Jergens Orchestra).

In high school these budding musicians listened to the greats of the time and did their best to emulate their styles, bands like Les Brown, Tommy Dorsey, Ted Heath, Count Basie, Bob Crosby and the Bobcats, and others. "I copied George Shearing and Errol Garner's piano styles," Jack explained. "Ironically, they both credited Jess Stacy's style as a major formative influence in their unique styles."

As other veterans returned from the war, they had their objectives well formulated.

Herb Suedekum, Red Weiser, Bob Rosenquist, Bruce Goodwin, Bill, Dick, and John Brandt, Homer Gilbert, Bill French, and the bands of The Blue Rhythm Boys, Martin Johnston, Don McNeely, Bill Ewing, Pete Propst, Jack Kinder, Elmo Donze, Frankie Ziebold, and others, provided a spectrum of dance choices. Even drummer George Josse played with Oscar Pettiford, and was the first cameraman for the *Kukla, Fran and Ollie* television show.

Herb Suedekum's nine-piece orchestra was the staple on Saturday nights at the Purple Crackle Supper Club in East Cape for almost twenty years. Members included Suedekum (bass), Buddy Vaughn (piano), George Josse (drums), Bill Brandt and Homer Gilbert (trumpet), Tom Wright (trombone), and John Quinn, Bill French, and Joe James, Jr. (sax). After Suedekum retired, Bill French fronted the orchestra for the remaining years. Phil Olson (trumpet), Gene Stiman (trombone), and Jimmy Leggett (piano), joined the band during the French years. Bill Brandt's trio ruled on Friday nights, and Jack Stalcup's Orchestra on Sunday nights.

The Crackle and Colony Club were two of the top midwestern night clubs in the country. They both featured American and Chinese cuisine, live dancing, big-name entertainment, and gambling out back in their small casinos.

Schultz says Martin Johnston deserves special recognition for the several outstanding bands he established. "Martin was a showman. He closely looked like the great Paul Whiteman and was quite an entertainer. In addition, he was a great trumpet player. He played with Alvino Rey his entire stint in the U.S. Navy, and also played lead-trumpet for the Glenn Miller Orchestra under the direction of Tex Beneke. One of the first outstanding local groups was a Johnston band featuring Sonny Stevens (sax), Buddy Vaughn (piano), Hal Campbell (bass), Paul Trovillion (trombone), and Hal McLaughlin (drums)."

Jack pays tribute to pianists of the time this way:

The stellar accomplishments of Jess Stacy partially obscured some of the pianists here in Cape. Tommy Chambers, a Central graduate, was music director for Warner Brothers Studio for over 20 years and a favorite accompanist of Frank Sinatra and Fred Astaire. Jerry Abernathy played like Earl Hines, replaced Henry Mancini in Tex Beneke's Orchestra, worked with Joe Bushkin and Buddy Ebsen, and is still recognized as one of the top jazz pianists in Southern California. Bruce Goodwin was also outstanding. Billy Simon played in a U.S. Air Corps Band, was a studio musician in Oklahoma City, composed the school song for Colorado University, and ultimately chaired the Department of Music at Bloomfield College in New Jersey. Clyde Ridge eventually migrated to New York City where he made piano rolls for the Aeolian Music Corporation and became a noted freelance jazz performer.

64

Bill Ewing was a truly great woodwind player. He was my junior high band instructor, and I performed with him for many years. While there's not room to do him justice, Schultz has a great story about Bill:

> The first time Ewing met Woody Herman was at the Colony Club in East Cape. He was introduced by Dr. Ent, a general surgeon and fine jazz baritone sax player from Cairo, Illinois. Ent and Ewing were life-long friends, and Ent had arranged for Bill to play for Herman. Bill began squeaking, missing notes, and skipping meter. Ent went ballistic, calling Ewing a decadent S.O.B., losing his medical composure in the process. To calm Ent in front of Woody, Ewing proceeded to play superb musical choruses on "Back Home in Indiana," never repeating himself, demonstrating the precocious mastery of his elegant capacity. Herman broke into uncontrollable laughter, hugging Ewing. He gave Bill his private phone number and told him to call collect if he ever wanted to join his "Thundering Herd."

Jack Schultz is a great jazz pianist/arranger. More of his attributes include his distinguished military career in the U.S. Army Band, playing on cruise ships, performing with "name" groups, appearances at Midwest Jazz Festivals, a distinguished career in education ending as Assistant Dean and Registrar of the Washington University Medical School, and still an active performer in the St. Louis Metro area. But he is such an encyclopedia of all these amazing '50s jazz musicians, there isn't space to do him or most of them justice. I'm indebted to him for helping chronicle these two decades of great jazz and big band musicians here in Cape Girardeau.

Schultz has a vociferous appetite for living and a great sense of humor. He's never at a loss for words. He wrote me a two-and-a-half page classic treatise on a subject close to the hearts of many men who have tried their luck at dancing in an attempt to please their wives, entitled "Managing a March Through a Minefield: The Dance Floor!"

It's hard to know how to end these chapters, but I'm going to have some fun with Jack. There are many funny situations in music, as in life. Here, in Jack's own words, is how he describes his acumen in sight-reading music:

> There were additional sources of trauma related to high school proms held in late spring in rancid gyms. The flower-laden facilities were enhanced by the wondrous aroma of over-priced corsages. All too frequently I would be side-tracked by an aspiring young lady of the senior class who was to sing her advanced senior recital piece she had been struggling with for several years. The complex piano accompaniment would be presented to me, which initiated a gastric reflux syndrome as I endeavored to communicate that I mostly

learned to play by ear. My constant companion in those days, Fred Goodwin, would go into uncontrollable laughter as he would listen to my chord structures and progressions as I struggled to do her rendition justice.

I bet he did.

L to r: Martin Johnston (trumpet), Billy Strain (piano), Don McNeely (sax), Sonny Stevens (sax), Alfred "Rooster" Jones (drums), Champ Gilliland (guitar). COURTESY OF JACK SCHULTZ.

Julian (Kaye) Porritt.

Julian (Kaye) Porritt

Julian Porritt, a multi-instrumentalist, began his love of big band music at the age of six here in Cape Girardeau. His first musical engagement at 16 began a lifetime voyage that would eventually take him to Hawaii, where he and his band were recognized as the premier orchestra throughout the Islands under the name of Julian Kaye and His Orchestra. It's no wonder, with his many appearances at the Hyatt Regency, Maui/Honolulu; Honolulu Mayor's Symphony Ball; Junior League Ball, Honolulu; Royal Hawaiian Hotel; Kahala Hilton, Honolulu; Kapalua Bay Hotel, Honolulu; Bayan Court Ala Mauna Hotel, Honolulu; Kuilima Hotel, Maui; Manna Lani Hotel, Honolulu; and other top hotels like the Fairmont, Mark Hopkins, and St. Francis in San Francisco, and even appearances at the Monterey Jazz Festival.

How about his performances with George Shearing, Johnny Mathis, Larry Elgart, Helen O'Connell, Red Skelton, Anita O'Day, Jess Stacy, Sammy Davis, Jr., Arthur Fiedler, Dizzy Gillespie, Andre Previn, Al Hirt, and more? I have a pretty good pedigree with my orchestra, but I obviously have a lo-o-ong way to go!

Julian grew up in Cape where his father was an agent for Metropolitan Life Insurance Company. His sister Barbara remembers, "We always had music in our home. Dad played sax and Mom played piano. Many, many evenings, our home was full of musicians and great big band music. Oh, the jam sessions were great fun!"

Julian graduated from Central High School and Southeast Missouri State, then enlisted and attended the Navy School of Music in Washington, D.C. He served in Japan and other countries, and even did a stint in the Navy Air Corps. After the war, he moved his family to Santa Rosa, California, for several years, and then on to Honolulu where he taught school for a year, opened a music store briefly, and then became a full-time big band leader for many years.

In his final years, he returned to Cape briefly where we reminisced about the glory days of the big bands. He reminded me of the old musicians' joke, "You know how to make a million dollars playing big band music? You start with two million!"

My orchestra music arranger, John Quinn, befriended Julian and assisted him here and at his final destination, Branson. He died at age 70 there, and John helped his family dispose of his many antique and expensive musical instruments and equipment to local schools and Southeast Missouri State University here in Cape Girardeau.

In addition, Quinn has catalogued Porritt's personal, voluminous music library of over 1,000 arrangements; 250 original Anson Weeks Orchestra arrangements; 200 South Coast Music Enterprises, San Carlos, complete big band arrangements; and a treasure trove of other big band arrangements awaiting a proper home to be decided by Quinn.

Major university departments of music would relish this personal history of the big-band era. Most likely, the collection will end up in the music department of Southeast at the River Campus where the Vincentians established a school of higher learning in 1843, a fitting tribute to Julian Porritt.

Jerry Abernathy.

Jerry Abernathy

Jerry Abernathy is a world-class jazz pianist currently performing in and around the San Diego/Los Angeles California region. His legendary technique is still held in awe by local musicians who were fortunate enough to perform with him in the few short years he was here in Cape Girardeau. When I asked him to explain his fast fingering, he answered, "My first impressions of pianist techniques, other than my father and mother, were from radio. I am self-taught. When asked why I use certain fingerings for improvisation, I quote Errol Garner and/or Art Tatum to wit: 'I use whatever method and moves that take me where I want to go.'"

Abernathy was born in Bernie, Missouri, in 1928, and showed promise as a youngster. His mother and grandmother played piano laboriously by note. "My father played by ear and showed me chord symbols in pop tunes," he remembered. "They agreed a neighbor lady should teach me. After two visits, she informed my family it was hopeless. 'He's a stubborn Missouri mule who'll do it his way or never!' I was 7."

He first came to Cape Girardeau in 1945 to attend Southeast, after graduation from Dexter High School, but quickly entered the Army Specialty Engineering Program and Infantry Officer Candidate School, Fort Benning, Georgia, where after two years, he landed in Sixth Army Headquarters, Presidio, San Francisco. "There I learned from seasoned, talented jazz musicians with studio chops and much experience in all phases of Bebop and Big Band."

He came back home in 1947 and again enrolled in Southeast under the G.I. Bill. He performed with some of the better jazz musicians in the area at that time, like Bill Ewing, Gardner Hitchcock, Jim Wedekind, Jerry Proffer, Skip Fosset, and others, in Southern Illinois gambling clubs like the Purple Crackle and Colony Club. But Jerry needed more, so he joined traveling bands. He explains:

> Remember this: the 1947-1954 period was the fading out of big bands, territorial bands, and club gigs. It was difficult to practice and perform your craft without locations to learn on the job. I branched out with short tours with orchestras such as Jules Herman, Bob Leighton, Vick Masters Quintet, Tex Beneke, Glenn Miller, and then back to Cape for another term in college. While with Tex Beneke, I asked, "Why did your piano-man bail on this good gig?" They said, "Henry Mancini went to Hollywood to get rich and famous." Guess what?

Back off the road, Abernathy taught at Franklin Elementary School in Cape for three years, and then moved his family to San Diego, California, to continue his involvement with jazz, performing with the greats at clubs and jazz festivals. His piano acumen has taken him to San Diego, San Francisco, La Jolla, the Sands Hotel in Las Vegas, Del Coronado Hotel, Sun Valley, Canada, Mexico, and more. His chronology of stars is long; here's an abbreviated list: Nat King Cole, Harry "Sweets" Edison, Danny Thomas, Shecky Green, Ray Brown, Herb Ellis, Joe Bushkin, Buddy Ebsen, Ray Brown, Mundell Lowe, Jack Sheldon, Tom Scott, Bill Watrous, and George Shearing.

Most of these men are the giants of jazz, a class well above the rest, and Jerry Abernathy is one of them. Not bad for a boy from Bernie who cut his teeth performing here in Cape, at Southeast, and across the river in the 1950s.

Oz Ramsey. COURTESY OF SUZANNE RAMSEY.

Oz Ramsey

Oz Ramsey rose from humble beginnings in East Prairie, Missouri, in 1926, to become San Francisco, California's premier big band leader for more than twenty years, just as Julian Porritt had become the premier band leader in Hawaii. Oz graduated from Anna-Jonesboro High School in Illinois and attended Southeast, where he played many percussion instruments with many of the outstanding musicians in this book in Southeast Missouri and Southern Illinois clubs.

He headed west from Cape and attended San Francisco State University where he graduated with a B.A. in music education. He joined the 573rd Air Force Band while serving four years in Korea. Upon his return from the war, he married fellow East Prairie native Earlene Ramsey in 1960, moved to Berkeley, California, and later settled in Lafayette, California, where they raised their three children. Oz taught music during the day in the Walnut Creek School District, and as a member of the musicians' union, played drums in various jazz combos at night.

Ramsey was an outstanding percussionist, multi-instrumentalist, avid record collector, audiophile, big band leader, and of course, jazz and music enthusiast. He led Oz Ramsey's Bay Area Big Band headquartered in Lafayette. Oz passed away in February of 2010. His big band is still performing and can be found and heard at: www.bayareabigband.com or just google Oz Ramsey.

Bob Swink.

Bob Swink

Bob Swink grew up in Cape Girardeau surrounded by many good jazz musicians. William Shivelbine was his first teacher at Franklin School. "He was firm, but right on. He'd admonish us, 'That's not fly sh— behind that note; that's a dot and you know what to do with it!' Fred Goodwin and I used to laugh a lot when other students would make mistakes and reap Mr. Shivelbine's wrath."

Swink said important music mentors, besides his parents, were O.L. Wilcox, Frieda Reick, and Glen Jacobs. After graduation from high school in 1948, Swink entered Southeast and played in the band and orchestra under Fritz Heim and Ms. Reick. About this time he was invited to join the Municipal Band under the leadership of Mr. Shivelbine and Elmore Kassel (my uncle), and also began playing in the dance bands of Tony Shearer, Pete Propst, and on the road with Thurlough Webb.

The Korean War had progressed to the point that Bob had to enlist or get drafted. "I chose to enlist in the Air Force rather than become a 'ground pounder,'" Swink laughed. After basic training in Texas, he was assigned to Holloman Air Force Base at Alamogordo, New Mexico:

> Upon my arrival, I immediately found that Hal Campbell, who had lived on Perry Avenue several blocks from my home, was a member of the 680th military band and leader of its big dance band. Hardly before I could unpack, he auditioned me and I was to play the 2nd trumpet book in the dance band. Before I had been issued a pass, we were on a plane headed to Albuquerque for a series of gigs!

Swink graduated from Southeast in 1956, and accepted a job in management with Montgomery Ward which took him to many states and communities where he continued performing for concerts, musicals, and dance gigs. He retired to Virginia Beach, where there are many venues to continue playing swing-dance music. The Melody Makers, a six-piece band, has been together for over twenty years, performing throughout the area. They played for the Grand Ball of the first International Korean War Veterans reunion and again for the Ball during the dedication of the National Monument in Washington, D.C.

In one of our conversations, Bob described his feelings on performing music; they are as poignant as I've ever heard. I know most musicians would concur: "To me, music is something that is born in you. It is as close to me as my love for my family and special people in my life. I am so thankful for this blessing. I'm thankful for the opportunity to pursue the art."

Dick Goodwin. COURTESY OF TIM DONAHUE.

Dick Goodwin

Richard Gordon Goodwin turned a one-dollar gig into an amazing music career as an American Society of Composers, Authors and Publishers symphonic composer, jazz trumpeter, big-band and quintet leader, arranger, owner of G.E.M. recording studio, Yamaha artist, Distinguished Professor Emeritus at the University of South Carolina, and the shining star of a unique musical family from Cape Girardeau that includes outstanding trumpeters, trombonists, pianists, bassists, vocalists, and music educators.

It all happened when Dick was to sing at the Cape Girardeau Municipal Band concert in Courthouse Park back in the mid '40s when he was about 4 years old. He sang "Some Sunday Morning, We'll Walk Down the Aisle." His parents were petrified that he hadn't bothered to learn all the lyrics, but he somehow sailed through the performance. The next day a man gave him a check for $1.00. He had his folks immediately open a bank account. As Dick remembered, "I got paid for singing the song even though I didn't even know all the words! From that day forward, I was hooked on music."

The Goodwin clan inherited a frontier quality that served them well in making their way in the world. Dick's grandfather Fred was an avid hunter. He could "hit a shot on the wing." As an amateur boxer, he was reported as being tough as a pine knot, even sparring with lightweight champion, Benny Leonard. He was a conductor for the Illinois Central Railroad. He admonished his family, "Never get between hobos and the open door in a railcar." He became a tailor and, in later years, a traveling salesman of women's ready-to-wear clothing.

Fred also possessed an aptitude for music. It was not uncommon for vocal music to flow at family reunions. He had a good ear, and his tenor voice easily blended with his three sons' voices in barbershop harmonies. In the family-friendly atmosphere, they would sing and sing. They were so good, they made each other cry. Dick's cousin Fred (recently deceased) enlightened, "They were really good, but the crying may have been induced by the whiskey consumed at those family gatherings!"

Tenacious productivity at work and musical acumen at home enabled the Goodwins to be successful in business and the arts. Dick's dad Gordon, who he is named after, was manager of a clothing manufacturing plant and played string bass and tuba. His mother Kathleen played piano and sang. His Uncle Van owned a Lincoln-Mercury dealership in Cape and played violin. His Uncle Bruce was supervisor in a cement plant, played in a dance band, and was a jazz pianist. One sister, Julianna, is an artist in Alaska. The other, Martha, is a retired school psychologist in Texas. Both sang and played instruments. Martha has two daughters (Katy and Amy), who are accomplished instrumentalists and singers. His first cousin Jeanne is a retired piano and choral teacher (with perfect pitch). His first cousin Fred was a jazz trombonist, bassist, and retired Dean of Humanities at Southeast Missouri State University in Cape Girardeau. Fred's son Mark is a fine trombone player and teacher, and Dick's daughter Gradi is an oboist and music teacher.

It's no surprise Dick inherited the family traits of intellect, tenacity, and talent. He had decided music would be his life's work, but an expectant wife and child briefly derailed his plans. Short on money, with a family to feed, he enlisted in the Coast Guard and substituted as director of the Guard's small band. Shortly thereafter, the director's job opened, and he tested first out of seven applicants in a very demanding two-and-one-half-day regimen for the position which he held for his entire four-year hitch.

He then enrolled in the University of Texas where he studied with J. Clifton Williams and Kent Kennan. (During our short time together in December of 2010, I discovered we both played Kent Kennan's Trumpet Sonata for our senior recitals; Dick at Texas, and me at Southeast.)

He described his Texas experience this way:

> What attracted me were orchestration, composition, and recording. As I was graduating in music theory and composition from the University of Texas, the the faculty encouraged me to finish the doctorate and take a teaching position there. I found I loved teaching, and I've had a successful run of it. But I now have the time and energy to concentrate full-time on my first love—composing, arranging, producing, and performing.

Goodwin taught music composition and theory at the University of Texas for over ten years and ran the jazz program, which he initiated. In 1973, he moved to the University of South Carolina, where he flourished as conductor of the university orchestra and head of the theory-composition area. His accolades include USC's prestigious Education Foundation Award, 2001 Elizabeth O'Neill Verner Individual Artist and Education Award (the highest honor awarded in the arts by the State of South Carolina), and numerous writer awards from ASCAP.

Goodwin has a great love of jazz. The Dick Goodwin Big Band and The Dick Goodwin Quintet perform throughout the U.S. and many foreign countries. He's played trumpet, string bass, and keyboards with many of the greats including Natalie Cole, Bob Hope, Johnny Mathis, Henry Mancini, Billy Taylor, Toni Tennille, Jimmie Durante, Isaac Hayes, Gregory Hines, Jerry Mulligan, Marian McPartland, Carol Burnett, and even the Ringling Brothers Circus.

Dick especially remembers two events. First was the honorary doctorate bestowed on trumpeter Clark Terry when Dick was at South Carolina. Terry, a staple on Johnny Carson's *Tonight Show*, performed "One Foot in the Gutter" the night of his hooding.

The other was when Goodwin was at the University of Texas trying to locate the great bebop trumpeter Dizzy Gillespie for an appearance at their annual jazz festival for university bands. Dick called everywhere, only to be told Dizzy was dead. Persistence paid off when Dick finally found him in Europe. Dizzy agreed to attend for a $350 fee plus travel expenses, even though his regular fee was five or six times that amount.

Two celebrities he particularly enjoyed working with were Bob Hope and Carol Burnett. Normally the "big name artists" just show up for a quick sound check, but Hope, always the perfectionist, continued to work on his timing with Goodwin during rehearsals for his show. "Carol Burnett was one of the nicest celebrities I've ever had the pleasure of working with," remembered Goodwin. "Harry Zimmerman was Burnett's music director/conductor and was on the podium for that concert." (Several years later, a classmate of Goodwin's at Cape Central, Bob Sisco, joined Zimmerman as a staff arranger for the Burnett show. Sisco's career is documented in a later chapter.)

It's hard to categorize Goodwin or his many genres. Besides performing, producing, recording, and teaching, he's written hundreds of works from jingle to opera, jazz band to symphony orchestra. And he does have a family life. His wife Winifred is an outstanding pianist, the principle keyboardist with the South Carolina Philharmonic, and staff pianist at the University of South Carolina. Daughter Gradi Evans is coordinator of fine arts at a private school in the San Antonio area. Son Richard is on the medical school faculty at the University of South Carolina and plays guitar. The Goodwin's have five grandchildren, three of whom are very active in music. So when I asked him what he was most proud of, he answered, "My two kids."

Dick's cousin (Fred's widow) Virginia, a piano teacher, describes Dick as "a very soft spoken, very modest person, with a sly sense of humor." Cousin Fred, on the other hand, described him, in a word, "Precocious. He can do anything!" When contemplating Dick's accomplishments, Fred exhorted, "Holy smoke, when does he sleep?" At one point, the South Carolina Jazz Society's newsletter, *The Cat's Meow*, stated: "Dick does so many things so well, maybe we ought to ask him to run for Congress!"

Dick's cousin Fred died December 5, 2010. Dick flew in from South Carolina for the service, and the next day we had a chance to spend the morning together touring Southeast's new River Campus. Dick remembered his Uncle Bruce, a fine piano player, as a major influence, along with cousin Fred Goodwin and Freck Shivelbine. "Uncle Bruce introduced me to many alternate jazz chords, and Fred and Freck taught me to listen more carefully to the likes of Jerry Mulligan (baritone sax) and Bob Brookmeyer (valve trombone)."

During our discussions, Dick remembered an evening in Academic Hall auditorium on the Southeast Missouri State College campus when he was very young. The

Sauter-Finnegan Orchestra performed their eclectic style of concert jazz to a packed house and a young fledgling musician. "I was blown away," Dick concedes. "They were spectacular! I was also fortunate to have mentors like Bill Ewing and Tony Carosello. They gave me the opportunity to perform in adult combos. While a band director in the Coast Guard in Cape May, New Jersey, I had the opportunity to hear and learn from the jazz greats, the big bands of the time, and of course, some magnificent symphonic performances in Atlantic City, Philadelphia, and New York City."

Wherever Goodwin performs, the superlatives flow, like "a jazz explosion," "superb technique and fine wit." In Venezuela, his jazz band was reviewed as "professional musicians of the highest caliber." In Guatemala, a newspaper said they were "Smash, Socko, Boffo." They were called "a true highlight" in Ecuador, and in Peru, they elicited "thunderous applause accompanied by shouting for more" (and etc.). One reviewer even said of Dick's Quintet, "They have eleven music degrees between them, but it doesn't seem to hurt their playing at all!"

His prolific volume of classical compositions, commissions, education seminars, conducting stints, and appearances at jazz festivals all receive similar accolades. Dick illuminates:

> I used to wear two hats: Gordon Goodwin for my classical work, and Dick Goodwin for the after-hours jazz character. We found while touring extensively in Latin America, audiences have many expectations when they attend a jazz concert. So we started programming a wide variety of styles, everything from Dixieland to our own compositions. We have carried that practice with us in our recordings, and have found that even hard-core jazz fans will embrace a lot of different kinds of music—as long as it is honest and played well.

In retirement from his university position, Goodwin is nowhere near the end of his musical journey. He says he hasn't given much thought of what to do next: "I'm too busy composing music and performing. Someday I might take the time to catalogue all my compositions, but I'm still in the writing mode at this point and plan to continue for some time. I seem to always have a number of commissions for classical pieces and a pile of arranging projects on my docket."

Goodwin maintains a hectic performance schedule. Always humble, Goodwin said, "At times I felt I stumbled from one position to another. But I seemed prepared enough to land the job." In one of our last conversations in preparing for this book, being a trumpet player myself who always admired Dick, I especially enjoyed his final comment before hanging up the phone: "Right now I'd better go do some lip slurs and long tones. I'm determined to be a better trumpet player!"

For more information on his activities, visit his web site at www.goodwinmusic. com.

Bob Dolle.

Bob Dolle

Bob Dolle has parlayed his grandfather's 130-year-old, $9 Sears & Roebuck catalogue fiddle into a lifetime of performing Western Swing music and into his induction into the Texas Western Swing Hall of Fame in San Marcos, Texas; the Pioneers of Western Swing Society Hall of Fame in Seattle, Washington; the Western Swing Society of the Southwest in Oklahoma City, Oklahoma; and the Western Swing Music Society Hall of Fame in Sacramento, California. Not bad for a self-taught musician who started playing chords on the piano at age 6!

Bob's older sister, Dorothy, would come home from piano lessons and practice her new songs. Bob would then sit at the piano, after listening to her, and repeat the songs without the music. "It used to make Dorothy mad as hell that I didn't need the lessons," laughed Bob.

Bob's first dance job was with the "Pop" Crites Band in Illmo, Missouri (about 5 miles south of Cape), at the age of 14. Zeb & Mandy was a duo from Arkansas that performed at a dive down at Illmo. Bob's dad would occasionally drive him down to "sit in" for a few tunes. They liked his piano style and recommended him to a popular Arkansas group led by Johnny Johnson. "I'll never forget when he came to our house to audition me," Bob recalled. "He was driving a '38 Olds." Johnson hired him, and Bob began playing piano, accordion, and fiddle professionally at the age of 16! His dad drove him back and forth from Cape Girardeau to Blytheville, Arkansas, appearing daily on radio station KLCN with Johnny Johnson and the Sandy Mountain Boys.

Bob formed his own 4-piece band in 1946 with himself on piano, Ralph Pickens on sax, Si Perkins on trumpet, and Don McLaughlin on drums. Over the years he attracted some of our best area musicians, including guitarists Jim Ham, Jerry Richardson, the great "Diz" Conrad, bassists Glen Kirchoff and Dave Green, and drummer Brad Lyle.

Bob's band played primarily for dances and concerts throughout Southeast Missouri, Southern Illinois, and Western Kentucky for several decades. They shared the "bill" in Cape with Mike Smith and the Runaways for many years for Fireman's Balls and Parade of Bands galas. They played the popular Travelers Protective Association (TPA) annual dance for 12 years. They even performed with Loretta Lynn. The band's style was influenced by swing, country, pop, jazz, big band, Dixieland, mountain music, and breakdowns—the iconic collection known as Western Swing.

Bob married his childhood sweetheart, Virginia, over 60 years ago in 1950. They have two talented children and four talented grandchildren who have excelled in music performance.

Their son Gary played tenor sax and violin; toured Europe with the Central High School jazz band on tenor sax; played guitar in Sing-Out Cape (where he met his future wife Patti) and the Southeast Missouri State University jazz band and musicals; tenor sax in the Golden Eagles marching band, concert, and jazz bands; received degrees in math and music, with distinction; and currently plays guitar, bass, and saxophone in his church's contemporary worship service. Gary's son Kris played in Lindbergh High School's concert, symphonic, and jazz bands; received Best New Member and Best Musician in the Lindbergh marching band; and was soloist in the Mizzou Jazz Ensemble. Gary's daughter Rebecca was soloist in school choirs, show choirs, talent shows, music reviews, and musicals in Texas and St. Louis; has recorded CD's; was finalist for the Matinee Idol Talent Search in Columbia, Missouri; and was selected from 1,200 in the first Branson Idol competition.

Bob's daughter Sherri played piano, flute, and piccolo in school. She is a teacher, and she and her husband David have two 11-year-old twins, Caleb and Clayton, who, in the Dolle tradition, take piano and violin lessons. Sherri sums up the family's sentiments when she says, "Thanks, Dad, for bringing music into our homes."

Since retirement in 1993, Bob and Virginia have a new musical life about half of the year as a result of discovering the Rio Grande Valley in their motor-home travels. Over one million "Winter Texans" converge on a 65 mile strip between Mission and Brownsville, Texas. In that 65 miles there are over 600 RV Parks! Bob and Virginia's park alone has over 1,000 spaces!

"We travel all over the country for about six months out of the year. The only state we haven't driven to is Hawaii! We flew there," Bob laughs.

Virginia recalled, "One day we stopped for gas when Bob heard of a cheaper place down the road and took off, leaving me and our dog Muffin. The gas station attendant asked what's going on, and I replied, 'Oh, he'll be back when he discovers Muffin is missing!'"

Bob plays keyboard and fiddle with the Texas Travelers, Village Dixie Band—a Western Swing band on the Rio Grande River—and for the past two summers with the Fun Valley Playboys at the Fun Valley RV Resort in South Fork, Colorado. He's performed at Turkey, Texas, for Bob Wills day; San Marcos, Texas, for the Texas Natural and Western Swing Festival; Tulsa, Oklahoma, at the famous Cain's Ballroom; Monterrey, Mexico, at the Hotel Rio; Canyon, Texas, at West Texas A&M University; Mena, Arkansas, for the annual Mena Western Swing gathering; Wichita Falls, Texas, for the Legends of Western Swing Music Festival; and Snyder, Texas, for the West Texas Swing Music Festival.

Bob is a member of the six-state Family Motor Coach Association and has entertained at many of their national rallies. There are 500 to 1,000 or more in attendance for these performances. In fact, most all of his performances are for many hundreds of Western Swing lovers. In addition, Bob and Virginia bring 1,000 visitors to Cape Girardeau each year for "Showcase" (a three-day Western Swing show) for the Western Swing Music Society of the Southwest, the world's largest society of Western Swing music. Bob is a director and member of their Hall of Fame.

Bob and Virginia Dolle.

In addition, Bob performs with Bob Cobb and the Swingin' Ambassadors, the Chuck Hayes Band, and the Western Swing Music Society of the Southwest Band. He takes several Hall of Fame members to Branson each July for a show at the ABC RV Park. And when in Cape Girardeau, he gives charity performances for nursing homes and our local Veterans home several times a week. His current Cape band includes Gene King, Bob Schwepker, and Gerald Kempher on guitars, Alice Koeppel on bass, and Bob on keyboards. The local *Southeast Missourian* newspaper did a special on Bob and his musical travels in November 2003. The article's appropriate headline read, "It's So Nice To Have You Back In Town."

His 2009 schedule had him leaving Cape after the 4th of July and performing:

> July 15–18 Oklahoma City: Western Swing Music Society of the
>   Southwest Hall of Fame
> July 19–29 South Fork, Colorado: Fun Valley RV Resort
> August 18 Goshen, Indiana: International RV Rally
> August 9–22: Mackinaw Island
> September–December: Cape Girardeau
> January–March: back to Texas

One of his biggest thrills was to perform with the original Bob Wills Texas Playboys. Bob feels fortunate to be able to continue to do what he loves to do. He tells young musicians, "Don't do like I did. Learn to read music, and practice hard." As Bob reflects over it all, he says, "I never get tired of traveling and performing. Virginia and I are going to continue as long as we're able. I thank God all my dreams have come true."

Bob Sisco. COURTESY OF BILLY SISCO.

Bob Sisco

My buddy Bob Sisco was like the Energizer Bunny, always wound up. He was in a hurry to get somewhere, and he did. In just a couple of years, he went from being a college sophomore to arranging musical scores for the popular Gary Moore and Carol Burnett weekly television shows, and for many "stars" of the day. As Don McNeely relates, "Bob was a musical prodigy. The old folks used to call exceptionally talented and bright people like Bob, *gifted*."

The Sisco family was devoutly religious. Sacred music was their forte. Bob's father was an accomplished, self-taught guitarist. Mrs. Sisco sang and played piano. Bob's younger brother Billy said his father "could play any stringed instrument."

In their younger years, Mr. and Mrs. Sisco traveled around the country with evangelist Reverend Muncie, providing music for tent shows. Their "Evening Light Trio" even had a thirty-minute Sunday morning live show on local country radio station KGMO.

In those days, their life revolved around Reverend A.J. Johnson's Evening Light Pentecostal Church on Mill Hill. The Siscos raised their children in that enviroment. The whole family performed for the services: Bob on alto saxophone, Billy on string bass, and Dad, a Gibson L5 guitar (Bill still has it). Mrs. Sisco played piano.

At age 14, Billy didn't know how to play bass. His dad would hold up his index finger for the one chord, second finger for the four chord, third finger for the five chord, and back to one. If there was an unusual chord, "Dad would make a zero with his thumb and index finger," Bill explained. "I just kept watching his fingers."

Bill remembered Bob banging pots and pans to the rhythm of songs on the radio at age four and five. In 1954, when Hirsch Broadcasting Company began broadcasting its CBS television signal (KFVS), "Mom and Dad couldn't decide whether to buy a piano or a television set, because they couldn't afford both," Bill related. "I don't know how they did it, but they bought both."

Bob began writing good musical arrangements for dance bands during his freshman and sophomore years in high school. Bill recalled, "Bob even made up four book reports on four fictitious books by four fictitious authors, and got A's on all of them, even though they didn't exist!"

When Don McNeely disbanded his orchestra in 1955, Bob purchased McNeely's music, stands, sound equipment, etc., and formed his own band. He augmented the McNeely book with his own arrangements. His band had four saxophones; two trumpets; a rhythm section consisting of a piano, string bass, and drums; and a girl vocalist. By 1956, he was writing original music and arranging "jingles" for radio and television commercials. I joined his orchestra as a high school junior in 1958. We performed throughout Southeast Missouri, Southern Illinois, Western Kentucky, and on *The Morning Show* on KFVS–TV.

We recorded many commercials for Versatile Television Productions, a subsidiary of KFVS–TV, in those high school days. I specifically remember Gristo Feeds, Blue Bell Meats, and Tuff-Nut jeans. Bob cranked out those arrangements prodigiously. Dr. Richard Moore remembers Bob as "the most single purpose-driven person I ever knew. As a kid, Bob could write complex musical arrangements like most people write simple letters. He was writing them for his band before he could even drive a car."

Bob spent two years studying music at Southeast Missouri State College in Cape. He had become restless with school when, in 1960, he ran across an ad in *DownBeat* magazine, for an orchestration position at the Westlake School of Modern Music in Laguna Beach, California. The school had a "who's who" of jazz alumni, including Bill Holman, Bill Perkins, Bud Brisbois, and Henry Mancini.

He called the school, miraculously passed a phone interview on the spot, and immediately left for California for an onsight interview. He was accepted as both an instructor and student, with no formal degree. While this is an unbelievable story to some, it didn't surprise us, because we had been performing his great dance band arrangements for years.

One would think with their conservative environment, Bob's parents would object to his dream of the secular entertainment world. Bill says it was just the opposite. He remembers, as if it were yesterday, his Dad saying to Bob, "There is only one Chet Atkins. Go find your own style."

Dr. Moore related a story about Bob's unique arranging ability. "As the rest of us were setting up for a dance one night, Bob wrote an arrangement of 'Laura' for the 9-piece band in about 30 minutes. During the first two intermissions he copied the parts, and we played the chart during the last set!"

As we laughed, I was reminded of a similar event. Bob and I were at the Colony Club listening to the great trombonist (of "Night Train" fame) Buddy Morrow's big band. They played a unique vocal arrangement of "Look Down That Lonesome Road." We liked it so much, Bob pulled out his manuscript book (which he carried with him all the time), I sang the riffs to him several times as he wrote, and he finished the arrangement also in about 30 minutes. When Bob left for California, I purchased his arrangements, stands, and equipment, maintaining the continuity of the Champ Gilliland, Martin Johnston, Don McNeely, and Bob Sisco orchestras.

The Westlake School of Jazz closed shortly after Bob arrived, so he enrolled in the Los Angeles Conservatory of Music and continued to study, arrange, and perform. He became the music director-conductor-arranger for Rusty Warren of "Knocker's Up" fame, and for the great organist and Decca recording artist, Earl Grant. His two years with Grant were critical. "I learned more about show biz from Earl than from anyone," Bob recalled. Bob's first arrangement for Earl, "Swinging Gently," sold over one million copies.

Bob settled in as music director for Frenchy's Theatre Night Club in Hayward,

California, outside San Francisco. He hit the big time for an arranger when he joined the staff of Harry Zimmerman. Zimmerman had the music contract for the popular *Gary Moore TV Show* and kept it when it transitioned into *The Carol Burnett Show*. Bob wrote many of the musical arrangements for both weekly series.

He continued freelancing for TV and motion pictures, including the *Andy Williams Show*, the *Red Skelton Show*, *Bonanza*, *Hollywood Talent Scouts*, Paramount Pictures, and Universal Television. In addition, he conducted for Billy Eckstein, The Andrews Sisters, and the Ink Spots. In those days, he also arranged for many stars. He told me once, "Debbie Reynolds used to call and wake me up at 2:30 or 3:00 in the morning wanting a particular arrangement. I'd finish it by 6:00 A.M. and deliver it to her by 8:00 A.M.!"

On my first honeymoon, my wife and I spent a week in Mexico City and Acapulco. We then flew to L.A. and spent four days with Bob. We watched two fascinating rehearsals of *The Carol Burnett Show* featuring Tim Conway and Harvey Korman. Big-band singers, Steve Lawrence and Eydie Gorme were the guest performers. I couldn't believe my eyes and ears. Here I was, sitting so close to some of my musical idols, I could reach out and touch them. Steve and Eydie on stage, and Elliott Lawrence conducting the CBS Orchestra with greats such as tenor saxophonist Bill Perkins in the pit. It was like I'd died and gone to heaven.

It was there I got a glimpse of the ordeal and pressure of producing a weekly TV show. Bob told it this way in an interview printed in the *Southeast Missourian* newspaper in 1962:

> The production schedule is grueling—with only one week to get music, script, actors, singers, dancers together and through rehearsals to the final taping. The musicians I work with all have bachelor degrees, and most have masters. They have to work on a production time schedule that demands discipline, organization, and most of all, reliability.

On June 17, 1975, everything came to a sudden halt. Bob was killed in one of those California freeway accidents caused by an unexpected sandstorm. Newspaper accounts reported, "Seventy mile an hour wind; no visibility; multi-car pileup; one fatality."

Bill told me, "Bob wanted to be another Henry Mancini, but due to the car wreck, we'll never know if he would have reached his dream." I've often wondered what path my life would have taken if Bob had lived. For me, those days with Bob were special. Bob's magnetic personality was infectious. Looking back, the three years I spent performing with him seemed like twenty.

At one of our monthly haircut sessions at his shop, I asked Bill to think back on all those years and tell me the most important moment in his relationship with his older brother Bob. Bill thought for a moment, and then said, "It was the day Bob and his buddies were going bicycle riding, and as they headed out the front door, he turned back to me and for the first time asked if I wanted to go along."

Several years after Bob's untimely death, I was in the lobby of the Hilton Hotel in Memphis, Tennessee, early one morning with my friend Don Staples. We were waiting for our friend Jim Tooke to drive us out to the Colonial Country Club to watch the touring golf professionals compete in the Memphis Open PGA Golf Tournament.

L to r: Mr. Sisco, Bob Sisco, and Billy Sisco. COURTESY OF BILLY SISCO.

As we were standing there, I heard gorgeous sounds coming from the piano in the lobby lounge. Someone was playing parts of Rosemary Clooney's hit, "Hey There," over and over. Each time, the chord progressions were different. Obviously, someone was experimenting with alternative chords, chords that fit the progression of the song, but different from the original standard version.

I finally looked around the corner expecting to see Tommy Ferguson, Memphis's, premiere jazz pianist. Tommy had gained that stature in the eyes of area musicians, just as Herb Drury had a similar reputation in St. Louis. I had performed with Tommy on several occasions, including a gig in Las Vegas with Bob Crosby's Orchestra.

Well, it wasn't Tommy. It was a young man in jeans and a t-shirt, slumped over the keyboard in deep concentration. While I generally don't interrupt in these situations, this time, I did. I asked him his name as he continued to play. He informed me that he was Carol Lawrence's arranger and conductor. They had performed at the annual convention of General Foods International the preceding night. Lawrence was TV spokesperson for them in those days. He was waiting for her so they could fly back to Los Angeles later that morning.

As he continued to play, it occurred to me that he was the right age (35-ish), right location (L.A.), right avocation (arranger-conductor), etc. So I popped the question: "Did you ever know an arranger in L.A. by the name of Bob Sisco?" He abruptly stopped playing, looked at me incredulously, and exclaimed, "Bob Sisco!" He quieted down and told me that Bob had been arranging a gospel album for The Archers, one of contemporary Christian music's earliest pop vocal groups, at the time of his death. He had completed the rhythm tracks and had begun the vocals. The producers were looking for an arranger who could finish the album. This young man got the job, chosen over two other arrangers. He took the job with the stipulation that "all proceeds go to Bob's widow and young daughter." He met Bob on occasion in studios, but didn't really know him. He remarked how strange it was "to hear Bob's voice on the tape—talking, giving tempos and other directions," as he finished the album. I never found the album.

Bob's brother Bill still plays good string bass. He performs only in church. We were in the same grade all through school and graduated from Central High School in 1960. At another monthly haircut session, he reminded me that The Archers came to Cape and honored the Sisco family with a memorial concert at our high school auditorium about two months after Bob's tragic death.

Dr. Richard Moore. COURTESY OF TOM NEUMEYER.

Dr. Richard Moore

Richard Moore, Bob Sisco, and my brother Don were the great influences on me in popular jazz music. Tony Carosello and Bill Ewing, my band directors in school, nurtured my talent, but the other three were the real inspirations to me.

Richard Moore was a prodigy of sorts. Starting at age 7, he took piano lessons from Dora Graham for 10 years in Fredericktown, Missouri. Here's Richard's account:

> Ms. Graham was a great influence. She exposed me to all kinds of music. She would place the music on the piano and play through it. I would listen, watch her hands, and then I would play it. For three years I relied on sight and ear. One day she asked me to identify a particular note; I couldn't. She was livid. She realized I had been faking it all that time. For the next six months, she grilled me with note spellers. I hated every minute, but it was the best training I ever received from anyone, and it paid great dividends later in my career.

Richard first played for Bob Sisco when Bob's orchestra played the Fredericktown high school prom in 1958, where Richard's father was the high school principal. When he came to Cape Girardeau from Fredericktown the following year to attend college, Bob hired him.

Richard was a disciple of the innovative jazz pianist Bill Evans. We had seldom heard a 6/9 chord with a Major 7th or a 13th with an augmented 11th that he weaved into standard tunes of the Popular American Songbook. Needing money for college, Bob helped get him a job at Shivelbine Music Store where Bob also worked. They became lifelong friends, collaborators, and performers. Richard recalled, "Sisco could sell anything, and he did. He could talk to anybody."

College wasn't for Richard at that time; he didn't like to go to class. One professor told him, "Son, you need to try something else." He did. He always wanted to fly, so he went down to the recruitment office on Broadway and enlisted in the Air Force. Everything went fine until he flunked his physical. He was color blind. That ended his flying days. They placed him in the Air Force Security Service. He graduated from the Russian Language School at Indiana University after becoming fluent in Russian. He was shipped off to Japan for one year, and as he puts it, "They stuck me on a mountaintop intercepting messages!"

He continued performing abroad and then was transferred back to the states in El Paso, Texas, for a year and a half. It was during that time he decided to quit music as a full-time avocation. Richard recalls:

I did a twelve week stint with Karen Dolan and her sister Lynn. Their father was an arranger in Hollywood. Lynn joined the Johnny Mann Singers and eventually ended up marrying Johnny Mann. We played five hours a night, six days a week. After that grueling regimen, I concluded I was going to get a regular 9-5 job. So I quit and enrolled in the engineering school at Rolla, Missouri, known as the School of Mines. (It was called that because it was located in the region of Missouri known as the Lead Belt.) I spent seven years at Rolla. And this time, I did a little better than I had years ago at Southeast. I actually went to class. I earned three degrees: a B.S. in Physics, an M.S., and a Ph.D. in Ceramics. I took a job with PPG Industries, but, once again, I wasn't satisfied.

Richard continued to play with various groups and jazz festivals with great trumpeters Clark Terry and Marvin Stamm through those years, and toured the Netherlands with the Jim Widner Big Band. By then he was a seasoned professional. As a result of some personal medical experiences, Richard left his job with PPG and enrolled in the medical school at the University of Missouri, Columbia. When Richard returned to Cape Girardeau in 1981, he was an M.D.

Richard and I have continued to perform together throughout our region since then. In one 6-month period, we collaborated in writing over 100 songs. Occasionally we perform some of them to enthusiastic crowds. We both maintain hectic schedules, but when we find the time someday, we will publish them.

Don Ford.

Don Ford

My brother Don started his music career on piano. He took lessons from Louise Eckardt, who lived around the corner from us. He hated the piano. Mom made him practice every morning before school, and I remember him sitting with her on the piano bench, crying as she led him through the various etudes.

But after a year or so, when he got a pair of drum sticks in his hands, he flew. His upbeat temperament and vociferous persona took over. He never doubted himself and always looked for his next challenge and his next adventure, throughout his life.

He set his drums up in the dining room, and we played along for hours with recordings by the great big bands and small ensemble jazz groups of the '40s and '50s: me with my trumpet and Don on his trap set. Blessed with superior intellect, he quickly became a great percussionist and terrific sight reader. He could play complicated drum scores at sight: meaning, he could play most music exactly correct the first time he saw it.

As a young boy, he gave lessons to most of the kids who became good drummers in our area. Bill Ewing, our junior high band director and a great saxophonist, started using Don as his drummer on dance jobs at the age of 13! The first was at the Cairo, Illinois, Elks Club. Shortly thereafter, Bob Sisco started using both of us in his orchestra at approximately the same time: Don at 13 and me at 15.

As related earlier, Bob Sisco was music director-arranger-conductor at Frenchy's Theatre Night Club close to San Francisco in Hayward, California. At one point, he auditioned several drummers for the house band, and wasn't satisfied. He knew Don was better than most of the drummers he'd come across in California, and he knew Don sight-read like a fiend, so he called him to come join the band. Don was majoring in mathematics at Southeast Missouri State College at the time. Dad gave his permission, the professors excused him from classes with no penalty, so Don spent the summer of 1963 in San Francisco.

There, he performed with name entertainers: The Gold Diggers, organist Earl Grant, Martin Denny, Dennis Day, the great accordionist Dick Contina, and others. In a newspaper interview, Dick Contina paid Don the ultimate compliment when he said, "Don is the finest drummer I've ever performed with, considering his age and experience."

Many drummers are good at either playing with small combos or big bands. Don did both with equal aplomb. It's one thing to support a small ensemble, but for a drummer to also possess the power and skill to drive and kick a 16- to 18-piece jazz band is rare indeed. Don elevated every group he performed with.

Besides excelling in music, Don had college degrees in math and language. He was teaching mathematics at Cape Junior High School when he was drafted into the army during the Vietnam War. He spent his three years playing every day in the band, and at night, performing with the jazz band and small combo in and around Fort Leonard Wood, out in the beautiful hills of mid-Missouri. During this time, he commuted between Crocker, Missouri, and Columbia (a three-hour drive) to earn his Masters Degree in Education Administration at the University of Missouri.

He and his wife Carolyn lived in a chicken coop that had been converted into small living quarters during WWII. Don commuted the seventeen miles to the army post each day. He told a great story about those days. The band was awakened in the wee hours one morning after being out most of the night playing for dance-parties on the base. "'Get your dress uniforms and on to the bus,' we were ordered."

> We drove for hours in our old bumpy school bus, not knowing our destination. By late morning, we arrived in downtown Chicago: sleepy, groggy, grouchy. As we got our bearings, we began dressing. We noticed the draw bridges over the Chicago River were being raised. A few minutes later, boats appeared. We were down in the Loop. All of a sudden the boats started shooting red, white, and blue water from their fire hoses. We began dressing more quickly, still not knowing what was going on, but sensing something special. We were escorted to the middle of the street. A few minutes later, about twenty motorcycles came screaming at us, followed by a convertible with, of all people, Mayor Daley. It was almost noon. About that time, a deafening twenty-one-cannon salute ricocheted off the downtown Chicago buildings. It was high noon. Magically, millions of people appeared everywhere, from the streets to hanging out of skyscrapers with confetti flying. At the same moment, a brand-new shiny white Cadillac convertible drove up with Neil Armstrong and the other astronauts who had just returned from the moon!

Don laughed as he recalled the scene, "You never saw a bunch of hungover, scraggly musicians shape up so quickly in all your life. We led the ticker-tape parade down the street." And he concluded, "Don't ever say Mayor Daley didn't know how to organize a parade!"

Donnie was a great drummer. I'll tell you how great. I've made this statement to various musicians over the years, and some who didn't know me too well or had never heard Don play, looked at me with more than a little skepticism: "Don could have taken drummer Ed Shaughnessy's place in Doc Severinson's big band on Johnny Carson's *Tonight Show*, and sight-read live most of the orchestra's charts. And they would have never missed a beat!"

I assumed the baton of Bob Sisco's orchestra when he left to pursue his music career in California in 1960. Upon his return from the army, Don joined Walter Joe and me in the family funeral business. Don contracted tuberculosis during that time in 1974. He spent six months in the sanitarium at Mt. Vernon, Missouri.

Upon returning, he left the funeral home, juggled his business career with Mercantile Bank in St. Louis, Southeast Missouri State University, and family responsibilities, and continued performing with me for the next 23 years throughout the Midwest. Highlights in those years were performing with Bob Crosby and his Orchestra on several occasions, Buddy Chilton's Orchestra in Chicago, Illinois, the Caesar's Palace Orchestra in Las Vegas, Nevada, Alvino Rey's Orchestra in Honolulu, Hawaii, and more.

Don's wife Carolyn remembers:

> Don was easily bored. He had 8 different jobs, each better than the one before, in over 30 years. He had an unbelievable effect on people with his zest for life. And music was the cohesion. He was always outgoing, enthusiastic, and interested in everyone else's well being. In his battles with tuberculosis and cancer, he was an inspiration to all around him. He was always the first to speak, the first to put people at ease. He enjoyed every day and looked forward to meeting someone new.

When I interviewed Dr. Richard Moore about his musical career, he reminisced about Don:

> Thinking back over my years of performing, Don was the best drummer I ever played with, and I've played with some great ones. He started at such a young age. I didn't appreciate his skills until later. He was steady as a clock. He played tasty fills. He was creative. He did things others didn't do. And through all those years, he was fun to be around because of his spectacular personality. He had to leave us all too soon.

Don passed away on August 7, 1997.

David McFarland. Hotel de Crillon, Paris, France.

David McFarland

David McFarland is one of my favorite people. He's made a living his entire adult life as a professional pianist. For over thirty years, he's gone from local lounges in Cape Girardeau to posh hotels in Paris, France, and continues sailing the seven seas on cruise ships.

His mother, Anna Jane (Lesem) McFarland, was his teacher. She began playing piano at a very early age and studied with Ruth Abbott and Professor Clyde Brandt at Southeast Missouri State College. She became an outstanding classical pianist and, in later life after raising her children, made her living as a professional pianist performing in places like North Dakota, Hot Springs, Arkansas, and even the famous New Orleans restaurant, Pat O'Brien's. She eventually ruled the piano bar at the Royal N'Orleans Restaurant in Cape for over 20 years.*

The McFarlands were a musical family. David's older brother Jim played fine alto saxophone and clarinet. Ann taught David the songs of the Popular American Songbook, instilling the importance of proper chord progressions and a keen sense of timing and rhythm. David also inherited her musical ear which helped him learn music quickly.

David's sister Jeanie said he was always playing the piano around the house:

> He could play beautiful music when he was very young. And he was always trustworthy, truthful, and responsible. He also had a knack of always being able to get around. As a kid, he was never afraid to jaunt out on his own. We would travel, and he'd set our itinerary. Even in New York City, he seemed to know where everything was. I always thought he would have made a great travel agent.

David started playing at the Blue Note Lounge on Broadway at age 18. He graduated down the street to the Royal N'Orleans for several years, and from 1971 through 1978, he played 5 nights a week in the lounge at the Purple Crackle night club in East Cape Girardeau, Illinois.

Many solo lounge musicians take liberties with music. Since they don't perform with other musicians, they don't have to be exact. Sometimes they don't follow the original chord progressions of the music, and most notably, they don't play with a good sense of rhythm. Not David. He's meticulous. He's right on, all the time.

David left Cape in April of 1980 for a music career that has taken him all over

---

* In the mid-sixties, Ann, Vi Ann Keys (sax/vocals), and my brother Don (drums), played a six-week stint at the old State Hotel in Kansas City, Missouri.

the world. He went to Miami, Florida, with the idea of playing on a cruise ship. His first audition was for the Norwegian Cruise Line, and they hired him on the spot. He was on the old *S.S. Norway* for three years. It has always been his favorite ship. "It was the first, and it's where I made most of my contacts for future work," David explains.

David always wanted to go to Paris, France. A friend connected him with an agent who booked musicians in small hotel chains throughout Europe. He sent an audition tape and was hired. He left the *S.S. Norway* for Paris. He stayed for six years. He first performed at the Nova Park Elysees Hotel and one day walked into the Hotel de Crillon, sat down and played, and again was hired on the spot. He stayed five years.

Since he performed in the evenings from 5:00 P.M. to 9:00 P.M., he studied French language, history, and literature during his first three years in Paris. He attended the famous Alliance Française, La Sorbonne, and Catholic Institute schools from 8:00 A.M. to 2:00 P.M.

"During the winter, it was pitch dark when I began each day," David explains. "But it was worth it. To really learn the language and customs, however, I frequented the markets everyday. The vendors were amazing. They taught me about fresh vegetables, fish, meat, poultry, fruits, and cheese."

He met and conversed with many celebrities in those days at his domain in the Hotel de Crillon's Salon de Tea, adjacent to the famous Restaurant les Ambassadeurs. Peter Falk, Mel Ferrer, Andrew Lloyd Webber, Catherine Deneuve, Arlene Dahl, Robert Mitchum, the late French composer Charles Trenet, French singer Line Renaud, Olivia de Haviland, Elizabeth Taylor, Gene Kelly, and many more stopped by.

> One day Gene Kelly came in for a drink and chatted briefly. I played a medley of songs from old MGM movie musicals that he really enjoyed. The next day he gave me a thumbs up when I surprised him with an obscure tune, "When I'm With You," I remembered from an old Shirley Temple movie. He was amazed I knew the song. He thanked me for not playing "Singing in the Rain" and exclaimed, "That's all I ever hear!"
>
> I played in the hotel's small bar on weekends. As I walked in to start playing one evening, I thought I saw Andrew Lloyd Webber and Sarah Brightman in a quiet corner. Having seen only a newspaper picture of Lloyd Webber, I wasn't sure it was him. So I played his mega hit "Memory" from the Broadway musical *Cats* to see if I would get a response. Nothing happened. Later in the evening as the room filled, someone requested "Memory," so I played it again. After returning from a break, the couple was gone. But there was a note on the piano: "Thanks for playing 'Memory' twice" from the composer— Andrew Lloyd Webber.

David still has the note.

Political figures, heads of state, and their accompanying security details were always around the hotel: people like Henry Kissinger, Jeanne Kirkpatrick, Yassir Arafat (the President of Palestine; he arrived by helicopter), Queen Noor of Jordan, Shimon Peres (the Prime Minister of Israel), Walter Mondale, P.W. Botha of South Africa, King Juan Carlos and Queen Sofia of Spain," David said. "Occasionally some of them would even stop and talk. You got the feeling at times, the de Crillon was the center of the universe! It always amazed me how ordinary these extraordinary people were."

David's favorite story is that on a late afternoon, conductor-composer Leonard Bernstein dramatically burst into the lounge with a spectacular white scarf around his neck. The Bernstein's room opened onto an inner courtyard where the doors and windows of the lounge David was playing were wide open. Bernstein exclaimed, "My wife and I have been up in our room listening to you play for the past hour. Who are you? Where are you from? What's your story? Your chords and changes are absolutely perfect. You play with such expression and feeling, and the way you play is exactly as the composers intended their songs to be played, mine included!"

"I was so flabbergasted, I could hardly concentrate on the conversation," David continued. "He was treating me as the celebrity instead of the other way around. Leonard Bernstein's praise put the cap on my whole playing career.

"I don't know what it is about Paris," David contemplated, "but people treat you differently there than they would anywhere else. I doubt if any of those people would have come up to me, just a piano player, in any other place except Paris."

David loves Paris.

David became restless and returned to the sea in 1989, and has remained there all these years. "I'm usually on one ship for three to five years, and then move to another," he explains. Ports of Call on the *S.S. Norway*, *Costa Classica*, and *Crown Odyssey* included Europe, the Mediterranean, Scandinavia, Russia, and the United Kingdom. For the past ten years, David has been on Royal Caribbean's *Grandeur of the Seas*, *Vision of the Seas*, and *Splendour of the Seas*.

With his incredible schedule in mind, I asked, "What's the toughest part of your job?" He answered, "*The confinement*. I'm on the ship for six months, off for four to six weeks, and back on for another six months, and then I do it all over again. I work primarily at night, playing the lounge and for the two dinner sittings. I get off the ship during the day and visit the various ports of call. If it wasn't for that, I couldn't do it."

While I have continued to stay in touch with David over time, a real treat was stumbling onto him in 2002 on a cruise of Alaska on the *Vision of the Seas*. Each afternoon at 4:00 P.M., he performed in the piano lounge. Each day the crowds grew as passengers learned of our hometown connection. On the last afternoon the group had swelled to over fifty. I had some fun.

I knew David could play one of my favorite songs, "Emily." It's a beautiful but obscure title song from Johnny Mandel's film score of *The Americanization of Emily*, starring James Garner and Julie Andrews. I stood and told the crowd, "No lounge piano player, from the Waldorf Astoria in New York City to the Fairmount Hotel on Knob Hill in San Francisco, knew the song I am about to request. (That's true.) If David can play the song, we will crown him King of the Piano Lounge!" David looked at me with a quizzical look, as if to say, *What are you doing to me?* But when I named the tune, he smiled, and in his inimitable, impeccable style, played the waltz beautifully.

David still sails the seven seas. Our latest conversation found him in Athens, Greece, where he related, "I've been a traveling musician since 1980, a lifetime really. It has been fun and interesting. And I hope to keep doing it for as long as I am able."

Jerry Ford Orchestra. Murray State University, 1960. L to r: Jim Rhodes, Jerry Ford, Jim Worley, Joe James, Jr., Elwood Fisher, Don Ford (back), Jon Kent Fisher, Vi Ann Keys, E.W. Kassel.

Jerry Ford Orchestra

I wanted to play trumpet the first time I heard one on our car radio when I was very young. I drove my dad and high school band director Tony Carosello nuts, insisting I had to play one. Tony finally acquiesced and started giving me lessons in the fourth grade. That started a lifetime love affair with music. I sang in Reverend Collie Shirrell's vocal quartet on KFVS radio when in the 5th grade, played in Erskine Miller's "Sacred Six" at the Church of the Nazarene in junior high, conducted the Maple Avenue Methodist Church Choir in high school, began playing in Bob Sisco's Orchestra throughout the region as a sophomore, won the Shivelbine Award as the outstanding musician at Central High School in May of 1960, and started the music department jazz program at Southeast as a freshman student in the fall of 1960.

Just as Bob Sisco bought Don McNeely's orchestra in 1955, I perpetuated the legacy by purchasing Sisco's orchestra in 1960, when he left to pursue his music career in California.

I don't pretend to be in the same category as the friends you're meeting in this book. I took the safe route and stayed home.

However, my musical organizations have done some neat things entertaining audiences throughout the Midwest. We've raised several hundred thousand dollars for needy people, churches, and not-for-profit organizations over these more than fifty years. We've been part of the marriages of hundreds of couples.

Jerry Ford.

I've personally performed with the orchestras of Bob Crosby, Dick Jergens, Ted Weems, Alvino Rey, The Caesars Palace Orchestra, Jack Stalcup, Herb Suedekum, Jack Kinder, Pete Propst, Bill French, Bob Rosenquist, Earl Myhre, Southern Jazz, and many more. I am still in demand as trumpet soloist, conductor, clinician, high school jazz and concert band judge, first-call musician for regional and national touring concerts and shows, and have played in Cape's Municipal Band since 1957.

Some Orchestra Highlights:
- Part-time fixture at the Purple Crackle and Colony Club in '50s, '60s, '70s
- Provided backup music for Bob Hope, Red Skelton, Kenny Rogers, Ray Stevens, Bobby Vinton, Dick Shawn, Shari Lewis, Ted Lewis, Guy Lombardo, and "The Rat Pack" from Las Vegas

- Five Inaugural Balls in the Missouri Capitol Rotunda—2003, 2005, 2007, 2009, 2011
- Four DuQuoin State Fair Labor Day Shows—2005, 2006, 2007, 2008
- Two Southern Legislative Conferences in Charleston, South Carolina–1998 and Kansas City, Missouri—1999
- Four Coterie Balls in Evansville, Indiana—2005, 2006, 2007, 2008
- National Convention of the National Ballroom & Entertainment Association, Casa Loma Ballroom, St. Louis—2007
- Lincoln Academy, Carbondale, Illinois—2008
- Numerous Muscular Dystrophy Association Telethons (KFVS–TV)
- Pit orchestra for twenty Jaycee Follies
- Several musicals, including *Sweet Charity* at the River Campus
- Twenty years welcoming the *Mississippi Queen*, *American Queen*, and *Delta Queen* to town
- Ten years providing over ninety dinner shows for the River Explorer when it docked in downtown Cape
- My combo still performs the last Sunday afternoon of every month at the River Ridge Winery in Commerce, Missouri.

During that time, I've had more than 150 musicians in my musical family. Yes, it's a family. I could write a long chapter about each of them, but that's for another time. Everyone in my orchestra is exceptional, has performed with major stars and shows, has an impressive resume, and most have college and graduate music degrees. I hope in the name of brevity, they will forgive me for short-changing them in this book. However, I can't write a book about music and musicians without including them:

Vocalist Pat Blackwell interpreted music of the big band era as tasty as you'd ever hear. She and her husband Joe performed with me for 45 years, and are chronicled in the next chapter.

John Quinn.

John Quinn, alto/tenor sax/clarinet/flute and arranger, is the *sound* of the Jerry Ford Orchestra. Patrons tell us occasionally, "You're the best band we've ever heard." While it takes first class musicianship to interpret them, it's Quinn's arrangements that are primarily responsible. John began playing around St. Louis in 1952; graduated with a music degree from Mizzou in 1958; played in the Third Army Band at Fort McPherson, Georgia, from 1959-61; was band director at Shawnee High School in Wolf Lake, Illinois, for 29 years; arranger/performer with the Bill French Orchestra at the

Purple Crackle Supper Club in East Cape, Illinois, from 1967-1978; and with the Jerry Ford Orchestra since 1968.

Dr. Dan Cotner, trombone, has been a Cape Girardeau institution for over 85 years. He raised his family literally all over the world, providing free dental care for thousands of people in underdeveloped countries through the Rotary International program. All four of Dan and Polly's children are dentists or dental hygienists. His community and philanthropic activities are too numerous to list. However, several that pertain to music performance must be acknowledged: trombonist in our Cape Municipal Band for 70 years; organist for various local churches for 70 years; pianist for our Downtown Rotary Club for 68 years; member of the St. Louis Theater Organ Society for 60 years; pianist, violinist, trombonist for the Cape Notre Dame High School Musicals for 43 years; and trombonist with the Jerry Ford Orchestra for 25 years.

L to r: Dr. Dan Cotner, Gene Stiman.

Gene Stiman traveled with Benny Goodman for three years in the '40s swing era; was band director in Salem, Illinois, for many years; lead trombonist for the Fabulous Fox Orchestra in St. Louis for 10 years, performing with over 400 of the greats of popular music; low brass instructor at Southern Illinois University in Carbondale, Illinois, for a decade; and with the Jerry Ford Orchestra for the past 12 years.

Beverly Reece. COURTESY OF CHEEKWOOD STUDIOS.

The same can be said of music prodigy, Beverly Reece. She began playing piano at age 2½, and singing music scores at age 3! She's played violin since age 7, and at age 13 had 35 piano students. As a freshman in high school she was one of only 2 students in the U.S. who scored a perfect 100% on the Harvard pitch and rhythm test. She has perfect pitch and a photographic mind. As a sophomore in high school, she accompanied Gloria DeHaven and played oboe with the Southeast University Orchestra. At Southeast, she accompanied over 200 senior recitals, 10 theatre productions, 5 years as concert-mistress of the orchestra, and toured with professor Paul Thompson and a Russian violinist that culminated in a concert in Carnegie Hall. She began playing jazz professionally with Bill Ewing at age 19, and later performed with distinction with the Jack Stalcup Orchestra for 10 years.

For over 30 years, Reece has been our area's premier piano instructor and church organist. Beverly is currently organist for Centenary United Methodist Church and Evangelical United Church of Christ here in Cape. She's a member of the Cape Girardeau and Paducah, Kentucky, Symphony Orchestras, and winner of numerous local and regional "fiddle" contests. Beverly is proficient as a classical concert pianist, as well as a great jazz performer with the Jerry Ford Orchestra.

Steve Williams.

Steve Williams, drummer (Cairo, Illinois), began banging on pots and pans at age 10. He played drums in high school and, during his junior year, played in the Columbia, Tennessee, Military Academy Jazz Band. Upon return to Cairo for his senior year, he played with the Rebel Rousers and the Penny Bagby Dance Band. Williams joined the army in 1961 and performed with top jazz players Buddy Prima (piano), Frannie Rice (sax), Steve Osgood (bass), Mae Sherman (vocals), and many more. Home from the service, he played in the bands of Bill Ewing, Joe Blackwell, Earl Myhre, Jack Stalcup, Herb Suedekum, Bill Brandt, Bill French, and Southern Jazz in Paducah, Kentucky. He's been featured with pianists Dr. Richard Moore, Alan Oldfield, and Don Heitler; saxophonist Buddy Rodgers, Carbondale; and for the past 15 years with the Jerry Ford Orchestra.

Narvol Randol, trumpet, stays busy giving of his time and talent for many community activities. He's played for at least 20 Notre Dame musicals and 7 or 8 Cape Central musicals; Municipal Band since 1971; Bill Brandt Orchestra at the Purple Crackle 5 years; backed Bobby Vinton, Red Skelton, Bob Hope, Ed Shaunessey, the Rat Pack, and others; continues to play "taps" at military funerals; Salvation Army Holiday Band with me, Dr. Dan Cotner, and others for over 30 years; and has been a member of the Jerry Ford Orchestra for over 25 years.

Narvol Randol. COURTESY OF SCOTT LORENZ.

Mike Goldsmith.

Lead alto saxophonist Mike Goldsmith is director of Jazz and Woodwinds Instruction at Mineral Area College, Park Hills, Missouri. He was director of bands and chair of Fine Arts at Fredericktown R-1 schools and former director of jazz combos and jazz studies at Columbia Hickman High School. He received his B.A. in Music from Truman

State and MEA from William Woods. He's an active performer, clinician, and adjudicator throughout the Midwest. With his hard, West-coast sound, Goldsmith is the best lead alto saxophonist I've ever had on the stand.

Lead trumpeters Bob Bartley, band director at Arcadia Valley High School in

Dr. Marc Fulgham.
COURTESY OF
CHEEKWOOD STUDIOS.

Ironton, and Dr. Marc Fulgham, instructor of trumpet at Southeast Missouri State University and principal trumpet for the Paducah Symphony for 21 years, provide the power, range, and wide sound required to ride herd over a great big band. Fulgham received his BME from Wichita State and his DMA from University of Colorado. He's performed with the Tulsa Philharmonic, Wichita Symphony, Springfield (Missouri) Symphony, Boulder Philharmonic, Mahlerfest Orchestra (Boulder, Colorado), and the Denver Chamber Orchestra. As a core musician of the Carson Four Rivers Center in Paducah, Kentucky, he's performed with Ray Charles, Frankie Vallee, Marie Osmond, Mannheim Steamroller, Amy Grant, and Cathy Rigby in the musical *Peter Pan*.

Mike Neville, tenor sax, started playing rock 'n' roll in the early '60s with Mert Mirly and the Rhythm Steppers, and Bob Kuban in St. Louis. As an FBI agent for 35 years, Mike traveled and played with groups in New Orleans, New York City, South Dakota, and in the '80s with the Bury Brothers at Stonewings Night Club in Minneapolis. His real claim to fame, however, was as an usher (his wife Marilyn at the guest book) at Tiny Tim's wedding! He's been with the Jerry Ford Orchestra for 10 years.

Michael Neville.
COURTESY OF PAT PATTERSON
PHOTOGRAPHY.

Jim Wall. COURTESY OF
MONICA TICHENOR.

Jim Wall, bass (Carbondale, Illinois), provides imaginative support in all styles, from swing to rock. The son of two professional musicians, Wall was exposed to music at an early age, with training on cello and French horn. His mother is a retired violinist in Chicago and his dad, a retired band director, was an orchestra tuba player. Wall became interested in the bass in high school and is regarded by many, me included, as the finest bass player in our two state region. A 20-plus year resident of Carbondale, Jim spent 20 years in sales, marketing, production, and promotion management in the commercial broadcast industry. Jim is currently a Senior Lecturer at Southern Illinois University, where he teaches in the Marketing and Management sequence in the Department of Radio and Television.

Eric Scott, trombone, performed in all the instrumental and vocal groups at Cape Central and Southeast Missouri State University. He's toured Europe with vocal groups and for 14 years has led the gospel quartet, New Beginnings. He plays local clubs with pianist Brett Yount, is music director at Westminster Presbyterian Church, and performs with the Jerry Ford Orchestra.

Eric Scott.

Paul Fliege.

Paul Fliege, alto, tenor, baritone sax and clarinet, has been band director at Jackson since 2001, teaching woodwind players of all grades. He received his BME from Culver Stockton and his MME from Southeast. Besides the Jerry Ford Orchestra, he performs with the Paducah Symphony, Heartland Winds, and Jackson Municipal Band. He and his wife Cecily have two daughters.

Tina Trickey.

Vocalist Tina Trickey brings a wide range of musical styles and experiences to our repertoire, from jazz to country to rock. A native of Cape, she participated in all Cape Central vocal groups and performed for most local churches, musicals, and shows. She moved to New York City where she became a print model for Revlon and transferred to Vancouver, Washington, as District Sales Manager for Revlon. There she performed with Chuck Berry, The Temptations, and concerts in renowned Pioneer Square in Portland, Oregon. Upon return to Cape, she reestablished herself as a premier vocalist for area performances.

Our newest member, Casey Janet Mills, graduated from Notre Dame High School in Cape and Murray State University in Murray, Kentucky. She's been singing on stage since age 5, in churches, school, and headlined in many of Mike Dumey's music productions. Casey was a finalist in CMT's Music City Madness and first runner-up in the Gaither Gospel Talent Competition. She has performed at Six Flags in St. Louis and starred for three years at the Badgett Playhouse Theatre in Grand

Casey Janet Mills.
COURTESY OF
CHEEKWOOD STUDIOS.

Rivers, Kentucky. She juggles her life among her family, working fulltime as a nurse, and performing in local and regional shows, as well as with the Jerry Ford Orchestra for special performances.

Bruce Zimmerman and Steve Schaffner, the Cape Girardeau region's best rock/blues guitarists/singers *rock* the house with us on occasion. Each has his own group and unique style. They are discussed in subsequent chapters of the rock 'n' roll section.

It takes a lot of work and dedication to keep a 14-piece orchestra together. The members drive; help make sure everyone gets to the job on time; secure motel/hotel rooms; set up the sound equipment, stands, lights, etc; and tear down and pack everything at the end of the evening. Great jazz musicians are like great athletes: they have to possess excellent intellect, good hand-eye coordination, a good sense of rhythm, a great ear, an awareness of their surroundings, discipline, dependability, creativity, teamwork, and a love for the art.

Several members out of the past have to be mentioned: Richard "Butch" Eggimann was a great swing pianist. The internationally acclaimed bassist Ray Brown seldom played a more lyrical line than Jim Worley of St. Mary, Missouri. The same can be said of trombonist Dr. Fred Goodwin, former Dean of Humanities at Southeast Missouri State University. In addition, pianists "Chips" Curtis and John Pyatt (St. Louis), Jim Rhodes (Jackson), Jim Leggett (Bloomfield), and Scott Blackwell (Cape); drummer Mark Hill; saxophonists Joe James, Elwood and Jon Kent Fisher, E.W. Kassel, Terry Kratky, Larry Sharpio, Sonny and Kerry Slinkard, Gary Rybolt, Richard Cortois, and Jim Finn all performed with me with distinction for many years. It takes a village.

Orchestra Personnel through the Years

(As many as I can remember!)

* Deceased

Trumpet

Bob Bartley – Ironton, Missouri
Bill Brandt * – Cape Girardeau
Tony Carosello – Cape Girardeau
Al Estes – Cape Girardeau
Jerry Ford – Cape Girardeau
Dr. Marc Fulgham – Cape Girardeau
Homer Gilbert * – Cape Girardeau
Billy Keys – Cape Girardeau
Josh LaMarr – Cape Girardeau
Matt Martin – Cape Girardeau
Nate Nall – Cape Girardeau
Narvol Randol – Cape Girardeau
Dan Smith – St. Louis
Scott Vangilder – Jackson, Missouri

Clarinet

Dr. Ted Borodowsky – Paducah, Kentucky
Bob Donze – Ste. Genevieve, Missouri
Jim Finn * – Herrin, Illinois
Paul Fliege – Jackson, Missouri
John Quinn – Cape Girardeau
Austin Sikes – Fredericktown
Pat Schwent – Cape Girardeau

Trombone

Ed Adams * – Cape Girardeau
Jacob Baggett – Cape Girardeau
Ray Cissell – Grand Rivers, Kentucky
Dr. Dan Cotner – Cape Girardeau
Dr. Fred Goodwin * – Cape Girardeau
Mark Goodwin – Jackson, Missouri
Terry Gockel * – Cape Girardeau
Brian Hardester – Cape Girardeau
Steve Linnes – Cape Girardeau
Eric Scott – Cape Girardeau
Gene Stiman – Ullin, Illinois
Brad Smith – Cape Girardeau/Oran,
   Missouri

Tuba

John Beaudean – Cape Girardeau
Ron Nall – Cape Girardeau
Ron Walker – Cape Girardeau

Vocalists

"Andrew Sisters" – Majhon Phillips,
   Sarah Orlovsky, Amanda Eads – Southeast
   Missouri State University
Pat Blackwell – Cape Girardeau
Vickie Boren – Cape Girardeau
Neal Boyd – Sikeston, Missouri
Sharon Clark – Carbondale, Illinois
J. J. Edmonds – Cape Girardeau
Betty Hearnes – Charleston, Missouri
Vi Ann Keys – Cape Girardeau
Quitman McBride III – Cape Girardeau
Joan Miget – Perryville, Missouri

"Mamanettes" – Pat Blackwell, Virginia
Boren,* Virginia Hill * – Cape Girardeau
Valerie Oestry – Cape Girardeau
Sharon Sams – Cape Girardeau
Lori Schaefer – Cape Girardeau
Steve Schaffner – Cape Girardeau
Tina Trickey – Cape Girardeau
Brodrick Twiggs – Cape Girardeau
Julie Wilkerson – Dahlgren, Illinois
Jim Worley * – St. Mary, Missouri
Bruce Zimmerman – Cape Girardeau
Casey Janet Mills – Cape Girardeau

Saxophone

Glen Chilton * – Poplar Bluff, Missouri
Rickey Crews – Cape Girardeau
Dick Cortois – Perryville, Missouri
Bob Donze – Ste. Genevieve, Missouri
Bill Ewing * – Cape Girardeau
Jim Finn * – Herrin, Illinois
Jon Kent Fisher * – Cape Girardeau
Elwood Fisher * – Cape Girardeau
Paul Fliege – Jackson, Missouri
Bill French * – Cape Girardeau
Mike Goldsmith – Fredericktown, Missouri
Jacob Herzog – Jackson, Missouri
Joe James – Cape Girardeau
Dr. Bob Jones – Cape Girardeau
E.W. Kassel * – Cape Girardeau
Josh Koehler – Jackson, Missouri
Terry Kratky – St. Louis
Bill McCaleb – Flat River, Missouri
Chris Deusinger – Cape Girardeau

Renee McClain – Cape Girardeau
Eric McGowan – Jackson, Missouri
Mike Neville – Cape Girardeau
Bruce Nunnelly – Cape Girardeau
John Quinn – Cape Girardeau
Buddy Rogers – Carbondale, Illinois
Gary Rybolt – St. Louis
Scott Rybolt – Dexter, Missouri
Ron Schnare – Cape Girardeau
Pat Schwent – Jackson, Missouri
Larry Sharpio – St. Louis
Austin Sikes –Fredericktown, Missouri
Bob Sisco * – Cape Girardeau
Kerry Slinkard – Cape Girardeau
Sonny Slinkard * – Cape Girardeau
Brandon Suedekum – Jackson, Missouri
Ralph Thomas – Jackson, Tennessee
Dr. Jervis Underwood – Cape Girardeau
Isaac Venable – Jackson, Missouri

Banjo

Joe Blackwell – Cape Girardeau
David Baldwin – Cape Girardeau

Guitar

J.B. Carney – Herrin, Illinois
Don Dickerson – Cape Girardeau
Kurt Morrison – Chicago, Illinois
Gary Presley – St. Louis
Dr. Jerry Richardson * – Cape Girardeau

Steve Schaffner – Cape Girardeau
Rep. Jim Siegfried – Marshall, Missouri
Chuck Sowers – Cape Girardeau
Will West – Jefferson City, Missouri
Bruce Zimmerman – Cape Girardeau

Organ

Dr. Richard Moore – Cape Girardeau
Kyle Lehning – Nashville, Tennessee
Terry Parker – Charleston, Missouri
Dr. Gary Miller * – Cape Girardeau
Mary Miller – Cape Girardeau

Beverly Reece – Cape Girardeau
Rebecca Gentry – Cape Girardeau
Dee Dee Reed – Charleston, Missouri
Helen Ueleke – Cape Girardeau

Piano

Richard "Butch" Eggimann * – Cape Girardeau
Jim Leggett * – Bloomfield, Missouri
Buddy Vaughn * – McClure, Illinois
Beverly Reece – Cape Girardeau
Dr. Richard Moore – Cape Girardeau
"H" Pruitte * – Paducah, Kentucky
Earl Myhre – Mounds, Illinois
"Chips" Curtis – St. Louis
Mike Michelson – Jefferson City, Missouri
Pete Propst * – Cape Girardeau
Jack Kinder * – Cape Girardeau
Jim Rhodes – Jackson, Missouri
"Bud" Miget – Perryville, Missouri
Mimi Kennison – Perryville, Missouri
Scott Blackwell – Cape Girardeau
Mel Goot – Carbondale, Illinois
John Pyatt – St. Louis
Vi Keys * – Cape Girardeau
Rep. Rachel Bringer – Palmyra, Missouri
Pete Parysek – Dexter, Missouri
Gus Populos – Carbondale, Illinois
Mark Trautwein – Cape Girardeau
Bill Gerhardt – Cape Girardeau
Jerry Bullock – Cape Girardeau
Brett Yount – Jackson, Missouri
Vince Huffman * – Murphysboro, Illinois

Bass

Joe Blackwell – Cape Girardeau
Jim Worley * – St. Mary, Missouri
Matt Pittman – Jackson
Joe Heuer – Cape Girardeau
Mike Wilkins * – Paducah, Kentucky
Jim Widner – Jefferson City/St. Louis
Richard Powell * – Sikeston/Jefferson City
Jim Parker – St. Louis
Jim Wall – Carbondale
Jim Fern * – Calvert City, Kentucky
Rep. W.T. Dawson – Jefferson City
Phil Brown – Carbondale, Illinois
Jarrod Harris – Cape Girardeau
Dr. David Green * – Cape Girardeau

Drums

Don Conner – Jefferson City, Missouri
Jay Contrino – Cape Girardeau
Mark Ellison – Perryville, Missouri
Don Ford * – Cape Girardeau
Keller Ford – Cape Girardeau
Ryan Harper – Jackson, Missouri
Denny Hill – Cape Girardeau
Mark Hill * – Cape Girardeau
Dean Hughes – Princeton, Kentucky
Brad Lyle * – Cape Girardeau
Craig Marshall – Cape Girardeau
Harry Martin – Cape Girardeau
Rich Oberto – Columbia, Missouri
Chuck Rapp – Cape Girardeau
David Thompson – Jackson, Missouri
Steve Williams – Cairo, Illinois

Arrangers

Bob Sisco * – Cape/Los Angeles, California
John Quinn – Cape Girardeau
Jim Rhodes – Jackson, Missouri
"Bud" Miget – Perryville, Missouri
"H" Pruitte * – Paducah, Kentucky

Master of Ceremonies

Dan Wiethop – Cape Girardeau
Jay Landers – Springfield, Illinois

Music has obviously been the focal point of my life while having a family, working in the family funeral home as a licensed embalmer and funeral director, directing a junior high and high school band, serving two terms on the Cape Girardeau Board of Education, two terms in the Missouri House of Representatives, running for the U.S. Congress, owning several businesses, authoring two books, and lobbying in the State Capitol for the past 25 years. And hey, I haven't played my last note yet!

Jerry Ford.

Jerry Ford Jazz Band. Cape Girardeau Riverfront.

The Mamanettes. L to r: Virginia Boren, Pat Blackwell, Virginia Hill.

The Blackwells

Joe and Pat Blackwell performed with me for 45 years: Joe on bass, Pat on vocals and, for a time, their son Scott on keyboards. In the beginning, Pat's dad made her cry for insisting she had to sing in front of his friends. That training took hold because she's been singing ever since. She took operatic voice lessons as a girl in St. Louis. She moved to Cape as a sophomore in high school, took lessons from Professor Brandt, and sang in all the school vocal groups. She memorized all the words to the top 10 songs on the weekly TV Show *Your Hit Parade*.

Pat's association with the Cape Choraliers lasted 25 years. While there, she formed The Mamanettes, a trio including Virginia Boren and Virginia Hill that performed famous McGuire Sisters' hits. They appeared on *The Breakfast Show* on KFVS–TV for four years, sang with the Choraliers at the 1964 World's Fair, and appeared in all 20 Jaycee Follies. Jack Kinder's band provided back-up, and they performed with him every Friday night in the Officer's Club at the Malden Air Force Base. The band consisted of Kinder (piano), Bill Crass (trumpet), Dennis Slinkard (sax), and Sherman Downing (drums).

Jim Rhodes of Versatile Television Productions hired Pat to perform television commercials—Jim Rhodes (piano), Jim Mulkey and Don Ford (drums), Bob Sisco (bass)—including Blue Bell Meats, Bunny Bread, Central Hardware, Burgermiester Beer, and King Cotton Meats.

Blackwell began singing with the Bob Sisco Orchestra in 1958. When Sisco left for California in 1960, her husband Joe formed a band that included himself (bass), Jim Leggett (piano), Steve Williams (drums), Glenn Chilton (sax), and Fred Goodwin and David Little (trombone). They played regularly at the Turquoise Club in the Holiday Inn at Poplar Bluff, and the Marion, Illinois, Country Club for five years.

Joe and Pat joined the Jerry Ford Orchestra in 1965 and continued until 2010. Their son Scott played with the JFO briefly and then went on the road playing rock 'n' roll for several years. He ended up in Nashville where he had a good career for many years recording with Tanya Tucker, Aaron Tippin, Sammy Kershaw, John Anderson, Joe Stampley, Joe Diffie, and others. He gave "Rascal Flatts" their name and wrote the title song for one of Kershaw's albums, *Honky Tonk Boots*.

Pat says there are many funny and unusual incidents that have occurred over the years. One more unexpected than most:

> We were playing at the Casa Loma Ballroom located close to where I grew up in south St. Louis. It was hot, and during one of my numbers, I passed out and fell between two saxophone stands. I was told Jerry just stood there looking down at me, and the band kept playing. Jerry told me later, as he looked

down at me, he thought I had come home to die! There was a doctor in the house who revived me, arranged for me to go to the hospital, where I stayed the night for observation. The next time we played at the Casa Loma, the doctor attended.

Joe and Pat's other two kids are also musically gifted. Their daughter Sally played sax and sang in musicals in high school. Their son Sam played sax in Willie Bollinger's band, Willie and the Challengers, and now plays harmonica on occasion. A former editor of the *Southeast Missourian* daily newspaper, Sam is the best columnist in our area and taught at Southeast Missouri State University, where he directed the college newspaper, *The Capaha Arrow*.

Recalling the past, Pat says

Everyone has to have a passion to be happy. Mine is singing and listening to jazz. I've been doing it all my life. The other night, Friday, February 11, 2011, I was at the River Campus listening to Southeast's jazz bands in concert. Those college kids were swingin' and groovin'. You could tell they were lovin' it, and so was I.

Pat Schwent.

Pat Schwent & Saxy Jazz

Pat Schwent has developed into a world-class saxophonist since she retired from 27 years as a high school band director in Jackson, Missouri. After performing with us on a regular basis for over 20 years, she's branched out on her own and formed "Saxy Jazz," a duo-quartet-quintet Motown Band ranging from 6 to 13 players, and is extremely popular throughout our region. She plays concerts with "name" entertainers, musicals, and other regional shows, which included a stint in Branson. Looking back, Pat remembers, "In the

early '80s, not many band leaders would ask a female horn player to perform with them. To Jerry, I am eternally grateful."

Pat grew up in a musical family in Ste. Genevieve. Her mother played piano with Elmo Donze and Herb Kist. Her Aunt Patty played drums and her sister Brenda, born with spinabifida and confined to a wheelchair, played guitar and sang. "My parents bought me a saxophone at age 12 and began teaching me the standard tunes of the era. Mom probably taught me over 100 of them," Pat recalls. At age 14, Pat joined the family group on sax and starred in the popular band, Brenda Kiefer and the Swing Tones, throughout their 2-state region for 25 years.

Schwent attended Mineral Area College and graduated from Southeast Missouri State University with a B.S. in music, and received an M.A. from Southwest Missouri State in 1971. She taught at Woodland High School from 1971 to 1975, and then began at Jackson.

Pat Schwent and Saxy Jazz. COURTESY OF CHEEKWOOD STUDIOS.

There she served with distinction, instructing all woodwind players in the Marching, Concert, and Symphonic Bands, and led the Jazz Band.

Pat credits her mom, high school band director Leo Miget, and her husband Tim for all their support. "Not many people have had the opportunities to do musically what I have done. I couldn't have done it without them. Because of them, I continue learning, studying, and practicing to improve my love of playing jazz."

Rock 'n' Roll

Rock 'n' Roll burst on the scene in 1955 with Bill Haley and the Comets' recording of "Rock Around the Clock." But almost immediately (1956-1957), the King of Rock 'n' Roll, Elvis Presley, exploded on the national scene with several No.1 hits, and the world has never been the same. The new phenomenon of "rock" features strong beats, pounding rhythms, electronic guitars and keyboards, and synthesizers. The new electronic age fostered styles of heavy metal, funk, disco, fusion, rap, punk, videos, and MTV. Rock ushered in the greatest commercial success of music in history.

Just as jazz spawned many outstanding musicians in its day here in Cape, rock has done the same with the younger set. This section of the book showcases the many talented people who have gained national notoriety thanks to rock 'n' roll.

Raymond "Tiny" Ford. LUEDERS STUDIOS.

Mike Ford. COURTESY OF
FORD ENTERTAINMENT & PRODUCTIONS.

Ford Entertainment & Productions

Mike Ford turned a small booking agency, started by his mom and dad in 1956, into a full-service, nationwide, entertainment and production company. Mike's dad, Raymond "Tiny" Ford Jr. started in the entertainment business when he opened two popular night clubs in the early 1950s: Tiny's Dance Land in Scott City and the Ozark Corral in Cape. As he showcased local rock 'n' roll and country talent and became familiar with regional booking agents, he gradually began booking acts himself for tours throughout the U.S. and Canada.

Ford booked Elvis's bass player Bill Black, and his famous Bill Black Combo, exclusively in the late '50s and early '60s. Narvel Felts was Tiny's first local "name" performer. Ford followed Felts with Mert Mirly, Fred Horrell, Dennis Turner, Billy Swan, Mike Smith and the Runaways, and others in our area, including my orchestra.

Ford published Billy Swan's first song, "Lover Please." It was recorded by local singer Dennis Turner and became a regional hit. Tiny took to the road with his Cadillac, big cigars, and Turner, to showcase the song and Dennis's talent, but Clyde McPhatter latched onto the song and made it a national hit. During this time Tiny began building his agency, booking acts in larger dance clubs in the Midwest. Tiny also began booking some greats of the time including Chubby Checker, Roy Orbison, Johnny Cash, Jerry Lee Lewis, and Neil Sedaka. Most of the original rock 'n' roll groups of our region credit Tiny as the one person who enabled them to have success in the music business.

After graduating from Southeast in 1971, Mike joined the growing family business. He continued the family tradition and, in 1987, changed the name to Ford Entertainment & Productions to reflect their newly expanded services. From talent acquisitions to fully produced shows, they have a diversified list of clients that includes: Huey Lewis and the News, Vince Gill, Natalie Cole, Kenny Rogers, Johnny Mathis, Bill Cosby, Olivia Newton-John, Shirley Jones, The Pointer Sisters, Billy Ray Cyrus, Jeff Foxworthy, The Doobie Brothers, Chicago, Barbara Mandrell, The Four Tops, Bobby Vinton, Willie Nelson, Waylon Jennings, Gladys Knight, Buddy Hackett, Anne Murray, REO Speedwagon, 38 Special, Styx, Wayne Newton, Randy Travis, Ben Vereen, Suzanne Somers, Lou Rawls, the Oak Ridge Boys, and many more.

Over the past 40 years, Mike has developed a unique stable of top-notch entertainers, including comedians, magicians, strolling musicians, big bands, rock 'n' roll bands, and after dinner speakers, covering every genre of entertainment. He's even introduced a Quick-Setup Hydraulic Mobile Stage, saving time, expense, and liability for major shows and venues. Ford Entertainment & Productions is truly a great American phenomenon.

Narvel Felts.

Narvel Felts

Narvel Felts raised himself out of the cotton fields of the Missouri Bootheel to become an international country and rockabilly recording artist and entertainer who has over 32 tours of Europe to his credit, and still counting. Born near Keiser, Arkansas, in 1938, and raised near Bernie, Missouri, Felts has recorded more than 30 albums and 80 singles for various record companies in his more than 50 years in the business. Seven of those singles have climbed into the Billboard Top 10. He's in this book because of his mentorship of Mert Mirly, Fred Horrell, Lou Hobbs, Billy Swan, and many others in our region.

"Felts was already a recording artist when the other pioneers of rock 'n' roll began," Fred Horrell states. "Narvel was first. He had a record contract, an agent, fans, and performed concerts around the country. I owe him a lot."

Back near Bernie, Felt's mother listened to country music on the radio. "We didn't have electricity in our home," Narvel remembers. "So we listened to what Momma wanted to hear on our battery-powered radio: Ernest Tubb, Hank Snow, and other stars of the Grand Ole Opry. That music rescued me from choppin' cotton! It was the only way for a kid to make money there. In the summers, I would earn fifty cents an hour choppin' cotton, and in the fall I'd earn three dollars per a hundred pounds pickin'. On a good day, I could pick two hundred pounds from sun-up to sunset. It paid for my first guitar and first car."

Felts entered a talent show at Bernie High School and was discovered by a disc jockey who just happened to be there. Narvel heard on the local radio station a message from the DJ, "If Narvel Felts is listening, contact KDEX immediately." He ran out of the house to tell his daddy, and they drove eight miles to a pay phone to call the station, where he got his first break. That break led him to become one of the original rock 'n' roll recording artists in the '50s and one of the top country artists of the '70s, with more than 70 international hits, including the 1975 Record of the Year, "Reconsider Me," and membership in the Rockabilly Hall of Fame.

His first single, "Kiss-a Me Baby," when he was 18, did fairly well on the charts. Roy Orbison helped him along the way. Orbison was instrumental in getting him a Sun Record deal. In a few months, Felts moved on to Mercury Records for 1957 and 1958. "Honey Love" got Felts on the Billboard Top 100 for the first time. He then released "Mountain of Love" and "I'd Trade All of My Tomorrows," with moderate success.

His major hit in 1973 was "Drift Away," No. 8 on Billboard's Hot Country Chart. It launched his "country" streak that continues to this day. In 1975, he signed with ABC Dot Records and enjoyed his biggest hit, "Reconsider Me," which showcased his soaring falsetto and high tenor range. The song reached No. 1 and was the second biggest selling record that year. Other top singles came along, including "Lonely Tear-drops," "Funny How Time Slips Away," and "Everlasting Love."

Felt's first band was really good. I've had people tell me over the years, "They had a great sound." I can attest to it because several of us who played in the Cape Municipal Band back in the '50s would go to Tiny's Dance Land in Fornfelt (now Scott City) after our concerts on Wednesday nights, have a beer, and listen to Felts. Members were Felts (vocals & guitar), J.W. Grubbs (bass), Jerry Tuttle (sax, steel guitar, and piano), Leon Barnett (lead guitar), and Bob Taylor (drums). Conway Twitty got Felts booked on tours of the Canadian Show Club Circuit in 1959. In 1960, Felts hired Matt Lucas to play drums. In 1963, Lucas had his own hit, "I'm Movin On." The band also toured Panama, Bermuda, and New Zealand.

From 1961 to 1967, Felts came off the road to join the National Guard in Poplar Bluff. With Tiny's help, he booked regional shows on weekends. He had a TV Show on Channel 8 in Jonesboro, Arkansas. The show gave him additional exposure over a wide area. Narvel's son, Narvel Jr. ("Bub") became a good drummer and toured Europe, Norway, Sweden, and other countries for several years with the band. One night, Bub was in a car accident near Campbell. Narvel remembers, "When the officer came to the door, he just stood there. I knew it was bad. He finally said, 'Narvel, he didn't make it.' I screamed at the top of my voice, and I've never quite gotten over it." Felts dedicates one of three songs in his son's memory at every performance: "Danny Boy," "Since I Don't Have You," or "Even Now."

Narvel Felts.

Felts lives with his wife of 48 years, Loretta, in Malden on Narvel Felts Avenue. I visited them on a Saturday afternoon in February of 2011 in preparation for this book. Felts told me,

> It wasn't easy. Back in the early days, skating rinks and drive-in theaters were fertile ground for rock 'n' roll bands. On August 7, 1956, I was featured singer in Jerry Mercer's band. We joined Roy Orbison and Eddie Bond on the roof of the concession stand at the Family Drive-In Theater in Dexter for our first big concert. Momma wanted me to finish high school, but I knew if I didn't take this opportunity when Mercer hired me, it would be gone forever. Music has completely changed my life. It's given me a career since 1956 doing something I really love to do. I've made a decent living and raised a family. I'm 72, and fortunate to have traveled all over the world and met a lot of wonderful people.

Felts continues to headline twelve to fifteen shows each year and also appears as one of our country's original rock 'n' roll and country artists with two national touring shows, "Legends and Memories" and "Country Gold." And he has tours of Europe booked in 2011. Not bad for a boy who began choppin' cotton in the Bootheel of Missouri almost 70 years ago!

Mert Mirly and the Rhythm Steppers. L to r: Charlie Thurman, Fred Horrell, Mert Mirly, Terry Heuer, Irving Wadlington. RHOTON STUDIO.

Mert Mirly and the Rhythm Steppers

Mert Mirly and the Rhythm Steppers was the first of an amazing group of rock 'n' roll bands in the Cape Girardeau area in the early '50s. Living in Chaffee, a stone's throw from Cape, Mert brought together the best rock musicians in the area at the time: Fred Horrell (bass/guitar), Charlie Thurman (guitar), Irving Wadlington (keyboards), Terry Heuer (sax), and Gene Casey (piano), Jerry Bass (bass), Bobby Bugg (drums), Dennis Turner (vocals), Mike Neville (sax), Chuck Sowers (guitar), and more, all performed with Mert from time to time.

Mert started playing trumpet in school. He later switched to drums when he joined the Welter 4 band for several years. He went into the army right out of high school, serving in Japan and Korea. He formed his own group in 1951.

Mert befriended and recorded with the Bill Black Combo in Nashville. Black had been the bass player for Elvis. Black's contacts, along with Tiny Ford Productions, enabled Mert to tour and perform in some in the major clubs throughout the Midwest. In fact, Mert was instrumental in having Dennis Turner record Billy Swan's "Lover Please" before it became a hit by Clyde McPhatter. Fred Horrell remembers Mert as a real bandleader.

> Mert was a good drummer and had management ability and experience. He was older, had a good job at N.O. Nelson, and was the only one with any sense! He took us under his wing and kept us in line. He was also the only one who had any money and could get credit and sign for equipment purchases. And he had a good, dependable station wagon for us to travel in.
>
> We had a real good band: Mert (drums), Charlie Thurman (guitar) and Bob Kielhefher (sax), and Gene Casey (keyboards), and me on bass and vocals. While we were all good, Charlie Thurman was the great one. Tiny booked us all over the area. Mert was a good showman and a great emcee. We not only provided good music, Mert entertained! Our real break came when Tiny booked Narvel Felts into the Canadian circuit. That opened up many venues for us, including Tiny's Dance Land on Wednesday nights. I started promoting the band and got us on Channel 3 WSIL Harrisburg and *The Breakfast Show* on KFVS Channel 12. We were the first rock 'n' roll band on KFVS!

When Mert left the road, Tiny remarked, "I'll miss the great guy, and I hope he will continue to drop around."

Mert passed away in 2010, leaving a legacy of nurturing many young musicians as leader of the first rock 'n' roll band in our immediate area. Mert's widow, Betty said, "Mert always expected the band to look good—white coats and pressed pants. He had a hard time handling the attention directed towards him. He always tried to deflect the credit to his band members." She reflected for a moment, and then remarked, "He was always just plain Mert."

Mert Mirly.

Fred Horrell.

Fred Horrell & the Flames

Fred Horrell has turned his sharp mind, energetic persona, and natural musical ability into a lifetime of musical performance and enjoyment for him and everyone in and around our area. Fred was a busy kid. He carhopped, pumped gas, set bowling pins, worked a paper route, clerked at a drug store, anything to make a buck. He was good in math, but didn't like music theory or reading music. He once remarked, "What will I ever need to know this for?" He loved to hear the sound of guitars and sang along with songs on the radio, not knowing in his late teens that his music would be broadcast over TV and radio to thousands of people, and he'd get paid for doing it.

Fred also listened to the new music of his generation, rock 'n' roll, with the likes of "Mystery Train" and "That's Alright, Mama." The styles of Elvis, Roy Orbison, Carl Perkins, and Bill Haley were paramount in his psyche. While he was a great high school football player, music kept churning in his head. He bought a 1956 Fender Telecaster guitar, took lessons, practiced, played with a few local bands, and with encouragement from friends, reluctantly entered a talent show at Onnie Wheeler's Ozark Corral. He won!

That was it. He formed his first band, The Corvettes. He sang with Narvel Felts and his Rockets, and then landed a job as lead singer with Mert Mirly and the Rhythm Steppers. They had a regular gig at popular Tiny's Dance Land in Fornfelt, Missouri, just a couple of miles south of Cape Girardeau. The group didn't have a bass, so Fred showed up one night with a new Fender Precision Bass. As he was tuning it on the stand, Mert asked, "What are you going to do with that thing?" Fred casually answered, "I'm going to play it." And he did, knowing if he didn't, he might lose his job.

Fred practiced at home a lot and became proficient "walking the bass" and singing at the same time. Leon Barnett, lead guitarist with Narvel Felts, complimented Fred "for nailing that bass playing to the wall." As the band got better, Fred turned his talents to promoting the group. He landed a regular spot on KFVS–TV's CBS *Morning Show* for the band. They became regulars on Lucky Leroy's ABC–TV Channel 3 show in Harrisburg, Illinois. With the TV exposure, Mert Mirly and the Rhythm Steppers appeared throughout our five-state area, and it led to higher paying jobs. They cut their first record in Chicago in 1959.

Fred left Mirly and formed his own band, Fred Horrell and The Flames, in 1960. Tiny booked them in Baltimore, Detroit, Arkansas, Iowa, Kentucky, Tennessee, and then into the Rainbow Inn in St. Louis for one night. They stayed 35 weeks. They packed the house each night with their professional sound, developed on the road, and held their own with their biggest competition, Ike and Tina Turner.

Fred toured with the Bill Black Combo for a time and also with Bruce "Hey Baby"

Channel, Roy Orbison, Gene Simmons, Lee Dorsey ("Ya Ya"), Charley Rich, and Jimmie Seals. While Fred loved performing, the strain of constant traveling got old. Billy Swan had taken the role as lead singer of the Flames in Fred's absence. Upon his return, Fred recorded Billy's first song, "Lover Please," immediately recognizing its potential. Bill Black and former Flames singer, Dennis Turner, recorded the song first and it later became Clyde McPhatter's smash hit.

The Flames expanded to include two saxes, keyboard, guitar, bass, drums, four singers, and continued performing throughout the Midwest for many years. Some of the outstanding musicians Horrell attracted were saxophonist Terry Heuer, bassist Jerry Bass, and keyboard player Irving Wadlington. The band propelled several members into the national limelight: drummer Bobby Bugg with famous sax player Ace Cannon, guitarist Chuck Sowers with Lee Mace, guitarist Charlie Thurman with Nashville artist Red Sovine, Ron Duff with Jimmy Velvet, Tom Stovall with Warner Brothers, Alvin Nunnally with Facts O' Life, David Kielhofner with Kris Kristofferson, vocalist Dennis Turner with the Bill Black Combo, and keyboardist Billy Swan, who wrote several huge hits including "Lover Please" and "I Can Help" and performed worldwide with Kris Kristofferson for over 25 years.

By 1972, Fred's carpet business had grown to the point that he could no longer justify the hours away from the business. He disbanded the group, only to reform after two long, sad years. "I just wasn't happy. I couldn't stand not having music in my life," he explained. He continued for another 10 years, backing his daughter, Kimberly (Kim Keele Kaminski).

In the 1980s, Fred started recording and producing country records in Nashville. His releases made the independent record charts and received extensive radio play throughout the U.S. Two made The Cashbox Top 100. They can be purchased on iTunes, E-music, Rhapsody, and others. He also promotes, produces, and records himself and others on his label, Capetown Records. He plays occasionally in local groups and resurrects The Flames for occasional reunions and charity causes. Fred looks back on those days with great fondness and pride. He says, "I wouldn't take anything for those days. We met a lot of great people and got to see places and do special things that most folks could never do."

When Fred's friend and fellow musician, Rockabilly Hall of Famer Lou Hobbs, presented the Certificate of Induction into the Hall of Fame to Fred, he rightly reminded everyone, "Fred was there at the beginning of rock 'n' roll, along with Elvis, Buddy Holly, and the rest." Fred responded, "I'm really proud to be listed right next to one of my idols and friends, Roy Orbison. He was a fantastic artist and great person."

I see Fred most Friday evenings when he and his wife Pat and friends Joe and Shannon Anders dine down by the river (Mississippi) at Port Cape Restaurant. He still has his ever-present smile and infectious laugh. I think it's because of his musical aptitude. There's something about many musicians that, besides craziness, emits a kind of gracious sensitivity. Anyone who knows Fred Horrell knows he does.

Vi Keys and The Dude Ranch Boys. COURTESY OF EDDIE KEYS.

Keys Music

A fortuitous change of pace four-week vacation gig in the lounge of the old Marquette Hotel in 1959 brought Vi and Eddie Keys from Kansas City to Cape Girardeau. That engagement lasted 14 weeks, then segued into 9 years performing in the lounge of the Purple Crackle Club and over 30 years operating Keys Music Store in Downtown Cape. Along the way, they raised four children, all musicians, and Cape has been the beneficiary.

Their journey started in the Dust Bowl of Oklahoma where Vi was raised with five brothers and three sisters. Her dad was laid off from the railroad and moved his family to rural Oklahoma to farm. Musically talented from birth, Vi would exchange a cool glass of water for a chance to play her brother's harmonica. She took up the fiddle and began playing for dances in saloons against her mother's wishes. She got a $2 a night job with a traveling band, where she met a good-looking young guitarist, Eddie Keys.

Vi and Eddie Keys. COURTESY OF *SOUTHEAST MISSOURIAN*.

They married in 1940 and moved to Joplin. When Eddie went into the military, Vi took her kids and joined both the Cole & Walters Circus band and a medicine show for one night stands in order to keep her family together. Upon Eddie's return, they eventually settled in Kansas City playing jazz and western swing for 15 years with Frankie Kay's band. And then in 1959, they made the fateful trip to the gig at the Marquette Hotel in Cape Girardeau.

In 1965, Vi secured a regional franchise for Hammond organs and opened Keys Music Store on Broadway Hill. It quickly became a haven for regional rockers. The business operated for 35 years, as son Eddie Jr. became a partner, and together they made it a success. Father Eddie formed a musicians' Union 818 affiliated with the national AFL–CIO, which enabled area musicians to extend their presence throughout our five-state region.

Vi Keys.

Their daughter, Vi Ann, was my first vocalist. As one might expect growing up in that environment, she sang all the genres well and played a great tenor sax. She met Herb Jimmerson, keyboard player and arranger, in Phoenix, and they traveled with their show band throughout the states, including Hawaii, and mostly in Las Vegas and Lake Tahoe. They both signed with Fantasy Records in San Francisco, Vi Ann as a singer and Herb as a staff producer, and stayed for four years. Two albums under the name *Paradise Express* are still available on the internet. They then started their own Production Company, Omega Studios, and signed and produced various artists.

Their son Eddie Ray played drums, bass, trumpet, sax, flute, trombone, and piano. His rock group, TUFA, was a staple rock band around Cape for 20 years. TUFA's personnel included Eddie on lead guitar/vocals, Chuck Hanna on keyboards/vocals, Allan Palermo on bass, and Wesley Gray on drums/vocals.

Eddie Ray's son Billy, a keyboardist and trumpet player, formed the rock groups Amethyst and Papa Aborigine. Amethyst lasted three years and included Keys (keyboards/vocals), Keller Ford (drums/vocals), Mark Wyatt (guitar), and T.J. "Machine Gun" Farrow (bass). Papa Aborigine lasted 10 years. Members included Keys (keyboards/vocals), Keller Ford (drums/vocals), Chris Ford and Jamie Pender (bass), and Alex Allen (guitar). Keys is currently a band director at Cape Central.

In Vi's later years, she entertained on a Hammond organ at the Holiday Inn Restaurant for 25 years. After a life of many hardships, she passed away in February of 2009, after giving years of enjoyment to people throughout the Midwest. I've never known any woman who persevered more than Vi Keys. I'll never forget her grit, her smile, her talent, and her enormous heart.

TUFA. L to r: Eddie Keys, Allan Palermo, Wesley Gray, Chuck Hanna. Courtesy of Eddie Keys.

Lou Hobbs.

Lou Hobbs

The amazing Lou Hobbs earned five cents a song standing on a crate in a general store at age 6 and turned his talent into a lifetime of performing Rockabilly, a melding of gospel, blues, and rock, throughout the U.S., Canada, and Europe. And he and his wife Nancy raised a family of five daughters, to boot. From 1962 thru 2000, Lou held 26 recording sessions in Memphis; Nashville; Muscle Shoals, Alabama; Cape Girardeau; and Jackson, Missouri, cranking out regional and national hits. In addition to touring nationally, he produced a weekly television show at KFVS–TV in Cape Girardeau for over 20 years that aired in our 5-state region as well as over 225 cable outlets.

Lou was born in 1941 "across the tracks" in south Cape, adjacent to the muddy Mississippi River bank. His parents were farm hands, picking cotton for a paltry living. Lou's mother was from a musical family who had a band, The Jewels, and a radio show on KFVS radio in the 1930s. Lou listened to Hank Williams sing on the radio and visited every day on his neighbor's porch to listen to Gerald Kaempfer pick his guitar. Kaempfer, a self-taught musician, had the reputation within his circle as being as gifted as anyone around Cape in those days.

Lou was the center of attraction, according to his brother Darrell. "Mom promoted Lou from the moment he entered first grade at May Greene School: churches, school assemblies, fairs, talent shows, any way to get him before the public."

I asked Darrell if Lou ever did anything besides perform music. He laughed, "Lord no. He went with me on a couple of service calls (Darrell's Cleaning Service) and spilled his bucket of dirty water all over our freshly waxed floor on one, and on the other, he stood on a sink to clean venetian blinds, and the weight of his body pulled the sink off the wall! He was generally all thumbs most of the time, but he sure could sing, play his guitar, and entertain folks."

In 1955, Lou became a regular on Onnie Wheeler's Ozark Corral radio show. After a couple of years, he branched out on his own with the help of another role model, friend, and mentor, Narvel Felts. "Buddy Buddy" Harris, owner of the Paradise Club in southern Illinois, signed Lou to a one-year contract and took him to Memphis to record. Harris had several hundred juke boxes located in clubs throughout five states, the perfect venue for promoting records and entertainers. The session was at Fernwood Records featuring Chuck Sowers (lead guitar), Rudy Gonzalis (bass), Paul Slinkard (drums), Lou on guitar and vocals, Bill Black offering advice, and engineered by Slim Wallis. The song was a Narvel Felts tune, "All That Heaven Sent," and the flip side was "Mama, Mama, Mama."

Felts connected Hobbs with Roland James of Sonic Studio in Memphis who engineered eight records for Lou between 1963 and 1966. He then toured the U.S. and Canada for the next six years. When Felts hit a big one with "Drift Away" in the mid-seventies, he convinced Lou to join and front his new band. That collaboration lasted for over a decade. Felts produced several records for Hobbs during this time, and after 20 years in the business, several of Lou's records finally made the Top 100: "Loving You Was All I Ever Needed," "We're Building Our Love On A Rock," "Another Place, Another Time," and more.

The year 1986 was pivotal. That's the year he launched his television show on KFVS–TV that lasted 20 years. The syndicated show featured stars like Johnny Cash, George Jones, Kris Kristofferson, Randy Travis, his high school buddy Billy Swan, and, of course, Narvel Felts.

For Lou, 1990 was also a very good year. Hobbs wrote, "Living on the New Madrid Fault Line," and he performed it live before an international group of news media that gathered the day Ivan Browning forecast another earthquake on the New Madrid fault. That exposure landed him on *Good Morning America, A Current Affair, Night Line with Ted Coppell, CNN Headline News,* and ninety other world-wide outlets. Record sales and bookings soared.

In 1994, Felts orchestrated a record deal for Lou in Germany, which resulted in two Top 10 records, "What's Wrong With Me" and "Back to Missouri." In 1998, Lou was diagnosed with Parkinson's Disease which slowly began to limit his activities. With his never-ending faith in the Lord, he recuperated enough to continue taping his TV show and briefly returned to recording.

Lou Hobbs. COURTESY OF DARRELL HOBBS.

In 1999, several of his songs hit the Top 10 and Top 20 in Europe, the most of any artist that year. In 2000, he toured England, filming acts at the Hembsy Rock 'n' Roll Festival for his TV show. Hobbs died in 2007, leaving a wealth of recorded music in the style he helped invent and popularize. He was one of the original members of the Rockabilly Hall of Fame, and anyone who knew Lou or listened to his recordings understood he truly was an original.

Billy Swan.

Billy Swan

Billy Swan had big dreams as a kid. His sister Joy reported that he used to say, "When I grow up, I'm going to be rich, famous, and drive a pink Cadillac." And he did. He followed his dreams to the heights of the country music scene as a composer, producer, and performer.

Joy helped raise Billy. Their parents died when Billy was 12. She said, "Billy was a quiet but determined kid. He was curious, always showing up at civic events like parades, service club dinners, celebrity appearances, celebrations, anything that was out of his normal routine. He especially loved Jerry Lee Lewis's songs like 'Whole Lotta Shakin' Going On' and 'Great Balls Of Fire'."

Billy later described it in *Rolling Stone Magazine*:

> Jerry Lee Lewis had the biggest impact on me. He was even bigger than Elvis. I dug that piano. "Whole Lotta Shakin' Going On" and "Great Balls Of Fire" were the greatest things I ever heard. And there was Buddy Holly. I remember, I used to get up in a tree and swing, singing "Oh Boy" as loud as I could.

Billy and I survived elementary, junior high, high school, and most of college together. We graduated from Central High School in 1960. In college, I was a member of the Sigma Chi Fraternity, and Billy lived at the Sig house on Broadway.

Our Bootheel area is a hot bed of high school basketball. It's a religion. In the '60-'61 school year, Billy was manager of Southeast Missouri State College's men's basketball team that went all the way to the NCAA Division II National Championship game before losing to Wittenberg of Ohio, 42 to 38. It was before shot clocks, and Wittenberg held the ball for most of the game. We thought we had the better team.

Billy's uncle, Sonny Stevens, had been a saxophone player in Don McNeely's Orchestra. McNeely was a well-known radio and television personality in the Southeast Missouri area at our local CBS affiliate station, KFVS. As a youngster, Billy would drop by and visit McNeely. "Don was always so nice. I'd follow him around the station. I got the biggest kick being there, watching him do live radio. . . . Man, that fascinated me," Billy explained. "Don is one of my heroes. What a gentleman."

In conducting interviews for this book, Don McNeely said to me one day, "Jerry, you know the first time I met Billy Swan was at the SEMO District Fair. I was doing a 'man on the street' bit for KFVS radio. I'd run out of people to talk to when I saw this little kid. I went up to him and asked his name. "The little boy quickly answered, 'My name is Billy Swan. What's yours?'"

Don laughed as he told the story and remarked, "I knew that little boy would go far!"

Billy had a good ear for melodies and kicked around singing in several local rock bands. He even hitchhiked to Chaffee, Missouri (15 miles from Cape), to rehearse with Mert Mirly and the Rhythm Steppers.

Billy always had a way with words. His high school English teacher, Mary Z. Reed, encouraged him to continue writing poetry. His Top 10 hit "Lover Please" began as a poem in Mrs. Reed's class. His itch took him to Memphis in 1961. Bill Black liked "Lover Please." He published it and convinced Clyde McPhatter to record it. It was a big hit. It would later win a Grammy when it was re-recorded by Kris Kristofferson and Rita Coolidge in 1975.

Billy commuted back and forth from Cape to Memphis and, for about five months in 1963, lived with Elvis Presley's uncle and aunt, Travis and Lorraine Smith. In August of 1963, he moved to Nashville, Tennessee. He was 21. As he stated many times, "I knew if I was going to make it in the country music business, I would have to go where the action was."

In those days, the Nashville music scene of recording studios, production houses, etc., were crowded into a small three or four block area around 16th Avenue, now known as Music Row. Billy took an apartment in the middle of the action above the Tally-Ho Tavern. There he bumped into many future stars from time to time, including Kris Kristofferson. The first time was in 1964 at one of those chance "Hello, how are you" meetings at Buckhorn Music, which was Marijon Wilkin's Publishing Company. "I just happened to be hanging out there at the time," Billy remembered.

He also began hanging out at the CBS recording studio, much the same as he'd done in Cape Girardeau with Don McNeely. CBS finally hired him as a gopher, more or less. He helped clean the studios between sessions, got food for engineers, erased tape, kept the coffee pot full, iced the sodas, and played a lot of ping pong with the musicians to pass the time. After a year or so, since he wasn't making progress, he decided to quit his job at CBS. As he was literally walking out the front door, Kris Kristofferson was walking in. Kris asked him, "Billy, do you know of any jobs?" Billy answered, "I just quit. You can have mine!" Billy took him into the office, introduced him to the manager, and Kris was hired. So Kris Kristofferson took Billy's job as a gopher at CBS.

Kris was a Rhodes Scholar and had a job teaching English literature at West Point. But he told Billy, "I prefer to hang around all you characters and write songs." Kris Kristofferson fell in love with Nashville and moved his family there a few months later (mid '60s). As Billy puts it, "Nashville and country music are very, very happy he did."

Several years went by. Billy signed with Combine Music, owned by Bob Beckman and Fred Foster. Fred Foster was a record promotion man who started his own record label, Monument, and produced some of the greatest records ever. Fred's biggest artist was Roy Orbison. In the '60s, Fred produced Roy's "Only The Lonely," "Crying," and "Pretty Woman."

Billy had come a long way from CBS. This time, at Combine, he sang harmony parts, played guitar, bass, keyboards, and anything else that was needed for the various recording sessions that included Dolly Parton, Boots Randolph, Joe Simon, Billy Grammer, and many more.

Kris Kristofferson signed with Combine Records about the same time as Billy. Billy was familiar with some of Kris's songs and helped him demo them from time to time. There in 1970, Kristofferson burst in one day shouting obscenities.

"I've got a gig in L.A. at the Troubadour Club, and my damn bass player got mad and quit," Kris shouted.

Billy replied, "I can play bass!"

That was the start of a collaboration lasting over 25 years, through 1992, that took them all over the world performing their songs. Billy fondly states, "Kris is one of a kind and I love him dearly, like a brother."

It was during those years (1974), when Billy wrote his biggest hit, "I Can Help." It went to Number One on the Top 40 charts and has sold over five million copies worldwide—and still counting.

Billy has many stories and memories of those days. One in particular stands out. He was at Combine Studio closing up around 11:30 P.M. one evening, when Kris burst in again, all excited about a song he'd written. Kris had just arrived in town from Morgan City, Louisiana, where his job was flying workers to the oil rigs off the coast in the Gulf of Mexico (he was a helicopter pilot).

"We've got to lay down some tracks so I can demo my song for Fred (Foster) first thing in the morning," he commanded. So Billy and Kris worked on the song all night and emerged the next morning bright and early at 6:30 A.M. The song was "Me and Bobby McGee."

They climbed the tree next to the studio to get into Kris's apartment which was in the building right next door to Combine. "He couldn't find his key, so we climbed through the window," Billy explained. Billy described the scene:

> When we entered, Kris went over to the closet looking for something clean to put on. Well, nothing clean was to be found. There was a pile of clothes in the corner of the closet, so Kris rustled through them and pulled out a blue cotton work shirt, popped it in the air a couple of times, put it on, and exclaimed, "This will do."

Billy noted, "I saw Kris get his cleanest dirty shirt, which became the famous line in another of Kris's big hits, 'Sunday Morning Coming Down'. The line goes; 'Then I fumbled in my closet through my clothes and found my cleanest dirty shirt'."

Billy met and married Marlu in Nashville. They had two daughters, Planet and Sienna, who have successful careers of their own. Sienna is currently traveling with Ringo Starr of Beatles fame. She plays keyboard and sings with his band. Sienna performed with Starr on *The Late Late Show with Craig Ferguson* on January 24, 2008, the night before Billy's sister Joy and I were going over Billy's chapter.

Billy's impressive discography includes releases on Columbia, Monument, A&M, Epic Country, and Bench records. His songs have been recorded by Emmylou Harris, Waylon Jennings, Loretta Lynn, Conway Twitty, Mel Tillis, Aaron Tippin, and others.

Billy moved back to Nashville from L.A. in 2003, after the death of his wife, where he's still active in the music business. His most recent project was as assistant music director for the movie *Great Balls Of Fire*, starring Dennis Quaid as Jerry Lee Lewis.

We had a reunion of sorts during Homecoming festivities in 2007, when Billy received Southeast Missouri State University's Award for Outstanding Achievement. I generally ask people like Billy to give advice to young, aspiring performers, but in Billy's case, one of his poems will do:

"Don't Ever Quit"

If you are losing and feel let down,
Don't turn your head and start to frown.
Put your chin up and try to win,
Keep on pushing again . . . again.

If the score's against you and you know not what to do:
Think and hustle, you still may come through.
Your score may start rising, surprising you.
You'll start to feel better, out of the blue.

Don't ever say, "You can never win"
You may start to believe it and hurt within.
There's nothing like winning, now use your wit,
And just remember—don't ever quit!

Tom Nolan of *Rolling Stone Magazine* once described Billy as "subtly ebullient." That depiction fits when describing his career. Billy humbly recalls, "It's been an adventure. For the most part, things just happened, as they sometimes do in life."

Kris Kristofferson and Billy Swan. COURTESY OF C.J. FLANAGAN.

Steve Schaffner.

Steve Schaffner

Steve Schaffner grew up in Cape Girardeau. His mother Barbara was babysitter for me and my younger brother Don. He graduated from Cape Central, received his BME from Augusta State, and his MME from Southeast Missouri State University. He has been orchestra director for the Cape Public Schools for over 20 years. Prior to his return to Cape, Steve was Orchestra Director and violin instructor at Davidson Fine Arts Magnet School in Augusta, Georgia.

Praised for his instructional leadership and commitment to music education, he's received many awards for his excellence as an educator, including the Edna C. Kinder "Excellence in Education Award" in 2003, inclusion in "Who's Who Among America's High School Teachers," and the 2006 Area Chamber of Commerce "Educator of the Year." He remains active in several regional, state, and national music associations.

Schaffner has toured the U.S. and Canada as a fiddler and guitarist with several world-renowned Nashville recording artists, including Narvel Felts for two years. He's directed and performed in Japan, England, France, Switzerland, Germany, Italy, Austria, and China.

Schaffner has played violin with the Paducah, Kentucky, and Southeast Missouri State University symphonies for 20 years. His string trio, Trio Girardeaux, is well established as our region's finest string ensemble, booked for many weddings and receptions. Members are Schaffner (violin), Melvin Gilhaus (violin), and his daughter, Stephanie (cello). Steve's popular rock/blues group, Manitou, features him on fiddle, guitar, and vocals; Derrick Irwin on keyboards; and Bill Bolton or Sid Gerlach on drums.

Being versatile and proficient on guitar as well as violin, he can be found performing on occasion with The Jerry Ford Orchestra, Pat Schwent's "Saxy Jazz," and other regional groups.

Most recently, he provided members of the string section for Mannheim Steamroller's Christmas Concert in St. Louis.

Bruce Zimmerman.

Bruce Zimmerman

Bruce Zimmerman began playing guitar in his family's band at age 9 and has never stopped. By age 14, he had recorded a session with Sam Phillips at the legendary Sun Studios in Memphis, Tennessee.

Zimmerman's dad farmed and played bass for 20 years in the house band of the Bootheel Jamboree in Bernie, Missouri. Mr. Zimmerman taught Bruce and his brother Dwayne to play guitars at an early age. By age 9, they were in the family band: Dad on bass, his sister Janice on piano, and the boys on acoustic guitars. At age 12, Bruce and Dwayne joined their cousins Mike (mandolin) and Darrell (lap steel), formed the Four Z's, and began playing dances around the area. Their ages were between 12 and 14.

After a while, they added drummer Jerry Swader and changed their name to The Blazers. They won a Ted Mack Amateur Hour contest and a chance to compete in the national contest. They never made it to the contest, but won a competition in Memphis that landed them the recording session at Sun Records. Bruce states, "I'm more proud that I was able to record at Sun Records at age 14 than I ever would have been appearing on the regional talent show stage."

Bruce started several bands in high school. Members included Ray Doan (drums), Bob Ash (guitar), Gene Hanners and Stan Hathcoat (bass), and Butch Smith and Steve "Whiz" Parker (guitars). Bruce graduated from Bernie High School in 1969, and began working in a factory 40 hours a week for minimum wage, earning $52.44 a week take-home pay. In 1970, Zimmerman got a call from drummer Don White of Poplar Bluff, offering him a six-night-a-week job at the Tijuana Club for $125.00 a week! "I quit my day job that day," Bruce laughed.

In 1972, he formed a band called The Next of Kin which started him on a 20-year career traveling around the country. Members of the original group were Ray Doan (drums), Clarence Kiefer (keyboards), Terry Zimmerman, and later, Al Scarborough (bass). During those years he played with Southbound, Dirtywork, Stampede, The Fad, The B'Nimbles, and too many good musicians to mention.

In 1981, Bruce, Paul Porter (drums), and Al McFerron and Anita Zimmerman (keyboards), toured six countries in Asia entertaining troops for the Department of Defense. In 1989, he formed a musical partnership with Doyle "Whitey" Hendrix known as Whitey & Slick, that lasted for several years until the untimely death of Hendrix to cancer.

In 1992, he formed Bruce Zimmerman and the Shysters that lasted for seven years. Since that time, Bruce has fronted Bruce Zimmerman and the Water Street Band. The group has appeared for over 20 years on Sunday nights at Port Cape Girardeau restaurant in Downtown Cape. Current members include Don

Greenwood (congas/percussion), Danny Rees (drums), Ken Keller (bass), Ralph MacDonald (sax), and Scott Bierschwal (keyboards).

Others who have appeared with The Water Street Band are Dean Winstead (bass), Kelly Keen (drums), Farrah McSpadden (keyboards), Wayne Griffin (guitar), Mike McElrath (guitar), Jeff Hankins (keyboards), Bob Camp (guitar), Chris Moore (bass), Brad Graham (bass), Paul Porter (drums), Stanton Hofthian (keyboards), vocals by Ruth Sauerbrunn-Winstead, and the late, great Willie Bollinger.

Mike Smith and the Runaways. L to r (back): Jack Ford, Steve Hornbeak, Ken Enke, Jay Moore. Front: Mike Smith. COURTESY OF KEN ENKE.

The Runaways

The Runaways was the most popular Top 40 rock 'n' roll band in and around Cape Girardeau from 1961 through 1993. Every generation or so, some really good rock groups appear on the horizon in Cape and then generally fade away after a few years. Not The Runaways; its 30-year run was an anomaly. It was their penchant for attracting the outstanding rock musicians in our area, nurturing promising young ones, and adapting to the ever-changing musical styles and tastes of the public.

While the band was a collaborative effort, Ken Enke was the driving force. His grandparents were musical, and he remembers his uncle George Perr teaching him a few chords on guitar when he was 7 or 8 years old. "Uncle George's musical style was definitely, 'cryin' in your beer' country," Ken laughingly recalls.

Ken and his buddies Brad Lyle and Ronnie Gray got the courage to enter a talent show their senior year at Cape Central High School (1961) and won the $10 first place prize. They used their winnings to pay Shivelbine Music Store the fee on the amplifier they rented for their scintillating performances of "Johnny Be Good" and "It's Only Make Believe."

Ken was hooked. He immediately laid plans for his own rock band. The corps of the group was fueled by five energetic, eclectic young kids with exceptional musical skills: Ken (guitar), Gordon Brumley (lead guitar), Brad Lyle (drums), Charley Fuerth (sax), and Don Griffaw (bass). Shortly thereafter, Mike Ford (Ford Entertainment) joined on sax, Tom Ward on guitar, and Enke switched to drums.

Their first gig was on the patio of the Bingo BBQ in Cape. They played once a week for a year at the Roll-O-Fun Roller Rink in Jackson, Missouri. Ten dollars or fifteen dollars a piece was big money in those days. They continued to experience moderate success over the next several years, appearing in saloons, dives, beer joints, long-road gigs, and occasional local parties.

Their big move came in 1966 when some of the original members went into the military. Jay Moore (bass) and Jack Ford (keyboard) joined the band, and they merged with Mike Smith and the Romans to become Mike Smith and the Runaways.

Equipped with Mike Smith, the best rock singer in our area, they took off. They played the motel lounge circuit in the Midwest off and on for many years and appeared at concerts opening for the likes of Chubby Checker, Joey Dee & the Starliners, Del Shannon, and Jerry Lee Lewis. They performed at 8 National Plumbers Conventions; 12 Sikeston Bootheel Rodeos with Tanya Tucker, Dottie West, and other national stars; and many major local parties including 25 annual Kiwanis Club '50s parties. All this while raising families and working regular jobs.

Mike Smith was with the Runaways for about 12 years. He started in church, singing gospel music. His first band, The Wildcats, featured Smith, Harry Martin, and Eddie Cook. Then he formed The Romans which featured Mike, Lee Ragland (drums), Jay Moore (bass), and Mike Ford (sax). And then the pinnacle was reached when he merged his band with The Runaways. Smith remembers the good times, good friends, and meeting good people. "When I was a kid, I was shy and didn't have much confidence, and I talked real fast. The Runaways taught me to be confident in myself and proud to be a professional. The experience gave me pride in myself and my music. It changed my life."

New blood can generate excitement and energy in any musical group. The Runaways was no exception. Members were always on the lookout for new material and new talent. Over the years they missed on a couple, namely, Billy Swan. Ken remembers, "We auditioned him and concluded, 'He will never make it!'" Billy joined Mert Mirly & the Rhythm Steppers, and later became a national celebrity composing and recording several hits, and appearing with Kris Kristofferson worldwide for over 25 years!

However in the '80s, they found several good ones, especially three young "phenoms"—Larry Seyer (nine Grammys), Tony Spinner (TOTO), and Steve Hornbeak (Lee Greenwood & Faith Hill)—who are chronicled in this book. Enke remembers each this way:

> We heard Larry Seyer was a great keyboard player. He was about 18, working in the local office of Southwestern Bell. Jack Ford was wanting to quit, so we auditioned Larry and hired him on the spot. We loaned him the money to buy a keyboard and a string machine. Mike Smith had heard rumblings of a very young, terrific guitar player, Tony Spinner. We asked Tony to come play a few licks for us as we were setting up to play at the local Elks Club. He was 15 and scared us to death! We hired him on the spot. He played the entire night with no rehearsal and did a great job. Steve Hornbeak came to us from right across the river (Mississippi) at Tamms, Illinois, at the age of 16. He was terrific and blossomed into a great pianist.

Looking back over the years Enke says

> It was great fun. We had a ball and even made a little pocket change. But I'm most proud of our alumni and especially Larry, Tony, and Steve. They were just kids when they joined us. We gave them experience, instilled the value of showmanship and how to play to the crowd; in other words, we taught them stage presence. I also know by our actions on and off the stage, and on the road, we showed them living the right way was not only important but key to any future success they might achieve. They have made us so proud.

The Runaways disbanded in the early '90s, succumbing to age, family and business obligations, and other interests. They occasionally reunite for charitable causes and recently gave a concert that raised over $5,000 for our local Humane Society.

Tony Spinner.

Tony Spinner

Tony Spinner picked up a guitar at the age of 8 in his hometown of Cape Girardeau, Missouri, and rose to be a world-acclaimed guitarist, vocalist, and integral part of the famous 1970s pop-rock band TOTO.

Music was always in the Spinner home. "We listened to Tom Jones and Elvis Presley around the house, and I really liked the Johnny Cash, Sonny & Cher, Dean Martin, and Glen Campbell television shows," Tony recalled. "I also started liking 50s rock 'n' roll and songs that told stories like Jim Croce's 'Bad, Bad Leroy Brown.' I really wanted to play the saxophone because it was always featured on those '50s songs, but I took guitar and piano lessons instead. My sister helped me with piano and guitar. Later, I tried out for the school jazz band on guitar. I didn't know the songs, so the first time through, I struggled. But after hearing it, I could play it the second time. The director stopped and asked me the name of a chord; I didn't know it. He then asked me to play a scale; I couldn't. He quickly figured out I couldn't read music and sent me on my way," Tony explained.

During high school, Tony and his buddies formed bands but couldn't settle on a name. They played in the style of Van Halen and Ted Nugent in local clubs and across the river in southern Illinois clubs, like the Hideaway. It was Chuck Berry who influenced him the most "because he was so expressive," Tony remembered. Jimi Hendrix and Rory Gallagher also were important to the development of Tony's style. "Rory Gallagher taught me not to try and impress people with fancy guitar licks, but to play from my heart."

However, Tony's "soaring guitar licks" didn't come by accident. His father Louis explains the remarkable story:

> I was extremely upset that Tony didn't want to go to college. Southeast Missouri State University is right here in our hometown. We had many discussions about it, but Tony insisted he wanted to play music. While many parents don't support their kids because they're upset the kids aren't doing the right thing or wanting the same things as they want, we decided to make Tony a bargain. We fixed up the basement for him and said, "All right, if you really want to play music, you'll have to work at it like a job. You will go down there and practice eight hours a day, five days a week." He did that and more. He practiced twelve hours a day, seven days a week.

Some of his school buddies and neighbors joined with him. As he got better, his dad took him to Shivelbine Music Store and bought him his first real electric guitar and amplifier. It was a black Gibson 335. "I still have that guitar," Tony recalls proudly. He then took seven or eight lessons from Allen Palermo at Keys Music Store. "All the guys at both stores were very supportive and helpful," Tony acknowledged.

After several months, his dad took him to the Ramada Inn to see and hear the outstanding show band, Terry Kratky and the Facts O' Life. The bass guitar player, Ed Weigle, invited them to come back the next day to hear Tony play. Ed confirmed to Tony and his dad that Tony was a good player and had a bright future. That vote of confidence was important to both of them, since Tony was primarily self-taught.

A major boost a short time later was when he joined the area's top rock group, Mike Smith and the Runaways, for two years.

In late 1981, Tony teamed up with Tom Koontz of the professional band Spiderwolf and began performing regionally. In late 1983, Tony moved to Jonesboro, Arkansas, to become a member of Doug Adam's 3 + 1 band, touring the Midwest for a couple of years. They went to New York as White River Monster, recorded and cut demos, and finally landed a contract with TimeWarner. The group fell apart when they discovered some of their copyrights and royalties had been ripped off.

Back in 1981, in Cape, while he was playing with Kevin Rellegert and his other buddies, his drummer Mark brought in an album entitled *Heavy Metal Guitar Hero's Volume 1*. It had a phone number on the back, so Tony called and made arrangements to send a tape to Mike Varney of Shrapnel Records, who was the producer. Tony said, "The tape was terrible, but Mr. Varney was nice and encouraging on the phone."

Out of the blue, 10 years later in 1993, Tony got a phone call from Mike Varney. "A friend called me and said I should bring you to California to record on a new project I'm working on. He has seen you perform in New York. And by the way, your name sure sounds familiar. Have we met before?" Tony, too embarrassed to admit he sent the tape as a kid many years before answered, "No." "Well, I'm sure our paths have crossed sometime." Then Tony confessed and reminded him of their brief phone encounter about the demo tape, and they both had a good laugh. Tony went to California and recorded three records with Varney through 1996.

Pat Travers was starting his new recording at the studio where Tony was finishing his new CD. Travers heard them mixing the songs and liked Tony's music. He asked, and Tony agreed to go on the road and tour with him in support of his new album in 1993.

Tony got another phone call out of the blue from Paul Gilbert. As he talked, he thought it was his dad's lawyer and golfing buddy back in Cape Girardeau. After a few minutes, he realized it was the great guitar player Paul Gilbert from "Mr. Big." He offered Tony a spot in his new band, and Tony jumped at the chance. They played at the Troubadour Club in Los Angeles and then headed off for a tour of Japan. Tony has toured Japan with Gilbert three more times since.

In December 1998, Tony got the big phone call. This time it was from a Nashville session drummer, Greg Morrow. Greg heard the road manager of Clint Black and

168

TOTO was looking for a backup singer for TOTO's upcoming tour of Europe, and encouraged Tony to audition. Tony didn't want to, because he considered himself primarily a guitar player. Greg was persistent and Tony obliged. He went to Los Angeles, rehearsed for two weeks, and toured with them worldwide for 10 years as a backup singer and guitar player. "I had no idea they were so popular," Tony exclaimed. "They are truly stars."

Tony Spinner.

Tony continues to have several irons in the fire. He has many performance credits to his name. He was asked to appear on tribute albums to Stevie Ray Vaughn (*Hats Off to Stevie Ray*) and Albert King (*Fit for a King*) by the Blues Bureau International label. He has recorded five albums, and is writing and recording songs for his sixth. He currently travels throughout the United States and Europe with his group, The Tony Spinner Band.

Tony's dream was to make his own music and be a rock star like Hendrix when he was a young boy. "I was lucky," he explains. "When you're a kid, most people tell you what you can't do. My parents let me try." Seeing the circus surrounding the many rock stars he's performed with over the past 25 years, Tony doesn't mind that he didn't become one. He's content with the freedom to make his own music and happy he can make a good living doing it. "That's all I ever wanted, to express myself through my music," Tony reminisces. "I love what I do and that's more than most people can say."

Larry Seyer.

Larry Seyer

Larry Seyer is a nine-time Grammy Award-winning fulltime producer, engineer, musician, and computer programmer, doing business as Larry Seyer Production Services in Austin, Texas. He got his start at a little recording studio (Kendall-Lee) in Cape Girardeau, Missouri. He's worked for over 300 artists during his more than 20-year collaboration with Asleep at the Wheel, working on several Grammy winning CD's while at the same time writing, recording, and producing his own musical material.

Larry's dad Lefty was one of thirteen children. After the Korean conflict, Lefty and his wife Ida Mae moved back to their little German Catholic town of Oran, Missouri, to start a family of their own in 1952. Larry was the first of eight children.

Kids in Oran played baseball, tag, hide-and-seek, cops-and-robbers, cards, kick-the-can, and any other games normal kids played back in those days, but not Larry. He wasn't normal. He wanted to play the piano located in the Seyer family living room.

That piano had power! The power was control—the piano came before all others. If any of the kids were watching TV or listening to the radio, and another wanted to play the piano, the piano ruled. The same was true of the guitar. If one of the kids wanted to play the guitar, they could play *anytime* they wanted, as long as it wasn't past bedtime. Larry couldn't wait to get home from the Catholic grade school to the piano and be king of the living room. As he fondly recalls, "I had an instrument and a captive audience. I could play anything I wanted, songs I had heard, or I could make them up along the way. It was fun." He did this for many years as he continued to grow.

Larry allied with buddies Charles Glueck, John Todt, Jimmie Schlosser, and Donnie Kielhofner to form a grade-school group called Mariner-V. His first real band that played for school dances and other parties in the area was called The Purgeons. It included Larry on guitar, Robert Menz on sax, Donnie Gilliland on drums, Richard Couch on tambourines, and Charles Taylor on bass. It was the first of several bands he formed from 1965 through 1972, along with The Road Runners, The Establishment, and Lunde Duff and Associates.

He eventually made his way to Cape Girardeau to record his band. At the studio, he met Jim Rhodes.* Jim was a short, thin, music teacher who owned the recording studio. He knew which microphones to use on each instrument, what level to record

---

* Jim Rhodes was the first piano player in my orchestra (1960). He performed off and on with my group for many years, and was piano accompanist for my senior trumpet recital in 1964 at Southeast Missouri State University.

the drums, how the balance of the instruments determined how the lead vocalist would sound, and more. Larry was in awe of the whole experience. "I *had* to know and learn *everything* about recording," he exclaimed. "I spent hours and hours with Jim, learning as much as I could."

The Vietnam War was raging, and Larry's draft number was 53. He joined the army for three years, was a member of the band at Fort Leonard Wood, and later transferred to the 82nd Army band in Stuttgart, Germany. He took advantage of the opportunity and began playing and recording with the bands. As he remembers, "Our duty was to foster goodwill between Germans and Americans, so we drank a lot of beer and played a lot of great music."

Upon his return from the military, he found Rhodes had moved to Springfield, Missouri, to work with the Ozark Mountain Daredevils, so he took control of the Cape studio. He worked diligently building his business. Musicians passed his good work from band to band, and he prospered.

In 1976, Mike Smith and the Runaways was looking for a keyboard player to fill in for them for some upcoming gigs. At that time, Larry's main instrument was guitar, but he jumped at the chance to play with one of the most popular bands in the region. He still counts that as one of the pivotal moments in his musical career. "Without the experience I gained while playing keyboards with The Runaways, my story might be totally different from what it is today," Larry explained.

He moved to Texas in 1978, to work with a band his friend Larry Franklin had formed, called Cooder Brown. While working with this band he met Wink Tyler of Austin Recording Studio and began recording-engineering local Austin groups. In 1986, he collaborated on an album with Ray Benson of Asleep at the Wheel entitled, *Asleep at the Wheel 10*. The song "String of Pars" won Larry his first Grammy. The next year he engineered and performed the classic "Sugarfoot Rag" with the Wheel on the album *Western Standard Time*, which won him two Grammys: one for engineering and one for performing (acoustic guitar).

Working closely with Benson, Larry branched out into scoring and re-recording movie films. They worked together on the movie *Wild Texas Wind* starring Dolly Parton, Gary Bussey, and Willie Nelson. Other film collaborations include Al Reinart with *For All Mankind* and Sam Um with *The Way* and *El Puente*.

In December of 1991, Larry was contacted by one of his clients who was forming an all-girl band. They were looking for a new producer to help with their new CD. Larry's reputation as a top-notch producer-engineer was well known in Texas by that time. He went to Dallas and spent two months working with the girls on songs, arrangements, and production points. After several weeks, Larry brought in one of his friends from Lubbock, Texas—Lloyd Maines—to play steel guitar as guest artist on the CD Larry was producing, and the Dixie Chicks' *Little' Ol' Cowgirl* was born!

Maines toured with the Dixie Chicks for several years, and his daughter Natalie became one of the three Dixie Chicks. This story and Larry's contributions to the group are in the Dixie Chicks' official book entitled, *Dixie Chicks—Down Home and Backstage* by James L. Dickerson, available on Amazon.com.

A short time later, Larry was asked to produce a CD for Austin artist Darden Smith at his TMPS recording studio in Austin. Lyle Lovett was a guest backup singer for the project. "I never dreamed Lyle and I would work on several other Grammy winning CDs years later with Asleep at the Wheel for their *Tribute to the Music of Bob Wills and the Texas Playboys* and *Ride with Bob*," Larry remembered.

In May of 1997, Larry was contacted by a friend at Walt Disney productions who was looking for an engineer to record Goldie Hawn singing "Hard Day's Night" with producer George Martin, for his final tribute to the Beatles, *In My Life*. "I jumped at the chance to work with such a legendary producer," Larry exclaimed.

In 2005, Larry contacted David Wilcock, a featured guest on *Coast to Coast AM*, about doing a music project collaboration. Since then, David and Larry have produced several music projects together, and now tour the world, performing selections from these projects at conferences they put together in cities such as New York, Toronto, London, and San Francisco. Larry writes the music and David the lyrics for these endeavors. Most of the instruments are performed by Larry on keyboards and guitar—with valuable experience gained from his time spent with Mike Smith and the Runaways in Cape Girardeau.

Not bad for a kid from Oran, Missouri, with Asleep at the Wheel.

Nine Grammy's ("Best Country" Category) with Asleep at the Wheel

1987	Instrumental Performance –"String of Pars"	Remixing & Engineering
1988	Instrumental Performance –"Sugarfoot Rag"	Recording & Mixing Engineer
1993	Instrumental Performance –"Sugarfoot Rag"	Musician
1993	Instrumental Performance –"Red Wing"	Recording & Mixing Engineer
1993	Vocal Duo Performance –"Blues for Dixie"	Recording & Mixing Engineer
1995	Instrumental Performance –"Hightower"	Recording & Mixing Engineer
1999	Instrumental Performance –"Bob's Breakdown"	Recording & Mixing Engineer
2000	Package – "Ride with Bob"	Recording & Mixing Engineer
2001	Duo or Group Performance –"Cherokee Maiden"	Recording & Mixing Engineer

He also recorded and mixed George Strait's *Box Set* that went Triple Platinum.

Steve Hornbeak.

Steve Hornbeak

Steve Hornbeak traveled the 20 minutes from Tamms, Illinois, to Cape Girardeau and began playing keyboards and singing with The Runaways, our premier, local rock 'n' roll group at age 16. They immediately recognized his terrific talent at that early age. The 3 years with The Runaways helped launch his 20-year professional career that led him to Lee Greenwood, Faith Hill, and beyond. Steve resides in Nashville, Tennessee, where he currently tours with Grammy Award-winning artist Richard Marx, and also operates a successful recording studio, 326 Productions in Anna, Illinois.

As a youngster, Steve remembers his family sitting around the piano singing church songs and harmonizing. "My mom showed me where to put my fingers on the piano to make chords." Steve was in band and chorus at Egyptian High School in Southern Illinois. "I would get picked to sing at homecomings and special events. It was the starting place for me getting serious about wanting to be in a band."

Hornbeak's years with The Runaways were an amazing time for him to grow as a musician. "Those guys took me in and taught me how to enjoy playing for a crowd. I became a much better musician because I had to keep up with them! They became my family and still are today." He moved to Tampa, Florida, at age 20, played with different bands for 4 years, married, and had a daughter Jaclyn, who is married and in medical school. Steve quipped, "I've always said a good retirement plan is having a daughter who's a doctor!"

His big break came when Lee Greenwood stayed in a motel where he was playing in Tampa. "I slipped a letter and a tape of some of my songs under his door. He came to the lounge that night to listen and ended up singing a couple of songs with us. Six weeks later he called and asked me to Nashville to audition for his band. I got the job and was with him for five years!"

Back to Tampa for a year and a half, Hornbeak began sending out feelers to return to the road:

> In 1993, I got a call about a new artist, Faith Hill.[*] I went back to Nashville, auditioned, and got the job that lasted almost 10 years. On that amazing ride, I played every major award show, all the major TV shows like Letterman, Leno, Ellen, Rosie, The Grammys, *Today Show*, *Good Morning America*, Billboard Awards, ACM Awards, Country Music Awards, Music City News Awards, and WB Music Awards. Others included *Regis & Kelly*, *Donnie & Marie*, *CMT Most*

---

[*] Faith Hill's first professional concert was at the Show Me Center, January 27, 1994, when she opened for The Oak Ridge Boys and Little Texas. She then returned the same year and opened for Alan Jackson on October 16, 1994.

Wanted Live, *Grand Ole Opry Live*, "CMT Faith Hill Special," ABC Faith Hill's Thanksgiving and New Year's Specials. We played every major arena and football stadium from 20,000 to 70,000 fans a night! I owe a lot to Faith and thank her for the years of great times.

I was doing a show on VH1 called *Divas Live* with Faith Hill. Elton John was on the show. I had to play right after him on his piano. I was standing about six feet behind him waiting to come out to play. He was doing "Rocket Man." I was close enough to tap him on the shoulder. When he finished, he got up, turned around, and said, "Have a good show," as he grabbed my arm. He then stood there and watched me play his piano. I still can't believe that happened!

Other entertainers Hornbeak has performed with include Jo Dee Messina, Billy Gilman, Vince Gill, Michael Bolton, Kenny Loggins, Tracy Lawrence, and Eddie Rabbitt. In addition, he's been featured in the 2000, 2002 issues of *Keyboard Magazine*; 2002, 2003 issues of *Yamaha Key*; and *Peavey Monitor* magazine in 1990, 1993, and 1996. Steve is endorsed by Yamaha and Peavey Keyboard Amps. He's toured Canada, Mexico, Australia, Greenland, Iceland, Scotland, New Finland, England, Norway, Italy, Germany, Turkey, India, Switzerland, Trinidad, Cuba, Dominican Republic, Ukraine, Taiwan, France, Bulgaria, Finland, Denmark, Russia, Ireland, and, of course, the USA.

Steve finds time to keep a busy recording schedule in his studio. His client list includes Richard Marx, Journey, Jessica Andrews, Billy Gilman, Dan Hill, Kelly Coffee, James Slater, Gary Burr, Stephanie Bentley, Marcel Chagnon, Tony Mullins, and many young aspiring singers. Steve's contemporaries have great respect for his work. Richard Marx describes him as "an exceptional musician and singer." Billy Gilman relates, "When I think of Steve, I think of two words: drive and passion." Jessica Andrews says, "Having someone in this town (Nashville) that you truly know will work to perfection, it's Steve."

"Sometimes things happen that you never thought would," Steve remembers. "After all the years touring and meeting famous people, nothing seems to make you stop and say, wow. I was a huge Journey fan, and saw them in concert in the '80s at SIU Arena, and knew that was what I wanted to do. It really hit me when I got a call that Journey was in Nashville and wanted to record at my studio. My studio was in my house, so when they knocked on the door and I opened it to see Journey standing there, well, it was surreal. They were great!"

Hornbeak has several projects in mind for the near future: writer, producer, Christian artist, releasing more of his own music, and continuing to build the studio in Anna, Illinois, to assist local artists in enjoying the things he's enjoyed. "Aspiring musicians must take it seriously," Hornbeak admonishes. "The competition is amazing, but it's great to play with great players."

Through it all, Steve says, "What a life I've had. I feel so blessed and thank God for the gift of music he gave me. Life is just beginning. I know God has a bigger plan for my musical gifts, and I can't wait to see what he has in store for me!"

The Contors. L to r. (back): Larry Lynch, Bob Beardman, Tom Mogelnicki, Rick Kerry, Bob Garner. L to r. (front): Winston Roads, Carson Ward, Al Williams. COURTESY OF TOM MOGELNICKI.

Tom Mogelnicki

Tom Mogelnicki was a pioneer in melding black and white musicians in the early '60s in St. Louis. Tom recalls, "My band, The Contors, was the first integrated rock band in the city. Our instrumentation consisted of guitar, bass, drum, two saxophones, and three black singers. I certainly didn't look at it as anything special; I just knew they were really good singers."

Tom started playing drums in his dad's polka band at age 12 because his dad contracted Parkinson's Disease. The band played for weddings, church picnics, and family celebrations. He branched out in the eighth grade and started a small rock 'n' roll band, performing in St. Louis area teen-towns. He formed The Contors during his sophomore year in high school, playing teen dances and weddings, and becoming the house band at the 2 Plus Two Club, a non-alcohol venue in Clayton.They even had gigs in East St. Louis from time to time. "My folks never knew the wide variety of locations I played or the stars I backed, like Ike and Tina Turner and Albert King. They were aware of some gigs at the Moonlight Lounge near Barnes Hospital with B.B. King," Mogelnicki recalls.

Music played a pivotal role in the integration of the St. Louis area. "Actually, by age 15, I was playing with all-black bands such as Gene Neil and Benny Sharp and the Sharpies in Gaslight Square. We had some success. One of our singers, Bonnie Lynn, was signed by RCA. We were asked to come to Nashville for her recording session, but we were in high school, and such a trip just wasn't possible."

People have asked Tom about his early days playing with black musicians in St. Louis. "It was really no big deal. We all considered ourselves musicians, not black ones or white ones," Mogelnicki said. "We respected each other's talents."

Tom came to Cape in 1965 on a scholarship to play football at Southeast Missouri State College, and simply never left. He formed several groups that performed in Cape in the '60s, '70s, and '80s: The Interns, The Soul Seekers, Orange Wedge, and Big Muddy. Tom and his friend Chuck McGinty even built their own sound system during this era. Then there was Conestoga Wagon and Hour Glass, which was popular at the Purple Crackle in East Cape. The Contors even rolled back around in the '90s for another eight years with some original members.

During all these more than 40 years, Tom's never really been out of the business. He still juggles his schedule to perform, returning to St. Louis and beyond whenever possible. At age 64, he's still going strong with The Generation Gap, his nine-member Motown, rock, funk band that's active in the Cape Girardeau and St. Louis areas. The band has performed with Chuck Berry and other national entertainers. Tom has played with Jeannie C. Riley, David Allen Coe, and others. He especially fondly remembers playing for Bob Kuban on the Admiral, and the Johnny Paulson Orchestra at the Chase Park Plaza Hotel, all on a Rogers set of drums he bought in 1968.

Mogelnicki talks about music this way: "When I get behind those drums, I'm in my own little world. All my problems go away. It's physically hard, but mentally relaxing. It's been my relief valve for 51 years."

Kent Goodson.

Kent Goodson

Kent Goodson began playing piano with local country, rock, and blues bands around Cape Girardeau and became country legend George Jones's pianist from 1982 through June 2011. He was leader of George Jones's Band, The Jones Boys, for the final fifteen years of their collaboration.

The Goodsons are sort of an all-American family. Scouting helped instill respect for family and community, and was the bond of the family in Kent's early years. His older brother Steve and his mom and dad were all active: his dad George, a scout leader, and his mother Jewel, a den mother. Mrs. Goodson said, "Steve and Kent were three and one half years apart. While they each had their own friends, they always got along well. They loved baseball and scouting." Kent and Steve both attained the rank of Eagle Scout.

Records from Bing Crosby to Hank Williams Sr. were played in the Goodson household. Steve began trumpet lessons in school when he was in the fifth grade. Kent followed suit when he reached the fifth grade. They occasionally practiced and performed together. Kent was 11 when Steve also began playing piano. Steve introduced Kent to his first chords on the piano and to the music of Ray Charles and Jimmy Smith. Kent listened to Ray Charles records until the needle wore through the grooves. He explained, "I slowed the records down to half speed and picked out the riffs note by note until I had them down."

When Steve started a rock 'n' roll band, Kent tagged along, learning from older musicians like Kenny Martin, Chuck McGinty, and Willie Bollinger. Kent remembers, "Everything seemed easy for Steve. He was outgoing, talented, popular in school, and always included me in his activities. Just by watching him play, I learned to love music."

Tragedy struck the family when Steve died in a car accident in 1968 in Scott City, Missouri, returning from a rehearsal with his band. The family was devastated. Kent was 15; his buddy, gone. At one point he told his mother, "You and Dad have each other; I don't have anyone."

Kent put his energy into playing music in the area with local bands through high school and college. They included The Jaguars, Ellis, and Easy Street. He worked with many musicians, like Randy Leiner, David Scheeter, Gary Nunnally, and the Sam Conrad Band. His mother recalled, "When Kent really wanted to practice on our old upright piano, he would hang a white sock on the door knob. That was our clue that he was not to be bothered: no phone calls, no visitors, period." As he honed his talent, his music tastes began moving toward the country sounds of Nashville: Floyd Cramer, Jerry Lee Lewis, Merle Haggard, and George Jones.

He graduated from Central High School, planning to major in music at Southeast

Missouri State University. He was turned down by a music professor who told him he didn't have enough classical music experience to major in music. So he majored in social work. He continued performing in the area and earned his college degree. His father helped him get his insurance license, and then he joined his dad in the family insurance agency. Kent related well to older people and was successful in the business. But after two years, he told his dad, "I've got to give music a try." His mom told me, "We really didn't want him to go. But knowing his love of music, we encouraged him." And his dad added, "I hope you won't change the way you are."

Kent Goodson.

At age 26, Kent placed an ad in a Memphis Musicians Union Office and landed a job for two years with a Nashville road band, which traveled in a broken down bus and stayed in motels reminiscent of the movie *Psycho*. The musicians were talented, and Kent learned a lot before the band broke up in 1979. Shortly thereafter, he got a break landing a job in Printer's Alley at The Captain's Table in Nashville, Tennessee.

The two years at The Captain's Table gave him the opportunity to rub shoulders with many musicians, singers, and songwriters. It paid off when George Jones's road manager, a regular at The Captain's Table, called Kent and asked if he would be interrested in the job as piano player in George's band. Kent jumped at the chance. He rehearsed with the band and left immediately with them for a gig in Virginia. The band liked his style, but George hadn't heard him play. "How will I know if I got the job?" Kent asked. The manager responded, "Oh, George will let you know before the weekend is over."

Kent was doubly nervous that evening. Not only was it his first big time show and he hadn't even met George yet, he was wearing a pink tuxedo he borrowed from the fiddle player while the rest of the band was wearing white. The former piano player had gotten mad for being fired and slashed the white tux that Kent was supposed to be wearing. Halfway through the show, as Kent was blending with the band behind

George in the up-tempo rockabilly hit, "White Lightning," he played his solo on the top two octaves of the piano with all he had. Kent recalled, "George looked over with excitement in his voice and yelled, 'Play it, Jerry Lee!' (Lewis).

"At that moment, I thought I had the job. It lasted over 25 years."

A real thrill for Kent was an evening on Johnny Carson's *Tonight Show*, when George and Ray Charles sang the duet "Friendship." The Jones Boys set up in the orchestra pit and began the rehearsal. There was no chart, so Ray went over and sat at the piano with Kent. Together, they worked out an arrangement for the rest of the band. Right before the taping, George whispered to Kent, "Let Ray play the tricky stuff." Kent gave George a smile and nodded, "OK." Kent told me, "After all, Ray had been teaching me since I was 11, so that special night was no exception."

The first time his family saw him perform with Jones was at the Performing Arts Center in Nashville. It was George's famous comeback concert. Kent's mother exclaimed, "I couldn't believe my little boy was on stage with one of country music's legendary performers. After the concert, Kent said that he knew Steve was looking down on us."

Their proudest moment, however, was when Jones opened the new 7,200 seat, multi-purpose Show Me Center on the campus of Kent's alma mater, Southeast Missouri State University, in his hometown of Cape Girardeau. Here's Mrs. Goodson's account:

> It was a packed house, and all our friends were there. Tanya Tucker opened the show, and then The Jones Boys and George Jones took the stage, with Kent at the grand piano. Kent's dad George and I were so proud. Kent looked so natural, sounded so good, and looked as if he really belonged there. I'll never forget it. After all, I'm his mother, his number one fan!

From the beginning, the Goodson family was always a close-knit team. George and Jewel traveled to many of Kent's performances over the years. "He's given us so much pleasure," Jewel remembers. "After one performance, my husband remarked to Kent, 'I'd like to take you up to the college and let that professor that turned you down see what you've accomplished in your music career!'" George died in 1998, leaving just Kent and his mother. Kent stayed with her for a couple of weeks, helping and teaching her the business of running the household. He still phones her everyday to make sure she's all right, and he returns home frequently. He obviously has never changed the way he is.

One of Kent's favorite stories happened one late night after a performance at the Houston Astrodome with Merle Haggard, the poet of the common man. His band The Strangers and The Jones Boys went back to the Holiday Inn to jam.

Merle always liked to hang out with the musicians, so he invited us up to his suite. We were jamming to Merle's hit song "Mama Tried," when I hit a high note on my harmonica. Merle's little Chihuahua, Tuffy, responded with a high, shrill-decibel howl. It happened several times. "Hush, Tuff, let the boy play," Merle commanded, to no avail. Well, nobody paid attention to Tuffy as the time passed. Someone forgot to take him outside and before long, Tuffy had to do his business, and some unsuspecting cowboy boot stepped in that pile of business! So Merle stopped the song, turned up his nose, and said, "Someone has stepped in Tuffy's poop: Boot check, boys!" A half a dozen guitar players laid down their guitars and began turning up their soles for everyone to see. "No, it's not me, Merle, I'm clean, guys," and so on. We finally went back to playing and forgot about Tuffy's business. I'll always remember that session in the wee hours of the morning and the great songs of Merle Haggard including, "I Take A Lot Of Pride In What I Am," "I'm Proud To Be An Okie From Muskogee," and "Boot Check, Boys."

Kent has traveled in all 50 states except Alaska, and many foreign countries including England, Ireland, Germany, Norway, Canada, and Switzerland, performing with Jones and the likes of Conway Twitty, Randy Travis, Lee Greenwood, Travis Tritt, Vince Gill, Lorrie Morgan, Aaron Neville, Roy Acuff, Merle Haggard, Tennessee Ernie Ford, Bill Monroe, Allison Krauss, Lee Ann Womack, and many other great country stars.

Kent is also no stranger to venues such as The Grand Ole Opry, *Hee Haw*, *The Jay Leno Show*, *The David Letterman Show*, *Music City Tonight*, *Austin City Limits*, *Nashville Now*, *George Jones Show* on TNN, *Farm Aid 85* and *86*, Carnegie Hall, and more.

He worked about eighty-five dates a year touring with George Jones, playing keyboards and harmonica. Kent has a studio in his home and continues to write songs, and does demos and production for several pet projects of his own. Kent has recently co-produced a spoken-word CD of baseball stories with Joe West, a veteran major league umpire. Kent composed and performed the background music for *Diamond Dreams*, the title of the CD. It was released in March 2008, and can be found at www.cowboyjoewest.com.

Through it all, Kent has retained the small-town soul he always possessed. During one of my meetings with his mother, she said, "Kent was always modest, and he's still the same, good person he's always been. He's honest, like his dad, and always helps people when they have a problem."

Kent explains, "I was lucky. There are a lot of good musicians walking around the streets of Nashville looking for work, while I've been able to make a living playing music and doing what I enjoy all these many years—and I still enjoy playing music around Cape with my old friends when I come home. Some things don't change. And that's a good thing."

He added these thoughts:

> My son Dillon was interested in music at an early age. He's graduated from DePaul University June 2011 and works in Chicago for The Chicago Loop Alliance. He plays drums, piano, writes and records songs with some of his college classmates. Over the years, he has gotten to know many of my musician friends in Cape. We occasionally jam with them when we come home to visit. Dillon has always been rather tall for his age. Doug Rees gave him the nickname Stretch Cadillac several years ago when he was introduced to sit in on drums at Tractors in Jackson. So many of the folks in my hometown area know Dillon by his blues name.

Kent concluded, "I'm glad I was able to pass the gift of music on to Dillon in the same way my brother Steve passed his love of music on to me." For more information on Kent's activities, consult his website www.kentgoodsonmusic.com.

Goodson recently concluded his 28-year association with legendary country singer George Jones. Kent spent the past 15 of those years as leader of The Jones Boys Band. Kent is active with various musical projects, including operation of his recording studio, and is excited about the next chapter in his career.

Local Bands

There are many good rock/blues bands performing in our immediate area today. Cape has always been a Mecca for music performance going back to the days of paddlewheel riverboats and Illinois nightclubs immediately across the river, fueled by gambling. Now with the demise of retail stores, the six blocks comprising the heart of Downtown Cape have become an entertainment district.

The many restaurants and bars give young talent a place to hone their craft. There must be 25 or 30 local and regional bands who perform regularly downtown. Just on one weekend—Friday, Saturday, and Sunday, February 4, 5, and 6, 2011—15 bands were performing downtown, country star Blake Shelton drew 4,500 fans at the Show Me Center, my 14-piece orchestra performed a floor show and dance for a corporate gala in St. Louis, and the next afternoon, the St. Louis Symphony played to a standing-room-only crowd at the River Campus on Super Bowl Sunday! In addition, 18 galleries had open houses at their traditional First Friday Night Receptions. Yes, art and entertainment are alive and well in Cape Girardeau, Missouri.

While sometimes it's unfair to single out specific groups, several local bands are exceptional and have elevated themselves above the rest over the past several years. And they have branched out into our region and beyond: Mid-Life Crisis, John D. Hale, and the Mike Renick Band. Each has their own distinctive style and draw large followings wherever they perform. Their popularity will continue to rise.

Mid-Life Crisis. L to r. (back): Chuck McGinty, Robb McClary, Al McFerron, Sissy Donahue, Dan McClard, Luke Landgraf. L to r. (front): Frank McGinty, Matt Coleman, Sally LeGrand. Not pictured: Darren Bergfeld and Billy Shivelbine. COURTESY OF THE PRINTING CO.

Chuck McGinty & Mid-Life Crisis

Chuck McGinty has been on our local rock scene for many years. He played with several groups in high school. The highlight of his music days was with the '70s group Fletcher, who had a huge following from Cape to St. Louis. He left the group when disco took over most of the clubs.

"I laid out when I got married, raised a family, and opened our jewelry store. After a short stint with the St. Louis group, Contors, in the '90s, my brother, Dr. Frank McGinty, wanted me to corral his buddies to start 'a real band!' Mid-Life Crisis was born in 2001 with Frank (bass), Luke Landgraf (guitar), Mike Pind and Dave Gerlach (vocals), Sid Gerlach (drums), and me (guitar/vocals). Shortly thereafter, we added Phil Wagoner and Sissy Donahue."

The band became very popular in and around Cape almost from its beginning. They were repeatedly booked for "Big Gigs" year after year as they added Al McFerron (keyboards), Dr. Matt Coleman (drums), and Sally LeGrand (vocals). Chuck wanted some brass, so they added Jim Edwards and Dan Berry (trumpet), and Robb Mc-Clary (sax). As Chuck proudly quipped, "Just what I wanted, a 10-piece band!" Doug Fowler helped with sound and technical issues until he moved away and was replaced by Maurice Leray. A.J. Stembel is the main "roadie." Several more changes continued, due to Robb McClary's death to cancer, Dan Berry's departure, and Jim Edwards's move from the area. Currently Bill Shivelbine (sax), Darren Bergfield (trombone), and Dan McClard (trumpet) man the horn section.

The future looks promising for the band. They continue to play to large audiences, have a loyal following, and, health permitting, will remain a major player in the music scene of our region and beyond for years to come. As McGinty proclaims, "It's always a blast." That's true for the band and their fans.

John D. Hale Band. L to r: Mason Watkins, John D. Hale, Cody Phillips, Chris Brotherton. COURTESY OF JOHN D. HALE.

John D. Hale Band

If you're looking for a raucous, edgy, country sound with a bit of southern rock and bluegrass thrown in, then you've come to the right chapter. The John D. Hale Band is just that, an original crafted sound from four creative, talented musicians: John D. Hale (guitar & vocals), Cody Phillips (bass & vocals), Chris Brotherton (drums & vocals), and Ryne Jackson (lead guitar, fiddle, harmonica, and vocals).

They released their first album, *One of A Kind*, in 2005. It climbed to No. 17 on XM Radio's X-Country Channel. With that success, in 2008 they recorded their second CD, *Lost*. The title track, "Lost," is an in-your-face "rocker," the style that's fast becoming the band's signature sound.

John Hale is no stranger to travel and touring. He started traveling with his parents, showing exotic animals from their 5-H Ranch north of Cape Girardeau throughout the country when he was a toddler. "I must have spent my entire kindergarten in Hawaii," John laughs.

> We always had music around the house. Dad occasionally played the radio! Mom and my sisters played the piano, and I liked the guitar. All the guys in the band grew up together working for Dad. We've been lifelong friends. I always liked the storytellers, Wayland and Willie, and especially Robert Earl Keen, outlaw bluegrass.

The band plays about 175 dates a year. Their agent is John Folk of Nashville, formerly of the Buddy Lee agency. He signed the group in 2009. They play festivals, concerts, old theatres, flatbed trucks . . . anywhere people will show up—10 or 10,000.

> We are happy doing what we're doing. We'd like a bus, but that will be awhile, so we'll just keep hustling. We like not having 8-to-5 jobs. We travel a lot, but still have time for family. Think about it. Many parents see their kids for an hour before they go to work and a few hours at night. We get to see our kids throughout the whole week. It's just weekends we're gone from them. And as long as people will come to hear us, we'll keep on touring.

John's experiences traveling as a young boy grounded him in the rural approach and subject matter of his songs. Armed with their original songs and some covers, they travel performing their energetic and rowdy showcase of American music to anyone and everyone who will listen. While they have attracted a large and enthusiastic following, I suspect they are just getting started as they continue to spread their unique sound to wider audiences. For more info, go to their website: johndhaleband.com.

Mike Renick Band. L to r: Blake Fisher, Zack Priester, Mike Renick, Bryan West, Wes Grabel. COURTESY OF ELAINE ROHDE PHOTOGRAPHY.

Mike Renick Band

Mike Renick has turned his love for rock, jazz, folk, acoustic guitar, singing, and song writing into a top original rock group in our region in just five years. Quite an accomplishment for an elementary school drummer.

Mike was born in Minnesota, moved to Clinton, Missouri, and landed in Cape Girardeau for good in junior high school. Marvin Gay, the Temptations, and Bob Wills and the Texas Playboys were always heard around Mike's house, "Especially when Dad was home," Mike remembers. "Mom and Dad were relieved when singing trumped my drum set!"

Singing came naturally. "It was my first musical instrument," Mike said. "Through grade school and musical theatre at Notre Dame High School, I've always enjoyed singing." Church, weddings, and a minor in music at Southeast Missouri State University followed, which included roles in the musicals *Sugar* and *Music Man*.

Renick studied the sounds of Sting, The Police, Dave Matthews Band, and Peter Gabriel. His first CD, *Diamond Eyes*, released in 2004, featured several outstanding Cape Girardeau musicians: Bruce Zimmerman, Danny Rees, Pat Koetting, and Ralph McDonald. In 2005, personnel solidified to include Bryan West (drums), Wes Grabel (sax), Blake Fisher (electric guitar), Pat Koetting (bass), and Scott Bierschwal (piano). New music was written in studio sessions, recorded, and distributed *free*. A whole new fan base emerged!

The band's signature sound features Renick's voice and original songs, and unique acoustic and amplified pulsating rhythms. MRB has caught the imagination of its loyal fans.

While the band cut its teeth in local bars and clubs, they branched out to St. Louis (The Pageant), Memphis, Columbia (Blue Note), Chicago, Durango, Colorado, and parts in between. They've performed with the Hipnecks, Steve Ewing from The Urge, and provided the warm-up for Sarah Palin at the Show Me Center in Cape Girardeau before a crowd of 10,000. The band continues to attract more and more followers as it expands its scope. A unique feature is their collaboration with classical violinist, Liesl Schoenberger (featured in another chapter), as they rock the house.

The band has its act together. "We have a strong passion for music. Our focus is being a better band and better musicians," Mike explains. They plan on continuing to write, perform, branch out further, and let as many people hear them as possible. They also know everyone won't necessarily like their unique style, which separates them from the typical cover bands. But Mike says, "I hope that whoever hears our music walks away respecting that we put an honest, thoughtful effort into our work" With that attitude, many more will hear them before they're finished.

Special Friends

This section runs the gamut from entertainers I've known all my life to new, young, performers with extraordinary talent who show great promise. Genres showcased here include jazz, rock 'n' roll, classical, pop, Broadway, folk, Christian, opera, and concert/stage performance.

The Bierschwals. L to r: Gary, Roger, Wanda, Scott.

The Bierschwals

The Bierschwals are one of my favorite musical families. Eddie, the father, played tenor sax in military bands during WWII. Wanda, the mother, possesses a beautiful, soft, lyrical, soprano voice. She began singing as a young girl in the junior quartet at General Baptist Church, then high school, and then the Cape Choraliers for many years, including in their appearance at the Seattle World's Fair in 1964. She's a 60-year member of Grace Methodist church choir and sang for our funerals at Ford & Sons Funeral Home for over thirty years.

Wanda's oldest son Roger is an outstanding vocalist and pianist. He began singing in church at age nine. He received his B.S. in Music from Southeast Missouri State in 1970, and his Masters in Music Education in 1978. He taught vocal music for 30 years in schools in New Madrid, Van Buren, Piedmont, and then St. Peters. Retired, he's released five Christian CDs, gives piano and vocal lessons, and performs regularly in the St. Louis area.

Gary started young like most of us. His first paying job consisted of free soda and popcorn. As he matured, he performed with many local and regional groups including The Mustangs, The Intruders, The Establishment, and King James Version. Members of the Cape groups included David Limbaugh, Richie Mitten, Lee Buckstein, Don Reece, Ron Duff, and two chronicled in this book, Larry Seyer and Kent Goodson. He attended Bandsman School in Norfolk, Virginia, and was transferred to Fort Ord, California, to play in the 28th Army Band, where he transformed himself into an outstanding, seasoned, professional drummer. Upon his return to Cape, there weren't many opportunities to perform, so he and his wife Becky packed up and moved to Kansas City, where he continues to perform.

Scott is a professional pianist. He began lessons at age eight and graduated from Southeast Missouri State University with a B.S. in Music Education in 1986. He's traveled with bands throughout the Midwest, Las Vegas, Gulf Coast, and the Florida Keys. He's a member of Noah's Rain and also performs with Bruce Zimmerman's Waterstreet Band. He has opened for B.J. Thomas, Joan Jett, and Paul Rodgers. Scott currently lives in Cape Girardeau and works at Shivelbine Music Store.

Sounds of Luv. L to r: Ronnie Meystedt, Mike Kohlfeld, David Headrick, Hollis Headrick, Brad Graham. LUEDERS STUDIOS.

Mike Kohlfeld

Mike Kohlfeld had a 10-year career as vocalist, bassist, and guitarist with several Cape bands including The Vulcans, Sounds of Luv, Rock Bottom, and Uncle Remus.

It all started with six years of piano lessons with Mrs. Hopper at age 7, and then a year of guitar lessons with Eddie Keys. "Mr. Keys did me a favor and let me play and sing a couple of times with him and Vi at the Purple Crackle Lounge when I was 14. It was a great thrill, and I was hooked," Mike recalls.

> My career with Kenny Martin's Vulcans was short lived. At age 16, I joined Ronnie Meystedt's Sounds of Luv. It was my first real taste of being in a rock band. Meystedt was a great guitar player. David Headrick played keyboards, Dean Winstead played bass, and Gary Garner played drums. Gary either broke a drum head or stick on every gig we ever played! Our personnel changed from time to time until the core settled in with Hollis Headrick on drums, and Brad "Boogie" Graham on bass. When Hollis left for college, Bill Bolton played drums. At that point we changed our name to Rock Bottom. We were really good, thanks to Meystedt's skill and passion, and traveled to Joliet, Decatur, Chanute Air Force Base in Illinois, and other good venues. By the way, Hollis was a terrific drummer and became Director of Weill Music Institute at Carnegie Hall!

Kohlfeld was primarily the vocalist in the bands he played in, until Randy Leiner, formerly of the Scott City group Chimes of Freedom, joined the group. He was an incredible vocalist, so Mike was relegated to the bass. They changed their name again, this time to Uncle Remus, and began playing three nights a week. "Randy was a joy to sing with. The harmonies we created opened up new avenues for our group," Kohlfeld remembered. Leiner ultimately moved to St. Louis and formed the popular Rockabilly group, The Melroys.

Kohlfeld has many memories of those good times and especially of the wonderful, talented musicians he had the opportunity to perform with. "I left to begin my career in the family business and have to be content with those memories, and I am."

Doug Rees.

Doug Rees

Doug Rees has been playing guitar and entertaining in our region for many years. He epitomizes what this book is about. As of September 2007, he's been a full-time, professional musician. He threw down sales jobs, carpentry, and was even a barber for several years, to follow his heart and his dream. He's a unique singer/songwriter who specializes in his own original material.

> As a child, I remember going to my grandparent's home in the Bootheel. There were instruments lying around everywhere. We were allowed to experiment with them, but if we mistreated them, we were reprimanded with an iron hand. My grandfather was a great musician and could play most any song after hearing it only one time. He played a lot like "Chet," and never knew a chord name or what note he might be playing.

Rees grew up in Jackson where he became "friends" with his guitar in school at age 13. Jimi Hendrix and the blues were some of his first influences. He signed a contract to play with upcoming star, Paul Plunkett and Crystal Blue in 1979, just three years out of high school. He moved to Nashville and played showcases and clubs until the money stopped. Along the way, he worked with Sammi Smith and other stars.

Doug and his wife Carol have been married 32 years. They have three children and eight grandchildren. During most of those years, Doug played on weekends with many local groups, including Bruce Zimmerman, Brad Graham, Gary Nunnally, Eddie Keys, Kent Goodson, Big Larry Williams, TUFA, The Runaways, and Santa Cruz, with Mark Rees, Roger Blankenship, Danny Tetley, and his brother Danny Rees. Doug's fondest memories, however, were playing with Vi Keys at the Holiday Inn from time to time: "I loved that lady."

As years went by, he started collecting original tunes and devoting his time to recording, pitching, and performing his songs. "I don't remember not playing," Rees states. "I credit my wife and family for somehow understanding my passion. Music has been with me since I was born, I think. It's not something I do; it's who I am. I cannot think of doing anything different."

Mike Dumey.

Robyn Hosp.

Mike Dumey & Robyn Hosp

One can't mention Mike Dumey without including Robyn Hosp in the same breath. They teamed up back in 1976 to quickly become our areas top duo-performers.

As choral director at the Cape Junior High School, Dumey has worked tirelessly to showcase and help develop hundreds of Cape's rising stars for nearly 40 years. There's no one in our area who has done more for budding, talented young people than Mike Dumey.

Since 1982, Mike has produced dinner shows: "Spotlight Tonight" at Port Cape, "Christmas with Mike and Robyn" at Deerfield Lodge, "Starz On the Rise" at Ray's Convention Plaza, and fifteen "Sounds of the Seasons" for Southeast Hospital. He's entertained at hundreds of civic and corporate events, with the Cape and Jackson Municipal Bands, at Schnuck's "Keeping the Love Alive," and on and on.

Church music has always played a large role in Mike's musical life. He was music director for 18 years at Grace United Methodist Church in Cape and currently serves in that capacity at Centenary United Methodist Church. Mike beams when he says, "It's been a blessing and a privilege to have worked with many wonderful Christian artists like Robyn Hosp, Liesl Schoenberger, Judith Farris, Jerry Ford, Dr. John Shelton, Mel Gilhaus, Wanda, Roger, and Scott Bierschwal, and many more. They are fantastic musicians, as good as you will find anywhere."

Dumey's passion continues on parade at his junior high Broadway musicals. Beginning with a small cast and crew for *The Little Mermaid* in 1992, from Schultz Seventh Grade Center, the casts and crews in his ambitious full-productions of *Annie*, *The Wizard of Oz*, *The Sound of Music*, and *Cats*, have grown to over 200! It's no wonder Dumey was honored as outstanding music educator in Southeast Missouri in 2006 by the Southeast Missouri State University Music Teachers Association.

Dumey was born in Jackson and received his B.S. in Music Education at Southeast Missouri State University. He and his wife Betsy are proud parents of two talented daughters, Lauren and Caitlyn, who star in Mike's productions. Cape's Music Man definitely keeps the music playing, to the delight of all of us.

Robyn Hosp is a true professional singer. She has that great pro-edge to her sound and pitch that's seldom heard in our area. She's equally adept at handling pop, country, jazz, and religious genres. For over 20 years, she teamed up with Dumey to entertain in their standing-room-only productions, "An Evening With Mike & Robyn," "Christmas With Mike & Robyn," and more, to give younger developing singers venues to perform and hone their talents.

Hosp started singing at an early age, prodded by her mother and grandmother.

"My grandmother took me to church every Sunday. I sat on her lap as she played an old pump organ and sang," Hosp remembers. "I can still hear Mom singing 'Somewhere Over the Rainbow' in the bathroom."

Robyn began trumpet and voice lessons in the seventh grade, but voice lessons quickly became her passion. She continued playing in the marching band, but as a senior in high school, won a spot in the All-State Choir and continued singing at school, in her community, and most importantly, at church. "Maybe it brought back the wonderful memories of Grandma and that old organ," Hosp reminisces, "but I've always felt most comfortable singing in church."

In 1976, Hosp began her lifetime collaboration with Mike Dumey. "Mike introduced me to the world of Broadway musicals," she says. She went on and sang at the Grand Palace at Six Flags. In 1980, she had the opportunity to sign with several recording companies when she auditioned at a Christian Artists Camp in the Colorado Rockies, but, not feeling comfortable with the professional music environment, Hosp declined. In the early '80s, she starred with Dumey at Port Cape in "Spotlight Tonight." The live band featured Scott Bierschwal and Brett Yount.

In 1999, she won a National Quartet Convention Talent Search and sang before 3,500 people at the Show Me Center in Cape Girardeau. Next she won at the Freedom Hall in Louisville, Kentucky, against over 200 contestants from around the U.S., performed before 22,000, and signed a recording contract with Daywind Records out of Nashville. She recorded three projects for Daywind as offers of tours and studio gigs came her way, but having her second child by then, she declined again. She explains,

> I've never regretted always placing family first. Upon his graduation from high school, my son told me how thankful he was for our sacrifices that enabled him to grow up in the same community, Jackson, and I've never looked back! I still perform locally, and that's fulfilling enough for me.

Robyn credits Nick Leist (band), Ernestine Kirk (choir), and her husband Ken as people who have made the difference in her life. "When I was little, my mom had a saying on our refrigerator door, 'One hundred years from now, it will not matter how much money you have, or how big your house is, or the kind of car you drive, but that you made the difference in the life of a child.' I hope I've done that. I want to leave a legacy."

Robyn Hosp definitely has.

Kristin Schweain. COURTESY OF REBECCA MOORE PHOTOGRAPHY.

Kristin Schweain

Kristin Schweain turned her dream of becoming a professional musician into reality when she starred with the contemporary Christian Pop/Rock group ZOEgirl from 2000 thru 2006. The trio burst on the scene in 2002 as the fastest selling debut artist in Sparrow Records history, garnering the Dove Award as Gospel Music Association's New Artist of the Year in the process! With more than 350,000 sales, they quickly became role models for a generation of American Christian girls.

Kristin's start was influenced by her jazz pianist grandfather Frederick Spies and her mother. "Mom was always playing music around the house," Kristen remembers. Schweain played piano at an early age, participated in band and choir in school, and wrote her first song, "I Need You," at age 18. She studied piano and voice at DePaul School of Music in Indiana, Missouri Baptist College in Missouri, and Belmont University in Nashville, Tennessee.

ZOEgirl came rather out of the blue. "It wasn't something I expected," Schweain explains. She was discovered by an agent for Sparrow Records in Nashville during a performance of her first band, Fleau. She was teamed up with Alisa Girard from California and Chrissy Conway from New Jersey. "We were all different, had different styles, and came from different areas of the country. I think that gave us a unique mixture that just clicked when we were together. It was magic," Kristin said.

Zoe in the New Testament means "life." Through their music, ZOEgirl talks about life in Christ. "It was an incredible experience that will never leave me. It gave me the opportunity to write, record, and tour with a ministry that made a huge impact on the lives of so many young women."

ZOEgirl released several albums and traveled with Christian artists Clay Crosse, Avalon, Natalie Grant, Newsboys, TobyMac, and Jump 5. They partnered with Big World Ventures for mission trips to Venezuela and Ecuador. They were also actively involved with Compassion International, which helped meet health care, nutritional, educational, and spiritual needs for over 600,000 children living in poverty in 23 countries. ZOEgirls' final album *Room to Breathe* was #1 on the Billboard Heatseekers chart.

Kristin has incredible memories of her many tours, but one stands out: the first night of Carman's "Heart of a Champion" tour in Memphis, Tennessee. "We stepped on stage to a crowd of over 10,000 people. It was terrifying AND incredible," she remembers.

Another memory wasn't so upbeat. After completing a show in northern California the night before, she boarded a plane on September 11, 2001. "I'll never forget the apprehension when the pilot announced we would be vacating the plane because of terrorists attacks. We rented a car and made the three-day trip back to Nashville, stunned like the rest of the country."

After seven years, the girls left Nashville, since marriage required more family responsibilities for all three members. Their last concert was in December of 2006. Kristin currently lives with her husband Ryan and two children back in Jackson, Missouri, where she's Associate Music Director of St. Paul Lutheran Church.

In June of 2008, Kristin released a solo album entitled *Days of Eden*. "I wrote and performed the songs on piano with just a touch of jazz. They are faith-based songs I've written at different times over the years. They are me, through and through."

When asked if there are opportunities in the future, Kristen says, "I'm the kind of person who likes to sit at the piano and tell a story. Maybe someday, I'll have the opportunity to do more recording. That's the moment you're actually sharing your heart with people."

Isabella

Alex Bettinger and four buddies from Perryville, Missouri, have turned an informal, jam-rock band, formed in January of 2008, into a budding professional group that had offers of record deals from two companies in 2009. "It's happened so fast," Alex states. "We've actually sold over 500 tunes on iTunes in our first week and a half. Members of Isabella are Alex Bettinger (drums), Tim Godlove (vocals), guitarists Joel Kapp and Josh Schindele, and Colt Buehler (bass). They all started music activities in school, Alex in Cape and the others in Perryville.

Isabella. L to r: Joel Kapp, Jake Tropf, Tim Godlove, Alex Bettinger, Colt Buehler. COURTESY OF JOHN LaROSE.

Alex started at Clippard Elementary and continued in junior high and high school, playing in marching and concert band. He studied at Southeast Missouri State University, where he excelled in the jazz band. The group practiced in Alex's basement and performed locally at Mississippi Mud House in Cape. They also were heard in venues in Farmington and St. Louis. Their big break came when, on a fluke, they entered Point Fest, a battle of thirty bands sponsored by radio station 105.7, The Point, in May 2009 in St. Louis. They won!

Things are moving at a fast pace now. They are self-promoting at this point. They've had two recording sessions in Cleveland, Ohio. They returned to Cleveland in August to finish their first CD. "We are all excited and very passionate about what small success we've had thus far," Alex says. "Our reviews so far have been great. We have high hopes and we're working hard, rehearsing, and writing new material almost every day. So, we'll see what happens."

More Friends . . .

Jim Rhodes.

Jim Rhodes began performing with Bob Sisco in 1957, graduated from Southeast Missouri State University in 1959, and was my original orchestra pianist in 1960 when Sisco left for California. From 1958 through 1967, he was the music director and animation artist for Versatile Television Productions, a subsidiary of KFVS–TV. He then opened Kendall-Lee Studio and continued writing, producing, engineering, and recording TV commercials, and taught in the Jackson, Missouri, school system. He sold his studio in 1976 and joined American Artists Studio in Springfield, Missouri, and a year later, on to Tulsa Studios in Tulsa, Oklahoma. He was lured back to Springfield in 1981 as President of Column Studios. Eight years later, The Great American Music Company hired Jim as music director of the Carolina Opry and Dixie Jubilee in Myrtle Beach, South Carolina.

Rhodes retired back to Jackson in 1991 and continues as an independent music producer and consultant. Over the years, he's worked on over 2,100 music and film productions, with clients like Roy Clark, Garth Brooks, Ronnie Dunn, Reba McEntire, Pat Boone, Ted Nugent, Boxcar Willie, Ozark Mountain Daredevils, and many more.

Jim Strong and I were members of the Central High School Class of 1960. He's a fine bass player, and I remember him most as bassist for the trio, Lee & the Lyrics, which included Leon Barnett (leader, singer, and lead guitar), Lee Ragland (drums), and Jim on bass. Strong first performed with high school buddies Ron Gray, Tom Ward, Paul "Corky" Weiss, and James "Footsie" Smith, after entering a talent show at Cape Central. Jim remembers, "I really didn't know much about the bass, but I faked it pretty good." They played at Teen Town, The Rainbow Room, and other local clubs. He later played with Cane Creek and Cecil Foutch, and in 1996, went with Nite Shift. Strong has played with Nite Shift for the past 16 years. The group includes Joe Lowes (leader, guitar, and vocals), Jack Ford (keyboards and vocals), Jim on bass, and David Barberis (drums and vocals). Strong's wife Bonnie laughs about their marriage, "We've lasted 44 years; pretty good for a musician!"

Nite Shift. L to r: Jack Ford, David Barberis, Joe Lowes, Jim Strong. COURTESY OF JIM STRONG.

Doug "Sonny" Blumer has turned an interest in acoustic country/folk music into a 30-year adventure of recording, performing, and traveling throughout the U.S. Sonny graduated from Central High School in Cape in 1973, and Southeast Missouri State University in 1978. After a four-year stint in the Navy, he located in San Francisco where, in between tours, he still makes his home. Sonny's acoustic honky-tonk group, The Westerleys, was formed in 1994 and appeared in many regional and national folk festivals, the Kennedy Center in Washington D.C., and the Grand Ole Opry in Nashville. Currently, he travels with his new group Mississippi Rider throughout the U.S.A.

Ted Miller.

Ted Miller, a fellow member of the Cape Central High School band, was a member of the French horn section of the Nashville, Tennessee Symphony Orchestra for 16 years. He taught music in schools around Nashville for 46 years and is retired in Portland, Maine.

Clyde Ridge was another accomplished pianist from Cape Central that my mom used to tell me about from her high school days. Unfortunately, I've not been able to find much about him other than he eventually settled in New York City in the '30s and '40s as a freelance jazz pianist. He must have possessed superior technique because he made piano rolls for player pianos for the Aeolian Music Corporation.

Jim "Jolly" Oliver, one of Cape's most popular personalities, settled in Nashville after his stint in the Marine Corp during the Vietnam War. He experienced success for many years there as a regional lounge-singer and songwriter on the Midwest motel/hotel circuit. "I was fortunate to keep working over a 13-14 year period, not an easy thing to do in Nashville," Jim remembers. "The road can be tough. But I played in more than beer joints and road houses. Classy supper clubs were my favorite. I could wear a velvet jacket and provide easy listening music for patrons. I traveled with Archie Campbell of Hee Haw fame, had one song,

Jim "Jolly" Oliver.

"East & West," recorded by The New Christy Minstrels, and another, "The Morning Girl," recorded by my lifetime friend Billy Swan. My biggest performance was before 2,500 in the Roy Acuff Theatre. When that applause comes roaring back at you, you never want it to stop."

At age 42, Jim decided to leave the road and get a more traditional job: insurance.

"There just wasn't enough stability for retirement," he surmised. He's been successful to the point that he's recently returned to writing music with Dennis Morgan, the Broadcast Music Incorporated (BMI) four-time award winner. He's also writing religious music that he performs in Nashville churches.

In our most recent phone conversation, Jolly seems content with his life and where he's been. As he put it, "Health is wealth, and with the Lord's help, I have some productive years left."

L to r: Brandon Sweeney, Nadir Maraschin, Stephen Limbaugh, Ian Schaeffer.

Stephen Limbaugh studied piano with Beverly Reece, graduated from Central High School, and transferred to California State University, Northridge, in 2004, after completing three years at the University of Missouri—Kansas City, where he studied composition and trumpet performance. He finished his composition degree and began writing alternative rock, his chosen genre, with another Cape Girardeau native, Ben Carter. Stephen received a private grant to record his *Concerto for Brass and Orchestra* in Moscow with the Russian Philharmonic Orchestra in December of 2005.

Back in Los Angeles he formed several different bands that won competitions at the Hard Rock Café and B.B. King's at Universal City. His group, Kingsley, signed with Wyman Records, released the album *Choices*, took it on a national tour, and had it subsequently released on DVD. *Digital Providence* is their latest release, slated for a tour in the spring and summer of 2011.

Kenny Martin has worked at Shivelbines for 41 years, plays and builds guitars, wrote a popular book on how to play the guitar entitled *Learning To Play Guitar Plain and Simple*, co-founded The Little Ole Opry outside of Burfordville, and is one of the funniest guys on the face of the earth.

The Opry started in a building provided by Jackson attorney Ken Waldron, to teach kids to play. Jeanie Hinck joined, along with Terry Hopkins, and together they built the Opry, where, for 25 years, 200 or more

Kenny Martin.

musicians and audience members performed every Friday and Saturday night. Since no talent was required, no one was turned away from the stage. However, Ken quipped, "Area musicians chipped in each week to pay me to stay away!" The house band included Ken (guitar and comedy), Chuck Sowers (guitar), Tim Hefler (keyboards), Vernon Fligg (drums), and Donna Mathes (bass).

Brad Lyle worked at Shivelbine Music Store for 40 years as a salesman and drum and percussion instructor. He was a good, dependable drummer who appeared with many local and regional bands, including *The Lou Hobbs Show* on KFVS–TV, Fred Horrell and the Flames, Mike Smith and the Runaways, Bob Dolle, Bob Rosenquist, my orchestra, and even Little Jimmy Dickens and other Nashville stars as they traveled throughout the area.

Brad Lyle.

Claire Syler. COURTESY OF CHEEKWOOD STUDIOS.

Claire Syler honed her talents in Cape Central musicals, became drama instructor at Belmont College, Nashville, Tennessee, and Education & Outreach Director for the Nashville Shakespeare Festival. Now married with one son, Syler is adjunct professor of Theatre at the University of Pittsburgh and active in community theatre productions.

Mary Bauer, a graduate of Cape Notre Dame Regional High School and a student at Southeast Missouri State University, has acquired an impressive music vita in a few short years: a top five finisher in Miss Missouri for two consecutive years, with the 2011 contest on the horizon; current Miss Jackson; and starred in several Mike Dumey "Sounds of the Seasons," "Sing America Sing," and "Starz on the Rise" shows. She's produced benefit concerts that raised $2,000 and $2,777, respectively, for St. Jude's and Miracle Network hospitals from proceeds from her CD, *Sounds of Hope*. She's performed the National Anthem at Kansas City Royals, Southeast Missouri State University, and University of Missouri baseball and basketball games; and finished high at the Mid-South Fair in Memphis. Her star is just beginning to shine!

Mary Bauer. COURTESY OF CHEEKWOOD STUDIOS.

Paige Kiefner, a senior at Saxony Lutheran High School and student of Judith Farris, is on her way to a fabulous career as an opera singer. Musicals caught her attention when she started singing and playing piano at an early age. "As I grew, I started placing a few classical pieces in my repertoire; I enjoyed the challenge. I was hooked," Paige recalls. "I love a challenge and succeed when I'm under pressure."

At a recent standing-room-only recital, Kiefner included demanding pieces by Schubert, Mozart, Puccini, Fauve, Barber, and Bernstein, generally reserved for older singers. As they left, her audience realized they had listened to a remarkable voice that's just beginning, and reveled at the thought of where she might go.

Paige Kiefner.
COURTESY OF
CHEEKWOOD STUDIOS.

"Paige has everything opera demands: the voice, the looks, the work ethic, the patience, the passion," Farris reveals. Paige begins the next chapter of her life this fall, as she has been awarded several scholarships to attend the Boston Conservatory of Music in Boston, Massachusetts.

Quitman McBride.
COURTESY OF Q WORK
STUDIOS.

Quitman McBride III starred in many musicals at Cape Central and productions of Mike Dumey, and is currently a freshman on scholarship at the prestigious Berklee College of Music in Boston, Massachusetts. I've featured him on several occasions with my full Jerry Ford Orchestra, and he receives standing ovations every time he sings with us. Look for great things from Quitman. Broadway is probably not too far off.

Jeff Nall (trumpet) and Eric Matzat (saxophone) both graduates of Cape Central, received their music degrees from Southwest Missouri State University in Springfield, Missouri. Both were members of Shoji Tabuchi's orchestra in Branson. Matzat was also band director at Branson High School for eight years and is currently President of Palen Music Company, with stores in multi-locations around the Springfield/Branson area. Nall is a freelance trumpet player, also around the Springfield/Branson area. He performs with the Springfield Little Theatre, Springfield Community and Jazz bands, churches, weddings, and other events. He also operates a landscape business.

Bullock Piano Salon

Thad Bullock purchased Martin Johnson's Piano Company at 813 Broadway in 1952, since Johnson and his bride wanted to start a motel business in Daytona Beach, Florida. For $1,500, Bullock received three pianos, an old upright, and all the materials and supplies. In 1955, he moved the piano salon and his family into a home he purchased at 1320 Broadway. Business was slow. His wife Ruby gave piano lessons. Bullock continued to play piano and entertain in various clubs as a one-man band.

As local neighbors began to object to the business in the family neighborhood, fate intervened in 1957. Local piano dealer and saxophonist, Don Heidbreder, sustained major injuries in a car wreck and was unable to work for many months. Baldwin awarded Bullock with their new piano and organ dealership. He moved the store to 705 Broadway and business flourished.

In 1960, Bullock moved his salon into the West Park Shopping Center, and business grew even more. In 1962, he partnered with the Whitby Brothers of Paducah, Kentucky, and opened Paducah Piano Center. After selling his interest in that business, he bought the Town Plaza Cafeteria and operated it for several years.

In 1969, Bullock purchased the Marquette Hotel in Downtown Cape and moved the piano salon once again, operating until 1994. His son Jerry, my lifetime friend, told me the most famous transaction his dad ever made was selling Nashville recording legend Chet Atkins his personal Baldwin grand piano.

Thad made several runs for the U.S. Congress. I asked him one time, why? His response: "You'd be surprised how many pianos and organs I've sold over the years with all that free advertisement!"

Bullock's son Jerry moved to White Plains, Maryland, and started Bullock Piano Salon East in 1964. For 37 years, his store has provided a full line of pianos, organs, musical instruments, audio equipment, student horn rentals, and music lessons. An accomplished jazz and blues pianist/vocalist, Jerry is a professional musician performing at local clubs and regional events under the name of the Byx Bullock Combo.

Classical/Broadway

It's no surprise we have an affinity for classical music spawned by our Western European ancestors. Christianity with its great cathedrals, royalty, and historic nobles sponsored the glorious instrumental and vocal music of symphonies, ballets, operas and their various forms, which provided the foundation for much of our secular music.

Classical music generally requires highly skilled and extensively trained musicians. While a couple of the musicians I've placed in this category may not fit our traditional definition of classical, they certainly have achieved their level of proficiency on Broadway and regional theatre through years of diligence, perfecting their talents.

JUDITH
FARRIS

Contralto

"Outstanding
vocalization and
characterization"
GANNETT NEWS

"Velvety of voice"
OPERA NEWS

Judith Farris

Where does one start with Cape's Diva, Judith Farris: The Kennedy Center, Lincoln Center, Carnegie Hall, Boston Symphony, The National Symphony, The New York Philharmonic? Or do we contemplate her renowned, sensitive interpretations of works by Johann Sebastian Bach and Gustav Mahler? Or her appearances with the Washington Opera, the Canadian Opera Company, the Connecticut Grand Opera, and the Mormon Tabernacle Choir. Or do we start at the corner of Good Hope and Sheridan Streets in Cape Girardeau where she and Billy Swan grew up next door to each other?

Her deep barreled contralto voice makes you think any minute she's going to grab an axe and split a rail. You see, the contralto voice has an unusually low, masculine quality. It certainly doesn't have the star power of the soprano and, therefore, doesn't command the adulation or the really big money in opera. As Judith says, "The only roles for Contraltos are the witches, bitches, and nurses!"

Her vocal tutelage includes Anthony Quinn, Peter Allen, Tony Randall, Betty Comden, Kaye Ballard, Marilu Henner, Matthew Broderick, Lauren Bacall, Tyne Daly, Cheryl Ladd, and many other celebrities. Judith describes stars in the heavens as, "Flaming balls of gas." She says, "However, the great stars on Broadway aren't that at all in my studio. They can be as insecure as many of us. They come to me to learn, to improve. They leave their egos at the front door."

Judy tells the story about when lyrists Betty Comden and her writing partner, Adolph Green ("Singing in the Rain," "On the Town"), Judy Holiday, and Leonard Bernstein were in their early collaborative days. One late afternoon, during a long rehearsal, they finally thought they had gotten the song right. Betty yelled, "Let's rent a hall before it's too late!"

Let's start at the beginning. Judy's aunt DeSha Day and her daughter Jo Donna encouraged Judy as a young girl. They observed her organizing plays and shows in her front yard, using the neighborhood kids. The Days were talented and active in the local arts community. Jo Donna operated a popular dance studio in Cape Girardeau. She and her mother arranged for Judy to take piano lessons from Louise Eckhardt at the age of 8.

Miss Eckhardt was a stern disciplinarian and task master, and Judy thrived and excelled in the environment. This five-year training provided an important foundation for Judy's future professional life. At 13, she was already giving lessons to younger kids. That year, when Judy visited Mrs. Eckhardt in the hospital, Mrs. Eckhardt told her, "I'm going to die, and I want you to teach all my students. You take my piano, my music, my books, all my equipment and continue." Judy obliged. Judy also began playing for school, church, and community groups. As she explains, "It was music that got me through my teenage years."

Red Star Baptist Church was another training ground in those days. She directed a children's choir, accompanied the vocal ensembles, and played for all the church services. There, in her formative years, she adopted the mantra of God's command, "Use your talents and they will grow."

Her high-school choir director told her to practice the piano, because "she would never be a singer!" So she attended Southeast Missouri State College as a piano major, thinking she would someday be a music teacher in the Bootheel. She needed the money to stay in school, so it was arranged that she would be the paid accompanist for the music department. Judy told me, "I never sang a note until college. All I ever wanted to do was play the piano."

Voice faculty-member Mary Lou Henry discovered Judy's singing potential in Class Voice during her freshman year. Judy adored her and took voice lessons from her for five years. It was the beginning of a lifetime collaboration between the two. Ms. Henry recalls, "I knew her as the best piano student in the department, even though she was only a freshman. I had no idea she had never sung before. The first time she sang for me in Class Voice, she was scared to death. She had a nice range and a very rich tone."

During her sophomore year, after Professor Doyle Dumas turned her down as the choir accompanist because he needed her in the alto section, Judy switched her major from piano to voice. "Judy told me she thought it would be easier," Ms. Henry remembered. She laughed, "Judy had no idea what was coming!"

Ms. Henry explained, "Great singers generally have a strong work ethic and discipline. It depends on each student and how badly they want to succeed. The demands are great. Judy worked hard. Her potential began to blossom. Her progress was a revelation to all of us."

Kent Jones, a university English teacher, took her to an opera in Memphis, Tennessee, performed by the Metropolitan Opera Company of New York City. Judy was blown away, "I didn't even know what opera was. I was dazzled by the magnitude of the spectacle. I was hooked."

Opera would be her passion.

Professor Jones then introduced her to the world-renowned opera star, Marjorie Lawrence, who was Artist in Residence at Southern Illinois University in Carbondale, Illinois. Ms. Lawrence bolstered Judy's confidence when she was the first to say, "Judy, I love your voice."

Judy studied with Mrs. Lawrence for one year. One day Judy arrived early for her lesson and heard awful vocal sounds coming from the student in the other room. To her shock, Judy heard Ms. Lawrence say the exact same thing to that student she had said to her months before, "I love your voice."

Judy was devastated. She thought, *I still can't sing.*

In August of 1970, Judy was given the opportunity to audition for a full scholarship to the Academy of Vocal Arts in Philadelphia, Pennsylvania. She had never been out of Cape Girardeau on her own in her life. She was scared to death. Travel agent Ricky Brasington made all the arrangements. Judy expected a school, but when she arrived at the Philadelphia Brownstone, she told the cab driver, "This can't be the right address." The cabbie responded, "It sure is." She rang the door bell and heard this strange buzzing noise. It happened every time she rang the bell. She was thinking, *Isn't anyone going to answer the door?* She didn't realize she should open the door herself during the buzzing; someone finally appeared to help her.

The school would only take 25 students. As she auditioned, she was thinking, *I can't leave Cape. I can't do this. Even though this is a full scholarship, I have no money. Please don't pick me.* They did.

The school didn't work out. It didn't take long for Judy to realize it didn't offer what she needed. They also would not let her audition for the prestigious Marian Anderson competition. So she left for New York City in December.

She found small singing parts wherever she could to earn money and survive. Over the phone, she got a job at a Jewish Temple. At the first rehearsal in the conductor's home, he asked her if she'd sung Jewish music before?

She answered, "Yes."

He asked if she knew Hebrew.

She answered, "Yes."

He asked her if she could sight-read Hebrew script.

She answered, "Yes."

That's when Judy became *Judith*. He loved the sweet Hebrew name, Judith. She faked her way through the rehearsal, and only one year later, Judith was soloist for the High Holy Day Services at Temple Emmanuel (the largest Jewish Temple in America) on 5th Avenue in New York City! Not bad for a little hayseed girl from Cape Girardeau, Missouri.

She went back to Philadelphia and entered the Marian Anderson competition. When she received the phone call back in New York that she had won, she remarked, "You must have called the wrong number!"

Her first real professional performance was in Handel's *Messiah* with a choir of former Robert Shaw Chorale members and the New York Philharmonic in Lincoln Center with Leonard Bernstein conducting. She loved the Chorale, first hearing it as a young girl in Academic Hall on the Southeast Missouri State University campus in Cape Girardeau at a concert provided by the Community Concert Association. "To sing with them was a personal milestone," she said.

Actually, the Shaw Chorale had disbanded, and Shaw's former assistant Tom Pyle moved to New York City to become a contractor for professional singers. His wife, Alice Parker, was the other half of the famed Shaw-Parker choral arranger team. Tom loved Judith's voice and hired her. Judith's career expanded as she went on to appearances with the Santa Fe, Tulsa, Toronto, Virginia, Detroit, and Fort Worth operas. Judith has performed in operas and with symphonies throughout the U.S. and Europe.

Her one shot at the Broadway stage was a hoot. Judith thinks conductor John Mauceri recommended her to audition for the role of Nettie in a new Rodgers and Hammerstein production of *Carousel*. She couldn't go at the appointed time. Jamie Hammerstein, Oscar's son, agreed to change it to meet her schedule. "I couldn't believe it," she exclaimed. She sang "You'll Never Walk Alone" for everyone: the producers, the cast, the entire Rodgers family, the entire Hammerstein family, and on and on. As she put it, "I must have sung the damn song 1,000 times!"

She got the part. The production used microphones. Judith had never used microphones. "In opera, you just go for it. You let it all hang out!" she explained. At one point in a rehearsal, she was having trouble with the microphone balance, so she asked the conductor, who by this time was at the back of the hall, "Is it loud?" He shouted back, "Is it loud? Jesus Christ, it's Godzilla! Turn the damn thing down!"

The inaugural performance was at the Kennedy Center Opera House in Washington, D.C. Many dignitaries were present, including Charlton Heston. The post performance reception was held on the lawn of the Smithsonian Institution. A reporter was interviewing all the cast leads, except Judith. She couldn't figure it out. She thought maybe the sound guy had turned her way down. After a couple of drinks, she assured herself she had done well. At the end of the evening, after most had left, the reporter finally came up to her.

"I'm sorry I haven't spoken to you sooner this evening," she apologized. "My mother died last week and 'You'll Never Walk Alone' was her favorite song, and your rendition moved me so. I knew if I came up to you, I wouldn't be able to talk without breaking down." The show never made it to Broadway.

Judith has received numerous prestigious awards including the National Arts Club of New York City Award for Contraltos, the Minna Kaufman Rudd Award, the Lucrezia Bori Award, and the Metropolitan Opera's Kathryn Long Grant, to name a few.

Judith's vast repertoire spans Pucinni, Purcell, Shostakovich, Tchaikovsky, and most other masters. She appeared at Carnegie Hall as the contralto soloist in the Verdi Requiem with Luciano Pavarotti as tenor. She's performed Haydn's *The Creation* with the New York Philharmonic with Zubin Mehta conducting. Her credits go on and on.

Critical acclaim follows her wherever she appears. The *Potomac News* described her rendition of Nettie in Rodgers and Hammerstein's hit musical *Carousel* this way, "'You'll Never Walk Alone' has never been more movingly or melodiously sung." The *Gannett-Westchester Rockland* proclaimed, "Her lullaby was an outstanding piece of vocalization in *The Consul*." The *Westport News* concluded in another performance, "Judith dominates the moment." *The New York Times* has described her as "wonderfully dramatic." And the *New York Daily News* has praised her singing on occasion as "superb" and "delectable."

A twist of fate occurred when Keith Davis, the renowned voice teacher in the New York Theatre scene, had three students receive Tony Awards one year. They credited him for their success. At that time, Judith was also his student. She called to congratulate him. He was frustrated with the notoriety, and told her he was too tired and too busy to accept new clients. "Everyone will be calling me now," he confided to her in his frustration. While Judith had been studying with him for only six months, he told her he was going to refer all new clients to her, just as Mrs. Eckhardt had done those many years ago.

From that point in time, Judith has become the voice teacher of choice for many celebrities as they transition from acting to the vocal demands of Broadway roles. Her specialty is achieving quick, positive, vocal results with professional actors and dancers. The proficiency of her piano, singing, and teaching skills, and the "use your talents and they will grow" philosophy, have served her well.

JUDITH FARRIS
Contralto

It is the communicative power of the art of music which provides the strongest motivation for contralto Judith Farris' singing. From roles as varied as Frau Mary in Wagner's *The Flying Dutchman* to Dolores in the world premiere of Villa-Lobos' *Yerma* at the Santa Fe Opera (in a production of *Yerma* which featured Frederica van Stade) and has included appearances at the Opera Theatre of St. Louis, Tulsa Opera, Fort Worth Opera and the Virginia Opera. She worked closely with composer Gian Carlo Menotti when she appeared as The Mother in recent productions of *The Consul* with the Chicago Opera Theatre and Connecticut Grand Opera, and recently performed in the Kennedy Center's production of *Carousel*.

Ms. Farris has appeared as soloist with many of the finest orchestras and recently performed the Haydn *Creation* with Simon Estes and the New York Philharmonic (with whom she recorded the Beethoven's *Choral Fantasy* on the RCA label). She has appeared as soloist with the Mormon Tabernacle Choir in Handel's *Messiah* and has been a frequent guest with New York's Musica Sacra.

Ms. Farris has received many awards and commendations including the Marian Anderson Scholarship, the National Arts Club of New York City award for Contraltos, the Minna Kaufman Ruud Award, the Lucrezia Bori Award, and the Metropolitan Opera's Kathryn Long Grant Award.

New York Debut Recital
Alice Tully Hall, Lincoln Center
Tuesday September 13, 1988, 8:00 p.m.
with Randolph Mauldin, piano
Works by Brahms, Korngold, Shostakovich, Schumann and Purcell
Tickets: $15.00, 12.00 and 10.00 (senior citizens and students half-price)
(212) 874-6770

TRAWICK ARTISTS MANAGEMENT
129 West 72nd St., NY, NY 10023
(212) 874-2482 FAX 204735 TAM UR

A big moment for Judith came in the fall of 2004. She came home to teach a master class at her alma mater, Southeast Missouri State University, and sing with the university orchestra. Everything went fine: rehearsals, class, everything. People were coming from the tri-state area, friends from far and wide; it was a sell-out. However, when she arrived the night of the performance, she was told by a campus cop there were no lights, no concert, the campus was completely dark! Everyone went home. Judith laughs when she recalls the event, "For once, I wasn't taken out by a reviewer. Instead, it was a *squirrel* in the transformer!"

It was at that time University President Kenneth Dobbins offered Judith the opportunity to return to her alma mater as Artist in Residence. She knew she would have to make sacrifices to her schedule, and told him she would seriously consider it if the logistics could be worked out.

Judith never expected to spend the amount of time she does at the University. But during her two-week stint as voice teacher for the production of *Guys and Dolls* in 2005, she was surprised at the respect the students showed for her, and the value they placed on all her accomplishments. That sealed the deal that President Dobbins had proposed several months earlier. She concluded, "It's all about them. I've come full circle. It was meant to be."

In reviewing her career, Judith is always amazed. She relates, "I never meant to do this. With my insecurities in performing, I don't know how it all happened. I just kept getting chosen!" She laughed and concluded, "At this point, you just keep going." Judith remains busy as ever, balancing two vocations as she commutes monthly from Cape Girardeau where she is Artist in Residence at Southeast Missouri State University's Holland School of Visual and Performing Arts in the Department of Theatre and Dance, to New York City where she continues her voice teaching.

Matthew Piazzi.

Through the years, Judith juggled her professional and personal career as a single mother, raising her son Matthew Piazzi in New York City. She's literally lived the lyrics of "You'll Never Walk Alone."

Matthew has carved a career for himself in The Big Apple as an actor and impersonator, with a penchant for imitations. He has 40 different actors and celebrities in his repertoire, including George Clooney, Joe Pesce, Arnold Schwartzenegger, Dean Martin, and Jerry Lee Lewis. His voiceovers are heard on television and radio commercials for Mazda cars, Domino's Pizza, Nyquil, HBO, and 10 video games.

Matthew was born in New York in 1977, and moved around a lot as a youngster, since his mother's career took them to many places in California, Michigan, and New

York. He spent his 5th and 6th grades in Italy with his father. He attended New York Military Academy, Cromwell, New York; Harvey School, Katonah, New York; and graduated from Darow School, New Lebanon, New York, in 1995. He made many summer trips back to Cape Girardeau to visit family and friends, and now that his mother has a home here, continues to spend more time in Cape.

Matthew attributes some of his success to meeting new people in those vagabond days. "To fit in, I listened carefully," he explains. "I discovered I have very keen ears and the ability to distinguish voices. By making a connection between the two, I can mimic them. I associate the pitch of the voice to a musical note, add gestures, and you have an impression!"

A big break came when he auditioned for the new television phenomenon, *America's Got Talent*, in 2008. He tells it this way:

> I'm a self-taught pianist. I enjoy "figuring it out." I have always been a singer. How could I not have been? I perform at house parties in New York City. I also have taken acting classes in scene study and technique. They all came together in the audition for that show. The producers immediately flew me to Las Vegas, where I made the top 40 and later the top 20 out of over 200,000. As the result, I have signed with two new agents and had preliminary discussions with ABC, CBS, and NBC about future projects and appearances.

When I asked him to describe his feelings about the experience, he replied:

> As the pressure mounted, we all had to adjust to 88 million people watching our every move. The adrenaline was flowing; we had to hold it together, stand and deliver. For me, it gave me additional confidence and the realization that I can do anything. I just have to keep working, keep getting better, keep my mind clean, and hope for the best.

Thomas Harte.

Thomas Harte

Thomas Harte, a successful freelance double bassist in Los Angeles, California, explains his musical beginnings:

> My intrigue for all things musical began as an elementary student at Franklin School in Cape Girardeau. I remember singing Mrs. Peyton's favorite tune, "We Shall Overcome," and getting upset when kids would change the lyrics to one of my favorites, "Yellow Submarine." I suppose I had respect for a composer's wishes even then. I loved rock 'n' roll! My dad had a collection of 45s, and I looked forward to Sundays and Kasey Kasem's Top 40 Countdown on the radio.

Thomas enrolled in orchestra class as a seventh grader because he didn't feel comfortable singing in public and he wanted to play football, so choir and marching band were out of the question. He chose the double bass because the music teacher told him it was too big to take home, therefore, homework was not required.

Junior high school brought a rock band, flippin' burgers at Hardees, and with the money earned, a used Les Paul guitar from Shivelbines. Thomas remembers, "That guitar made me feel like a real musician." Piano lessons followed with Beverly Reece, but still no classical thoughts.

The shift toward classical music began as a junior in high school when he accompanied his father to London, England, for a semester in a teacher exchange program. Thomas was surrounded by music: rock concerts almost every week by legendary bands such as The Ramones, Sonic Youth, The Pixies, and The Grateful Dead. However, it was his newfound exposure to classical music that would have the greatest impact. He explains, "Though I was seeing numerous rock concerts, I was getting to see even more classical performances while in London." One of the highlights was a killer performance of Beethoven's 5th Symphony by the London Symphony Orchestra at Royal Albert Hall.

Upon return from London, Thomas began to take classical music and playing the double bass more seriously. Steve Schaffner, orchestra instructor at Central High School, helped prepare him for an audition in the Missouri All-State Orchestra. Since he was still a relative novice, Beverly Reece helped him find the pitches on the fingerboard for the 3-octave E-minor scale requirement. Thomas was thrilled when he was accepted to the orchestra.

At that point, Harte's focus began to narrow. He started taking lessons from Dr. Sara Edgerton at Southeast Missouri State University, received a scholarship, enrolled as a music performance major, and began practicing four to six hours a day. "I was the only double bass player and didn't really know how a bass was supposed to sound, so I emulated Ms. Edgerton's cello sound as my goal. I've always felt this helped me progress much faster than had I been around other bassists."

The support of Southeast music faculty members Paul Thompson, Gary Miller, Robert Freuhwald, and Robert Gifford encouraged his enthusiasm. During his freshman year at Southeast, when he was asked to join a Faculty Chamber group and perform a solo recital, he completely committed to becoming a professional musician.

At the end of that first year, Dr. Edgerton arranged for an audition for the Eastern Music Festival in North Carolina. That year drew bassists from schools like Indiana University, Oberlin, and Colorado University. "For the first time I was going to be among other bass players, and I fully expected to be at the bottom of the pack. To my surprise, I was the top bass player there and voted to play principal bass, including a chance to play the solo in Mahler's First Symphony."

Upon return, Thomas was fortunate to be accepted as a student by the St. Louis Symphony's new principal bassist, Erik Harris. The intensity of lessons from Harris and Dr. Edgerton helped make his decision to transfer to a music conservatory. He narrowed the list to Indiana University School of Music, the Curtis Institute, and The Juilliard School of Music. He was offered scholarships at Indiana and Juilliard, and chose Juilliard.

As a member of the Juilliard orchestra, Harte played under the baton of Leonard Slatkin, David Robertson, Robert Spano, and Kurt Masur. The highlight of his Juilliard experience came when he toured Japan and Korea with the orchestra. The orchestra was made up of the top players in the school, and today many are now soloists, studio recording musicians, concertmasters, principals, and section members of the world's greatest ensembles. Thomas tells of the Asian experience:

> Every hall from Tokyo to Seoul was as good as Carnegie Hall. The people's love for classical music there was so inspiring and supportive. I'll never forget an afternoon concert at an all-girls school. When we played the opening four notes of Beethoven's 5th Symphony, you could hear the students gasping with excitement.

After five years in New York City, Thomas and his wife Leah moved to Houston, Texas, so he could focus on auditions for major orchestras. Opportunities for teaching and performing began to fill his schedule. He performed with orchestras in and around Houston, San Antonio, and Shreveport, Louisiana.

In 2002, he accepted a position at the University of Southern California's Thornton School of Music as a Visiting Scholar, performing with the USC Orchestra and teaching private lessons to double bass students. Within a couple of years, he won auditions for jobs with the Santa Barbara Symphony, The New West Symphony, San

Bernardino Symphony, and Long Beach Symphony. In addition, he has performed with the Los Angeles Philharmonic, Los Angeles Opera Orchestra, the Pacific Symphony, San Diego Symphony, the Cabrillo Festival of Contemporary Music, and Festival MOZAIC, among others.

Harte holds Bachelor and Master of Music degrees from The Juilliard School in New York City as well as an Artist Diploma from the USC Thornton School of Music. He's been fortunate to study with some of the greatest bass instructors in the country, including Homer Mensch (The Juilliard School), Paul Ellison (Rice University), and David Moore (USC and the Los Angeles Philharmonic).

Always versatile, Thomas has performed and recorded with a diverse range of artists including Sting, Andrea Bocelli, Josh Groban, El Debarge, Taylor Swift, Steve Vai, X Japan, Florence + the Machine, and Rihanna. He can also be heard on various soundtracks for TV, film, and video game scores. His performance with Sting on the *Tonight Show* with Jay Leno was a huge highlight. Thomas remembers, "The orchestra was made up of some of L.A.'s top studio musicians, and the energy level was off the charts!"

Recording at Capitol Studios in the world famous Capitol Records building has been another thrill for Harte. "One of the first calls I received was to work with legendary guitarist Steve Vai for a short animated film. When I arrived at the session, I looked through the music and realized the score was based on Deep Purple's 'Smoke on the Water.' That was literally the first guitar lick I ever learned, and now I was playing it again, this time as a professional."

As a classically trained musician, working as a studio recording musician in Los Angeles has been an unexpected and welcomed opportunity for Harte. Working with both pop and rock 'n' roll artists has fulfilled his childhood dreams. As Thomas tells, "There is nothing else I would rather do.

"As a double bass player, the two most important things in my life are my supportive wife and a great bass. I met my wife Leah in Cape Central's orchestra when we were 16 or 17. She has always been supportive and encouraging to me, and I can't imagine having gone on this journey without her." Leah remembers, "We just fit. He makes me laugh, and we've had a lot of fun over the years."

Harte remembers,

> Leah has been an important part of each step in my career and was an integral part of the discovery of my right instrument. At Juilliard, I began searching for a bass that would be well suited for the next chapter in my studies. String players can go for years, if not a lifetime, searching for the right instrument. With my search only three weeks old, Leah and I walked into Koistein's Violin Shop in Long Island, New York, on a Friday night when Mr. Koistein had just received an old Italian bass. I played three notes on it that felt better

than any three notes I had ever played before. Leah said, "I think this is the bass for you." It was a huge investment, and thankfully, with the help of my supportive parents, I have been playing that bass ever since.

Harte says he enjoys the challenge of being a double bass player in Los Angeles playing so many types of music with so many different players.

I thrive on the excitement and unpredictability of it. Getting an 8:00 A.M. call for a recording session in Hollywood the same afternoon will never get old! I often think back over my Juilliard teacher's career and how similarly, I got to play both orchestrally and as a studio recording musician. I hope Mr. Mensch would be proud of me and the career I've had thus far. As I say to my colleagues when they ask me how I'm doing, "If I've got my bass in my hands, I'm doing great!"

I asked Leah to sum up her feelings about Thomas's career.

I knew as soon as Thomas found his love for the double bass, there could be no other career for him as a musician. I don't really even think he had a choice in the matter. From my observation, musicians are just born vessels from which music flows. We moved from Missouri to New York City, eventually making it to Los Angeles, and through this journey, I've gotten to witness first hand that it takes an immeasurable amount of dedication to pursue one's dream to become a professional musician. It has been tremendously inspiring to watch Thomas's journey of perseverance as he followed his passion. As I've observed, you can tell much about a musician's personal character as it is so often reflected in the way he makes music. When I hear Thomas play his bass, I am so moved to hear such care, passion, attention, love, and dedication flowing through those low notes. Those words describe his bass playing, but I am even prouder to say those words also describe him as a person.

Sally Merriman.

Sally Merriman

Sally Merriman, born in Lincoln, Nebraska, and raised in Cape Girardeau, lived in Israel for seven years as a bassoonist for the Tel Aviv Opera Orchestra, the Haifa Symphony Orchestra, and the Israel Chamber Orchestra. She returned to the Boston area in 2000, where she is a freelance bassoonist performing with such groups as the Boston Ballet Orchestra, the Rhode Island Philharmonic, Nashua Symphony Orchestra, Opera Boston, Boston Philharmonic Orchestra, Radius Ensemble, Portland Symphony Orchestra, and Boston Classical Orchestra. She has also performed with the Boston Pops Esplanade Orchestra and the Boston Chamber Music Society.

Merriman started studying piano at age 7 and clarinet in 7th grade. At Cape Central, she enjoyed brief stints on tenor and baritone sax, xylophone, and electric bass. But when she heard the St. Louis Symphony in concert in Cape Girardeau, the bassoon section caught her attention. She acquired substantial acumen on bassoon rather quickly at Central. She performed with the Cape Municipal Band and the orchestral and wind ensembles at Southeast Missouri State University before graduating high school in 1986.

Sally received her Bachelor of Music from the North Carolina School for the Arts in 1989, where she studied with Mark Popkin and freelanced with the Winston-Salem Symphony and the North Carolina Symphony Orchestra. She then studied at The Juilliard School with Don MacCourt and moved to New York City in 1989. During one of the many festivals where she performed, she met Israeli composer Odod Zehavi who recommended her for a position with the Tel Aviv Opera Orchestra. She was accepted and arrived in September for the start of the orchestra season. She recalls,

> My timing wasn't the greatest. I arrived four months before the Gulf War started! There were air raid sirens requiring gas masks and sealed shelter rooms for safety. Some elderly neighbors kept mistaking my practicing in my apartment as air raids, not the best compliment I ever received! Due to the heroic efforts of Mrs. Harte, our travel agent, she got me out of Tel Aviv in a few days, and I was back in the good ole U.S.A. After things quieted down, I went back and stayed for seven years.

Sally now lives in the Boston area, and besides freelancing with area orchestras and ensembles, she stays busy working at Rayburn Music in educational sales, has a small reed-making business, and has developed acumen in playing baroque and classical bassoon, which requires different instruments than the modern bassoon.

Donna Smith. COURTESY OF LISA CROSBY.

Donna Smith

Donna Smith turned a musical childhood of piano lessons, school and church choirs, vocal competitions, hard work, and determination into a successful operatic career in New York City.

Donna was born in Cape Girardeau to a family of some musical ability but no formal training. Singing church hymns and Southern gospel music were a big part of her initial musical experience.

"Dad loves bluegrass and took us to festivals in the summertime. I didn't really appreciate it then, but I have come to respect it. After all, the bones of opera and bluegrass are similar; they are both based on storytelling. My junior high choral teacher, Jeanie Tjaden, was the first positive influence. She gave me solo opportunities and encouraged me to keep singing. But the teacher that truly influenced me and changed my life was my voice teacher from Southeast Missouri State University, Louisa Takahashi."

Her first big break came while at Southeast when she auditioned for The Rome Festival. Donna was asked to sing the lead soprano role of Pamina in Mozart's *The Magic Flute*. That summer changed her life. Her parents were surprised when, upon her return, she informed them she would pursue her career in opera. "They have always been extremely supportive. I wouldn't have been able to pursue this career if they had not been. It's just too hard, if you don't have that level of support," Donna relates.

Two more summers in Rome followed, along with extensive travel throughout Europe. During this time she also entered the Metropolitan Opera National Council Auditions for young aspiring singers. She was first runner-up in the district and placed third in the Midwest Regional.

Donna studied at the New England Conservatory of Music in Boston and was fortunate to be accepted in the Manhattan School of Music to study for three years with Ted Puffer.

This experience solidified her technique and inspired her to start auditioning for opera companies.

Just as she was preparing for auditions, she had an accident that left her with a nearly dislocated cervical spine, jaw, and head injury. It took a year of rehabilitation to physically recover and two years to regain her voice. Don Marrazzio, a friend and fellow opera singer, encouraged Donna to begin singing again. It was a slow and tedious process, but gradually they rebuilt her voice. "Don is a huge part of why I'm singing again," Donna explains. "I owe him more than I will ever be able to repay."

A year later, armed with her new voice and more confidence, she flew to St. Louis and competed again in the Metropolitan Opera competition. She won first the Midwest Regional finals in Tulsa, Oklahoma, and on to the semi-finals on the stage of the Metropolitan Opera House in New York City.

"When the competition began," she said, "I was definitely nervous, but I relaxed a bit after I started singing. We sang for a small audience of artistic directors, donors, managers, our family members, and a panel of judges made up of some of the top names in opera. I didn't advance to the finals, but I was pleased with how far I had come in the previous year or so."

Opportunities began to come her way, first by participating in the Young Artist program with Opera Theatre of St. Louis. "They took a chance with me, and I will always be grateful to them," Donna says. For the next four years, Donna continued on the Young Artist path, gaining valuable experience working with professional singers, conductors, and directors at several opera companies across the country. "It was only then I realized how much of a team effort opera really is. Singers are only a small part of a very large puzzle. None would be possible without every conductor, director, seamstress, set designer, stage hand, makeup artist, and stage manager to make a really great show."

Donna is a busy working musician, performing, teaching, and living in New York City. She travels where her performances take her: Utah Opera, Dayton Opera, Opera Theatre of St. Louis, Glimmerglass Opera, American Opera Projects, and more, with over 30 roles in the past several years including: Blonde in *The Abduction from the Seraglio*, Norina in *Don Pasquale*, Adina in *L' Elisir d' Amore*, Taumannchen in *Hansel und Gretel*, Suor Genoveffa in *Suor Angelica*, Lauretta in *Gianni Schicchi*, Josephine in *H.M.S. Pinafore*, Venus in *Orpheus in the Underworld*, Strolling Girl in *Death in Venice*, Ana Lucia in *SHOT*, and more.

She has also covered main stage roles such as Gretel in *Hansel and Gretel*, Pat Nixon in *Nixon in China*, Lucie in *Lucie de Lammermoor*, Eurydice in *Orphée et Eurydice*, and Yum Yum in *The Mikado*.

On Monday, February 14, 2011, she wrote:

> I'm leaving for a production of *Little Women* with Utah Opera, then immediately off to Dayton Opera as a last minute replacement of Marie in *La Fille du Regiment* . . . over 100 pages of French to memorize in a month . . . in between rehearsals and performances in Utah. Things are a little challenging right now, but I'm not complaining!

Liesl Schoenberger. COURTESY OF MATTHEW FRIED.

Liesl Schoenberger

Liesl Schoenberger has elevated her violin studies beginning at the age of 2½ into a Master's Degree from Indiana University, an Artist Diploma from Yale University, and a reputation as an international virtuoso performer. In between, Liesl has won the hearts of her followers with her dramatic and lighthearted recitals, concerts, and appearances. She is comfortable with Brahms and Ysaye sonatas, Kreisler and Dvorak delicacies, and down-home Texas-swing fiddling.

"Mom enrolled me in a Suzuki String program from an ad she read in the *Southeast Missourian* newspaper. My parents also exposed me to swimming and dancing. But by the age of five or six, the violin stuck," Liesl recalls.

She was a normal girl growing up, but she recognized that her schedule was different with all the traveling. She took lessons for nine years from Mimi Zweig, making the weekly 600-mile trip from Cape Girardeau to Bloomington, Indiana.

Liesl loved Notre Dame High School: choir, musicals, and various clubs. Her most satisfying accomplishment in those days, however, was passing her driver's test. "I can play until my head spins, but learning to parallel park in my dad's '93 Ford conversion van was my biggest thrill in high school," she proudly admits. "I really wanted my driver's license."

Her parents were musical. They never pursued their talent, but Leisl said her dad was a good singer, always imitating celebrities on the radio. "He had a beautiful whistle and a stunning, great ear," Liesl remembered. "Mom appreciated music and tinkered around on the piano some."

Liesl has won many fiddling contests, performed in Carnegie Hall and the Grand Ole Opry, toured Europe, and released three CDs. She is a four-time winner of the Indiana State Governor's Cup in bluegrass and old-time fiddling. She was winner of the Missouri String Teacher's Association Competition, Blount-Young Competition, National Federation of Music Club's Young Artists Competition, Paducah and Mississippi Symphony Young Artist Concerto Competitions.

Hats were her trademark. "They set me apart, they were my 'hook'," she explains. "When you're in competitions with many artists, you can get lost in the fog. I needed a way to be easily recognized. People started calling me 'the little girl with the sunflower hat'. It's now become a tradition. I wear all kinds of hats when fiddling."

Great achievement in any field of endeavor generally takes time, commitment, and hard work. For Liesl, reaching her level of performance hasn't been easy. Her father Dr. John Schoenberger stated, "Seeing her grow and develop has been amazing. Her mother and I have enjoyed every minute of it." He laughed as he remembered the time when Liesl won her first fiddling competition at age 9 against

8 men with considerable experience. "The next year they suddenly instituted a junior category!"

Liesl is accustomed to glowing reviews when she performs. In a recent interview with Brandon Christensen, accomplished violinist and creative director of the Symphony Series at Southeast Missouri State University's River Campus, where Liesl recently gave a standing-room-only recital, he said, "Liesl is an incredible talent. I wouldn't dare try to take away from her considerable *thunder*!"

Rudi Keller, *Southeast Missourian* reporter, described Liesl's rendition of Eugene Ysaye's Sonata No. 3 in D minor "Ballade" this way, "Her fingers flew over the strings as the music's high and low moods created soaring contrasts, with the notes coming so fast at times, it seemed to be the soundtrack of a movie chase scene."

Buddy Spicher, of Nashville, Tennessee, says, "Of all the hundreds of fiddlers I have heard over the years, Liesl has the finest tone of any. The sound of her violin is absolutely amazing and she uses it to its fullest."

Liesl was an adjunct instructor of violin at Southeast Missouri State University in Cape Girardeau during the spring of 2010. She taught classes, served as concertmaster of the school orchestra, and was string chamber music coordinator. During the summer, she performed at the Yellow Barn Music Festival in Putney, Vermont. She then returned to Yale in the fall to complete her degree.

Liesl is about finished with her formal training at Yale studying with Ani Kavafian. She received her Artist Diploma in December of 2010 and is touring with pianist/composer Eric Genius in Texas, Louisiana, and Florida. She will continue touring and will pursue her Doctor of Musical Arts in the fall. She's being drawn in many directions. At one point she told me, "There are so many paths that could open up. That's the beauty and scariness of being in this field. I could teach, go on to my doctorate, or maybe join a rock band."

It looks like the rock band will have to wait. Her doctoral degree is next on her menu.

Roger Seyer.

Roger Seyer

Roger Seyer is a troubadour. At an early age, when he watched old movie musicals like *Singing In The Rain*, *Oklahoma*, and *Carousel*, he knew he wanted to sing and dance. He went to the public library and studied musical scripts to see how they fit into plays. But Roger remembers, "Growing up in Cape Girardeau, the prospect of performing on Broadway seemed very far away, more of a pipe dream."

His dad Joe said Roger learned to get along with people as a young boy. "He had to, with me, Mom, five brothers, two sisters, and one small bathroom." Mrs. Seyer was one of eight children, and Mr. Seyer was one of twelve. When the Seyer clan gathers, it's quite a sight. Mrs. Seyer reports cooking Thanksgiving dinner for 42 in 2007. There was plenty of competition around the house. All the kids were talented. Roger's brother Chris said Roger was always singing around the house, and they would yell, "Mom, make Roger stop!"

Roger's first performance was in the ensemble of *Mame* at Notre Dame High School, even though he was in the eighth grade at St. Mary's Elementary School. Director Cindy King said, "Roger's voice was so mature, so vibrant, so alive at that young age, I had to place him in the ensemble. I needed his voice." Mrs. King remembered that Mrs. Seyer gave her permission, "As long as it didn't interfere with his basketball!"

Once in high school, he hit his stride performing lead roles in the musicals *Guys & Dolls*, *West Side Story*, *Once Upon a Mattress*, and *Barnum*. "I had a very positive experience at Notre Dame," Roger said. "Our director Cindy King was a wonderful influence. She exposed me to the vast musical theatre repertoire and helped instill confidence in my abilities."

Roger's brother Chris remembers when he was a senior and Roger was a sophomore, Roger beat him out for the lead of Tony in *West Side Story*. "I was disappointed," Chris said, "but not upset. Roger was the better person to play the role."

Roger's high-school guidance counselor told him, "Your chance of making it to Broadway is one in a million." With fire in his belly, Roger knew the path he wanted to pursue. He responded, "I don't care! I know if I don't try, I will spend the rest of my life wondering *What if?*"

After a long search, he chose Milliken University in Decatur, Illinois, to further his talents, primarily because they were one of the few schools in the Midwest to offer a Bachelor of Fine Arts Degree in Musical Theatre. In that environment, he knew he could start performing immediately and gain the first-hand experience he needed if he was to grow.

"The theatre program was small, more like an acting company than an educational situation," Roger described. "Everyone was involved in acting, dancing, building sets, doing load-ins and strikes." During those years, Roger starred in *The Crucible, Road, West Side Story, Charlie's Aunt*, and *Can-Can*.

Dr. David Golden, chairman of the program, challenged Roger to stretch and grow in ways he didn't know were even possible. In later years, Dr. Golden developed a class about Roger's success on Broadway, and it's still part of the program's curriculum. Roger says, "The most important event at Milliken, however, was meeting Kari Gorz, the woman who would eventually become my wife."

In 1988, he began a busy two-year stint doing summer stock at the Little Theatre on the Square in Sullivan, Illinois. There he appeared in productions of *Sugar Babies, Joseph and the Amazing Technicolor Dreamcoat, Seven Brides for Seven Brothers, 42nd Street, My One and Only*, and *The Wizard of Oz*. Roger describes it this way, "It was great training. We did five major shows each running two weeks." Here was the schedule:

Rehearsals for children's theatre show or technical theatre work call	10:00 a.m.
Lunch Break	1:00 p.m.
Rehearsals for next main stage production	2:00 p.m.
Dinner Break	6:00 p.m.
Report for Show	7:30 p.m.
Curtain Up	8:00 p.m.
Curtain Down – Show's Over	10:30 p.m.

"It was exhausting, but I was doing professional theatre and loving it."

After several more years honing his talent and developing his tenor voice in regional theatre in St. Louis; Chicago, Illinois; Falmouth, Massachusetts; Sanibel Island, Florida; and others, Roger finally bit the bullet and headed to New York City in 1993. He described it this way:

> Two weeks before I was supposed to get married, I flew to New York for a week to do some auditioning. I had only ever been to New York once before, so the prospect of going there on my own was pretty daunting. My wife and I were intending to move there after our nuptials and I wanted to get a head start on perhaps securing a job.
>
> I made it to several auditions that week. I went to my very first New York audition straight from the plane. I brought my luggage with me to the audition, went to just about every audition that I could fit into my schedule. And the week was very productive.
>
> I got three job offers as a result of auditions that week. One was for a dinner theatre in Ohio, but the pay wasn't very much; one was for a performing position on a cruise ship sailing out of Singapore for six months, but I didn't

think my soon-to-be wife would appreciate me traveling to the other side of the globe for six months immediately after our big day; and the final offer was for the role of Charlie Brown in *You're a Good Man, Charlie Brown* in Florida. That's the one I accepted. The theatre's producer also offered my wife a job in the box office, so we set off for Florida after our wedding day.

After being there for seven months, I returned to St. Louis to do my first season at Stages St. Louis in Kirkwood, Missouri. My wife took a job stage managing for the same Florida producer at a theatre he ran on Cape Cod for the summer. I joined her at the end of the summer on the Cape as a replacement in the show that she was managing.

Once the gig was over, we drove to New York to find a place to live. The first apartment we looked at was one that we liked, but we were afraid to make a move on it because we thought we owed it to ourselves to do a little comparison shopping. We saw several more apartments that following week, but none that we liked as much as the first. We called the agent who had originally shown us the place and were happy to find that the apartment was still available. When we told that story to our New York friends they always tell us how lucky we were that such a great place was still available.

We also got an early bit of bad news. The two people who had agreed to help us move into our new home, in fact, the only two people we knew in New York, called to let us know that they had both received a last minute plea to appear in a staged reading of a new show. Now we had no one to assist us in moving into our new third floor walk-up.

The next day after many hours, many boxes and many, many trips up and down three flights of stairs, we finally had all of our belongings in our new home. It was a great place. We stayed there five years. But when we finally decided it was time to move to a different place, the first thing we did was call movers!

Considering he had no agent, Roger had a rather meteoric rise. He auditioned, auditioned, auditioned. He only got bit parts in several musicals until 1995. He hit the big time when he was chosen to become a cast member of Cameron Macintosh's production of the mega hit *Miss Saigon* at the Broadway Theatre. He enjoyed a five-year run through 2000 with *Miss Saigon* on Broadway.

We've all heard stories about people being in the right place at the right time. I love Roger's humble account of how he got the job: "I auditioned for the role on several occasions over a year or so. During this time, I had also auditioned for a four-week run in *The Will Rogers Follies*. I got that part, and three days before I was to leave for rehearsals, the *Miss Saigon* call came out of the blue. I really don't know how I got the role. The guy I was replacing was about my same size. *Maybe I fit the costume!*"

Roger Seyer as Valjean.

His next big role was in *Les Miserables*. He was in *Miss Saigon* and auditioning for the *Les Mis* role simultaneously. The shows had the same casting director. She told Roger to go to the open call. Two weeks later they called him in, and he auditioned. They wanted him to learn the coveted role of Valjean. Six months later they called him in for a work session on the material. (Remember, all this time the show was running on Broadway with various cast changes from time to time, and Roger was appearing in *Miss Saigon*.) He never heard anything.

Nearly a year went by when he got a call to come to another work session. He obliged. Again, he heard nothing from the casting director. He was driving to St. Louis after visiting family in Cape Girardeau one day when he got the call. They wanted him to come to yet another callback, *now*. "I can't. I'm starting rehearsals for another show tomorrow . . . in St. Louis," he replied.

Eight weeks later after returning to New York, he got the call again. This time he was able to make the callback. This time, he was hired. He was cast as one of the students, Feuilly, and he understudied for the role of Valjean. His tenure with *Les Miserables* lasted over three years.

Roger's account on touring with *Les Misérables*:

> I absolutely loved it. I guess I've got a bit of wanderlust in my soul because I love going to new places and experiencing them first hand. Getting to do that on the company dime made it all the more sweet.
>
> I was in the original Broadway run of *Les Misérables* when it closed in May of 2003. Rumors had been circulating that the National Tour would take a summer hiatus, might replace some of the company with members from the Broadway company, and the return to touring in the fall of 2003. I was one of the people asked to tour.
>
> My wife was in a work situation that she wasn't really fond of, so we decided that she should quit her job and tour with me. We packed up everything in our apartment and put it in storage (or I guess I should say that the movers

did). Since the company would not pay for her transportation, we decided to pack the Jeep and drive from place to place.

I'm really glad that Kari got out of her job to come with me. And we probably couldn't do the same thing now that we have our son, Declan. It was a once in a lifetime opportunity.

During our discussions, I asked Roger what was his most thrilling performance as of this date. He said, "There were two."

Number one was the first time I went on for the role of Vaijean on Broadway in 2001. I flew my parents up for the event. My father said that several people in back of them were upset when my name was announced as the understudy who would perform the role of Valjean. My parents didn't say anything, but of course, they were upset with the reaction. At the conclusion, my dad turned and asked them how I did. "He was absolutely marvelous," they responded. That's when he told them I was his son.

Number two was at the Fox Theatre in St. Louis, where I had seen so many great shows and performances in my young years. I once again got to go on for the role of Valjean in the National Tour of *Les Miserables.*"

It was indescribable to have several hundred of my family, friends, and supporters there to hear me sing "Bring Him Home." I will never forget it.

Life begins at 40, and Roger is now 40. The troubadour has slowed down for a while. In his new life, he's a stay-at-home Dad, helping raise his one and a half year old son, Declan. He expects to continue performing, but right now, he has more important priorities: family.

When I asked him if he would have done anything differently to this point in his career, he answered, "I would have probably spent more energy promoting myself. It's a business, and I didn't understand that for a long time, because I was having so much fun performing."

When asked to give advice to young aspiring performers, he immediately responded "Go for it! I stayed too long in the wings trying to prepare. When I finally got to New York, I realized I had the talent and tools to succeed all along."

In that regard, Roger has established a website designed to help young, aspiring performers get through the pitfalls of a professional career in New York City. Log onto the site at www.broadwayliving.com.

There were many special moments writing this book, none more poignant than when I delivered the first draft of Roger's story. He had flown to Cape on Monday for the Thanksgiving holiday. We met at Panera Bread Tuesday afternoon and reviewed the preliminary information he'd e-mailed me a week or two earlier.

Wednesday evening, I pulled up to his folks' house on South Sprigg Street around 6:30 P.M. It was dark. I knocked on the outer back porch screen door. The light through the glass in the kitchen door exposed them, so I brazenly entered the porch and knocked again.

I was greeted by Roger's mother, "Oh, Jerry, come on in. No one ever knocks around here." Roger's little son was sitting on his lap, and his wife, parents, and in-laws were around the table eating Domino's Pizza. We exchanged pleasantries, I delivered the draft and, feeling like an intruder, excused myself.

As I reflected on the scene I had just left, *it hit me*. Here was a kid, who wasn't a kid anymore, humbly sitting with his family, his son on his lap, quietly enjoying pizza. No one knew he was in town. Most have never known or even heard of him. The town was oblivious this night to one of its own, who has sung on the great stages of America. My thoughts reflected back to the scene in the kitchen: *If there is an American Dream, this surely is one.*

Chris Talbert. COURTESY OF TAYLOR HOOPER PHOTOGRAPHY.

Chris Talbert

Chris Talbert is a marathon man. For more than 26 years, Chris has chased his dream to be an actor and singer, with moderate success. He declares, "I'm in it for the long haul."

Chris remembers that music was always in the Talbert home. "After they put the kids to bed, Mom and Dad would retire to the downstairs den. Dad would sing songs from Broadway musicals, and Mom would accompany him on our piano. It always struck me they both were really good. My parents loved all the old MGM musicals on television. The film *That's Entertainment* was a family favorite. I remember thinking, *That looks like fun. I think I could do that.* In the fifth grade talent show at Alma Schrader, I garnered enough courage to sing my first solo, 'Mañana.' I promptly forgot the words. My music teacher, Mrs. Cantrell, leaned over the piano and fed them to me."

Chris's mother, Bettie, said all three sons were exposed to music at an early age, and Chris, in the middle, was always trying to keep up with his older brother. "Chris was tall, talented, and handsome. He was born aggressive; always independent, energetic, and at times, argumentative," she reported. "The boys were painfully normal!"

Eighth grade was pivotal for Chris. "Our teacher took us to the school auditorium to see the classic movie, *To Kill A Mockingbird*. When Gregory Peck admonished the jury in his summation, 'in the name of God, do your duty,' I thought, *My God—I want to be a lawyer*, never knowing in a few short years I would realize that what I really wanted to be was an actor!"

Chris's senior year in high school at Cape Central was a busy time. Though he'd never been in a play before, Chris landed the leads in *Hello Dolly* and a little obscure play, *The Silver Whistle*, for which he won the Best Actor award.

Upon graduation, he enrolled in Vanderbilt University in Nashville, Tennessee, as a pre-law major. He never seriously considered pursuing a career in acting, but in between many, many hours of study, he appeared in eight college theatrical productions; basically, one each semester. A natural leader and organizer, he also found himself producing dinner shows during the summer months at the Port Cape Girardeau Restaurant in Cape Girardeau.

Chris moved on to law school at Southern Methodist University in Dallas, Texas, and turned his focus on the demanding first year. It didn't take him long to discover the school's arts program was as good as advertised. Even though he was studying like crazy, he mustered the courage and knocked on Professor Thomas Hayward's door unannounced. Mr. Hayward had been a star at the Metropolitan Opera in New York City for several decades before becoming an instructor at SMU.

He liked my voice, and I studied consistently with him for three years until I graduated from law school. Nevertheless, I knew it was so very difficult to break through as a Broadway performer, so I took a job in beautiful Austin, Texas, with the large development company Trammell-Crow, specializing in real estate law.

Soon thereafter, the savings and loan crisis of the early '90s hit Austin pretty hard. Work in commercial real estate diminished drastically. I knew commercial real estate wasn't what I really wanted to do with my life. I realized if I was ever going to give the stage career a shot, it would have to be now. So I picked up, moved to New York City, and enrolled in the American Academy of Dramatic Arts. The academy is the oldest acting school in New York, with alumni like Grace Kelly, Kirk Douglas, Robert Redford, Paul Rudd, and Kim Cattrall. The first-year class had 180 students. The second was pared down to 60, and I made the final cut to 20 the 3rd year. It was during this time I earned my equity card performing in 4 shows over 12 weeks at the 2,000-seat Casa Mañana Theatre in Fort Worth, Texas.

Over the years, Chris has watched his brothers and several college friends use their talents to become financially successful. Here's Chris's reflection:

I'm doing what I love. It's my passion. Money is not the focus of my life. So much sacrifice was involved during my first several years in New York. I lived in a bunch of dumps like the one room, 250-square-foot-flat in New York City. It had no kitchen. I only had a hot plate, a small refrigerator, and actually washed my dishes in the bathtub. More than once I loaded my possessions into a storage unit while doing a show out of town, only to return and move into a bedroom sublet to me by a stranger.

Even the best actors can go a long time between gigs. An example was in 1997 when I auditioned and signed with famed agent Beverly Anderson. She said I was perfect for the role of Raul in *Phantom of the Opera*. Ms. Anderson had placed several clients in the role. However by then, the casting directors had a long list of qualified actors to fill the roles, and I never got the chance to audition.

Though I've been cast in smaller, recurring roles on the soaps, I've been up for leading roles on *All My Children* and *The Guiding Light* to no avail. The last couple of years, I've had several callbacks for the long running shows, *Chicago* on Broadway and the *Fantasticks* off-Broadway, but again, the list of quality actors is long. Sometimes actors have six to eight callbacks over a number of years.

Still, life in New York has been very rewarding, and I've had encounters with celebrities over the years. My very favorite was in the mid '90s when the American Academy chose me to be an escort for stars who attended a black-tie fundraiser at the Plaza Hotel in honor of five-time Tony Award winner Julie Harris. Later at dinner, I was asked to bring a young Alec Baldwin his coat as he planned an early exit to the event. He looked at me and said 'Do me a favor and take my coat' as he got caught up in conversations with fellow actors. As I followed him around, I got to converse with Jason Robards, Charles Nelson Reilly, Charles Durning, and others. (I think they thought I was Mr. Baldwin's brother!) I remember most Christopher Reeve and his wife Dana, since it wasn't too long before his tragic accident.

Chris on "green screen" movie set for the film "The Call."

Chris finally decided *once and for all* he was really going to stay in it for the long haul. His luxury and salvation is his law degree. It helps him hang on.

> I'm a contract or temp-attorney. It has given me the freedom to audition. I practice commercial real estate law for large firms in Manhattan when they need to staff up for multi-state work. They send me on special assignments along with dozens of attorneys for a week, a month, or parts of a year or two. I was featured in a *New York Times* article on the subject of temporary attorneys who were pursuing other dreams. I then return and audition, audition, audition. When I'm fortunate to land a part, upon return to New York City, the process starts all over again. I've had small reoccurring roles in soap operas *The Guiding Light*, *As The World Turns*, and *All My Children*; appeared in *I Do, I Do* in the Catskill mountains where I had free time to hike with my wife and dog; Sky in *Guys and Dolls* in Birmingham, Alabama, and Sarasota, Florida, and numerous other regional shows.

Currently (the Fall of 2011), Chris is playing the role of Luther Rosser, the defense attorney, in the musical *Parade* at historic Ford's Theatre in Washington, D.C., again opposite veteran Broadway performers. Chris just provided the vocals for the leading role of "George" in the premier studio recording for a new musical, *Lily*, to be presented in New York City during 2012.

In one of our sessions for this book, we discussed *Guys and Dolls* composer Frank Loesser's occasional trips to Cape Girardeau to visit his in-laws Hessie and Eileen Sullivan. Chris remembered his dad pointing to the Loesser's big black limousine as it rounded the corner near his home at Robin Hood Circle and Sherwood Street. In the early nineties, Chris had the good fortune to meet Mr. Loesser's wife Jo Sullivan and his daughter Emily in an acting class he was attending in New York City under William Esper, the distinguished acting teacher.

Chris's parents are proud of his accomplishments. Bettie is present at most of his performances. "He has the best of all worlds," she explains. "He has a wonderful wife, he earns a good living in law in a tough town, he has the talent to elicit applause and standing ovations, and he's doing what he loves." His father Tim, a successful cardiologist in Cape Girardeau, appreciates Chris's concern and empathy for others. "He's always been a caring person from the time he was young. Even now, Chris continues to provide *pro-bono* legal work for fledgling actors."

Chris has overcome some long odds. Most actors' careers are fleeting. But through it all, his energy and persistence have served him well. Chris reports the quality of his auditions continues to improve. "I'm juggling my family, my law career, and my passion to perform. As hectic as life is, I'm happy."

Acting is definitely in Chris's blood.

It's inexplicable. Once on stage when you have moved a crowd full of strangers, you have to find a way to do it again. When you've experienced that, especially when you know the audience really loves the show and your interpretation of your role, you're hooked. A true artist is most alive when he can practice and hone his craft, just as an athlete does with his sport. Any sacrifice I make for it is nothing compared to the sacrifice I'd be making if I gave it up one day. I think actors learn to build their lives around it, as my wife Shelby does for her own love of acting. Otherwise, no matter how much wealth I might acquire, my life wouldn't make sense; something would always be missing.

Neal E. Boyd. COURTESY OF *SOUTHEAST MISSOURIAN*.

Neal E. Boyd

Neal E. Boyd, "The Voice of Missouri," had planned to perform at my "50 Years of Music" benefit concert, Palm Sunday, March 16, 2008, but a little television show called *America's Got Talent* got in the way.

Neal has skyrocketed onto the national scene with his powerful yet tender emotional delivery of songs in his operatic style on the wildly popular, zany, NBC television show, *America's Got Talent*. He was tabbed as a favorite to win from the beginning by judges Piers Morgan, Sharon Osbourne, and David Hasselhoff, when he stunned them and the national TV audience with his eye-popping rendition of Puccini's "Nessun Dorma." It seemed to come out of nowhere, catching everyone by surprise.

When Neal reached the Top 20 episode, Morgan replied, "He's got a brilliant chance." Osborne commented, "What a Superstar." And Hasselhoff exclaimed, "You blew me away!" Neal received similar accolades throughout each episode.

Neal's penchant for opera didn't occur overnight. He caught the bug at age 13, when he discovered a *Three Tenors* CD in his hometown of Sikeston, Missouri. He wore out the CD mimicking Luciano Pavarotti, Placido Domingo, and Jose Carreras. He studied at Southeast Missouri State University in Cape Girardeau and the University of Missouri–Columbia, receiving degrees from both schools in May 2001.

Neal was a frequent soloist at Southeast and Mizzou, performing scenes as Alfredo in Verdi's *La Traviata*, Nemorino in Donizetti's *L'Elisir d'Amore*, The Duke in Verdi's *Rigoletto*, Fenton in Verdi's *Falstaff*, and Lennie in Floyd's *Of Mice and Men*. In addition, he performed full-scale collegiate performances as Ferrando in Mozart's *Cosi Fan Tutti*, Eisenstein in *Die Fledermaus*, and The Negro in *The Roar of the Greasepaint—The Smell of the Crowd*. Chris Goeke, Chairperson of the Department of Music at the Holland School of Visual and Performing Arts at Southeast, remembered Neal as a high school senior. "When he auditioned for us, Neal's voice was mature, warm, and powerful without being unnaturally so. That is to say, he did not have to force it to make it what it was."

While at Mizzou, Neal often made the 30-mile drive down to Jefferson City and performed with Mike Michelson and me at the Ramada Inn on Wednesday evenings. Michelson has been the pianist in the Library Lounge for over 30 years. In my role as a lobbyist in the Capitol, I generally play my trumpet with Mike on Wednesday evenings to keep my chops in shape. Neal would occasionally sing with us. He continued during his semester as an intern in the Capitol for Representative Paula Carter of St. Louis. I secured Neal a spot in a historical pageant during Governor-elect Bob Holden's Inauguration festivities, January 8, 2000, in Richardson Auditorium at Lincoln University in Jefferson City. As usual, Neal brought down the house.

With Neal, what you see is what you get. He really is the humble kid from Sikeston that America has fallen in love with. He's sweet and always flashes that infectious smile. His size is only outweighed by his talent and great voice. Karen Michelson, Mike's wife, describes Neal as "soft hearted, and always full of laughter." He's performed concerts throughout our area in churches and schools. In 2000, he won the National Collegiate Artist Voice Competition of the Music Teachers National Association, sang in Carnegie Hall in 2001, and the Kennedy Center in Washington, D.C., and attended the New England Conservatory of Music in Boston, Massachusetts.

After college, he knocked around performing wherever he could secure a gig and moved to St. Louis to sell insurance for AFLAC.

However, nothing prepared him for the fame he's received on the national TV stage in *America's Got Talent*. Week after week he persevered, making it through the competition into the final five. "It's been a wild ride," Boyd says. "I never expected these kinds of accolades."

Sikeston, Missouri, is kind of a second home to me. My wife raised her family there, and I have made many friends and acquaintances over the years in music and politics. I sat in my living room the night of *America's Got Talent*'s final show, Wednesday, October 1, 2008, switching the TV channels between the Chicago Cubs–Los Angeles Dodgers baseball playoff game and Neal's show. Blake DeWitt, another Sikeston product, plays for the Dodgers. They beat the Cubs, and Neal won the contest. Sikeston never had a better night!

When Neal was announced the winner as the "Best New Act in America," I cried. I called several friends who know Neal, and we celebrated over the phone. I've known and appreciated Neal all these years. There is no one more deserving. He will make a great professional entertainer, a great ambassador for Sikeston and the State of Missouri, and a role model for thousands of young people.

I talked to him a couple of days after the show and asked him what it felt like on that stage when Jerry Springer announced his name. "It was a dream come true, because I really never expected to win. At that moment, I knew my life would change forever."

Neal's new life started Friday, October 17, 2008, when he headlined his show at the MGM Grand Hotel & Casino in Las Vegas, which along with $1,000,000 was part of his first-place prize. His first album *My American Dream* was released June 3, 2009. He returned home Wednesday, June 24, 2009, to Sikeston to share billing with Kenny Rogers in a concert benefiting the Kenny Rogers Muscular Dystrophy Center. Over 3,000 people attended.

> I felt right at home. I was used to singing in school, at church, and an occasional local show for maybe 300 people. This was my first time singing at home with a microphone for 3,000! It was also special because as a kid, I loved "The Gambler." To share the stage with Kenny Rogers fulfilled one of my childhood

dreams. I didn't have long to savor the event because I immediately flew back to New York, and by the end of the week, I was in Los Angeles. But I still think about how special that night was. It was for a good cause. It felt natural because I'm not a star to my friends, but I am in the eyes of some old girlfriends!"

Neal's life is a virtual whirlwind these days, promoting his debut CD. In one 3-week period he was in Dallas, Houston, New York, Boston, Miami, Orlando, Atlanta, Chicago, Atlantic City, back to Chicago, Washington, D.C., Quantico, Virginia, and Bethesda, Maryland.

He's receiving great support from veterans. "God Bless the USA" has become the anthem of the CD. He's having some fun along the way. "Walking through airports is great. Everyone seems to know me, and occasionally they break out in applause," Neal reflected. "California Governor Arnold Schwartzenegger even remarked after I sang an impromptu version of 'God Bless the USA' before one of his speeches, 'That was amazing. If I had that kind of talent, I would never have been the Terminator.'"

Neal is working hard to change his lifestyle. Dieting and exercising are now on his daily menu. "I'm doing everything I can to take advantage of what's come my way. I love singing more than ever, but with things moving so fast, I have to be ready to stay new and unique. It's early in the game, but movies, Broadway, TV sitcoms, and additional CDs are possibilities," he states.

When asked what lasting benefit *America's Got Talent* gave him, Neal answered, "It changed my life in a split-second. The show will help me realize my dream of making opera mainstream. I think what I'm here for is to move people with my voice, and I know that has already happened."

And then he added a challenge to young, aspiring musicians: "Dare to dream bigger than people say you are supposed to."

Neal E. Boyd is living his big dream.

Variety

These last nine friends are hard to categorize. Eclectic is probably an appropriate description of their special talents. Although they are not specifically musicians, I just felt that they should be included.

Robbie Robison.

Robbie Robison

Robbie Robison graduated from Cape Central High School in 1950, worked on the Mississippi River, and a year later joined the Navy serving on several submarines in the Atlantic and Pacific Oceans. He remembers his years in the Navy as "my first experience working with men who were resourceful, self-confident, and unflappable under pressure." He returned to Cape, earned a B.S. and M.A. degrees at Southeast Missouri State University, and knocked around as a teacher, football coach, and construction supervisor. He got his feet wet booking local music acts in what would become his lifelong avocation: public relations.

In 1970, Robbie left Cape Girardeau to promote nationally known country and popular-music celebrities in Nashville, Tennessee. "I had moderate success working with Fred Burch, Buzz Cason, Lee Stoller, Shelby Singleton, David Allen Coe, and others. I even had a few songs published, and Charlie Pride recorded a few. I left the music industry in 1976 and formed the literary agency of Bob Robison & Associates." Here's how he says it happened:

> I had made a lot of contacts of all kinds in Nashville in my first few years. It was great fun working side-by-side with fun-loving, creative, talented entertainers, publishers, and producers, all characters in their own right. As I was talking to Sgt. Barry (Green Beret) Sadler right before I left for a three-week tour of Europe with Carl Mann, I told him, "If you haven't sold your book by the time I get back, I'll start a literary agency and sell your book." He didn't and I did! We did 30 books together.

Since that fateful day, Robbie has built one of the most successful commercial agencies outside of New York and Los Angeles. He maintains a select list of producing writers who have among their credits Emmys, Sylvanias, Peabodys, Spurs, Paperback Originals, Military Writers, and Pulitzer nominations. Works of his writers have appeared on the *New York Times* best seller list, *Publishers Weekly*, *Library Journal*, *USA Today*, and others.

"I'm very proud of my association with Captain William R. Anderson, who took the crew and *USS Nautilus* under the North Pole in 1958. That feat is still considered one of the top three maritime adventures undertaken by mankind. I worked with him on his bio, *The Ice Diaries*."

Chet Hagan was another of Robbie's favorites. Hagan was a veteran writer and producer in Nashville for over 500 shows, including NBC, Roy Acuff, and others. "I called on him to pitch an idea for a TV show and came away as his literary agent. We were together for 20 years until his death."

One of the shows for NBC at the Rhyman Theater gave Robbie a very special treat.

"I got to have breakfast with Roy Rogers. I idolized him as a kid, having watched all of his movies over the years. He was one of the most polite stars I ever met. He kept asking me about my life and what I did. I thought later, *He still doesn't know he's Roy Rogers.*"

Robbie then reflected upon his younger years here in Cape Girardeau.

> The people in Cape were and are still very dear to me. Their influence, to a great degree, was the primary driving force on how I looked at life as an adult. Jerry, I've known many politicians, but none wiser than your dad, Doc Ford. I worked for Tiny Ford (no kin) tending bar while in college. I learned a lot about people from him. I financed trucks for Charles N. Harris. He should have been mayor of Vegas! I worked for Governor Hearnes in Jefferson City for a spell and became very close to the Dean of the Lobby Corps, John Britton. Britton became a fulltime habit. Tuck Priest was one of the most colorful persons I've ever known, and his son, Jerry, is one of my lifetime friends.

Kevin King. COURTESY OF DENNIS CARNEY PHOTOGRAPHY, INC.

Kevin King

Kevin (Propst) King is the original flim-flam man: a magician, mentalist, and one of only a couple of professional double-talkers in the country. Having a conversation with him leaves one dizzy. His appearances at corporate functions, concert openings, and charity events leaves his audiences asking each other, "What did he say?"

King grew up in Cape Girardeau, and from the time he was a little kid, he was intrigued with magic. His dad bought him a gag gift for a Christmas party when he was 13-years-old. He went to the library the next day, began reading every magic book he could get his hands on, and went to the local magic shop, The Fun Shop. "From that time forward, that's all I've ever done," Kevin explains. "I was hooked. I performed everywhere people would have me: birthday parties, anniversaries, school shows, churches, everywhere." One time he even decked his closest buddy for making fun of him while showing him a card trick.

John Mehner, Executive Director of Cape Girardeau's Chamber of Commerce, remembers, "Kevin was always good at what he did. I always thought he would end up a great magician. He was always doing crazy magic tricks. We went through school together, and one year in Central study hall, we got very bored. We invented a game called *Dad-Gum Ball*. We wadded up a piece of paper, wet it a little, and then flicked it into the goal formed by the other's index and little finger for one point. We passed away many hours that year."

Bill Coomer, a Cape Girardeau magician, was a great help and inspiration to Kevin. Coomer taught him, mentored him, and took him along to shows for experience. After graduation from Central High School in 1977, Kevin branched out. He befriended the famous ESP clairvoyant David Hoy, of Paducah, Kentucky. Hoy appeared many times on radio and TV, confounding his audiences with his apparent supernatural powers and insights.

Kevin learned much from Hoy. Hoy had established himself world-wide on radio, television, and in the country music industry as a great after-dinner entertainer. Kevin began making appearances at celebrity golf tournaments in and around Nashville, Tennessee. At one of those events in April 1981, David Hoy became deathly sick. Kevin rushed him to a local hospital where, shortly thereafter, Hoy died.

At Hoy's funeral, many of the Nashville stars told Kevin, "David's gone; you need to come to Nashville." To his surprise a few weeks later, Perry Como called for him to entertain at his celebrity golf tournament. Chet Atkins and Dinah Shore followed, and his career took off. Kevin has performed at over 300 celebrity golf tournaments over the past 30 years. It filled the axiom of being at the right place at the right time. However, Kevin appropriately describes it as "when preparedness meets opportunity."

King performs regularly from Nashville to Las Vegas to London and beyond. He's appeared with many celebrities, including Chet Atkins, Eddy Arnold, Garrison Keillor, and even co-hosted a network television special starring Johnny Cash, entitled "The Winning Hand," in 1984. One of the great privileges of Kevin's career came when the family of Chet Atkins asked him to be the final speaker at the legendary guitarist's funeral after the other two invited friends, Eddy Arnold and Garrison Keillor, completed their eulogies.

Johnny Cash and Kevin King.

My cousin Pete Poe is director of the SEMO District Fair and president of the Missouri State Fair Association. He's familiar with many stars and has seen well over 100 of their performances over the years. "Kevin King is the most unique performer I've ever seen," Poe admiringly says. "King has propelled himself from Clippard Elementary School in Cape Girardeau to Nashville, Las Vegas, and all points in between. Several years ago, I contracted him to be the entertainment for our Fair Board's annual Christmas party. Kevin came in, stationed himself at the front door, and welcomed all 155 guests into the room. Thirty minutes later, he went on stage, looked around, and miraculously, one-by-one, called all 155 by THEIR NAMES!"

Al Kelly was the first nationally recognized double-talker. He began appearing in the '50s. Also back in those days, Durwood Fincher was know as "The Mumbler," but his style was different than Kelly's. Contemporary jazz trumpeter Clark Terry became famous in Doc Severinson's Orchestra on *The Tonight Show*, starring Johnny Carson. His nickname was "Mumbles," as he vocally "scatted" through legendary jazz choruses.

King has perfected the old art form into a mesmerizing, jargoned, complicated, soliloquy that's difficult to comprehend. "I like to think of it as charming, enchanting, mumbo-jumbo! It's a hit with audiences when I perform as an after-dinner speaker."

King is currently working on a new "character" he thinks will take him to an even higher level, with potential for television and movie roles. He continues to live in Nashville—still traveling, performing, and mystifying his audiences.

Matt Buttrey. COURTESY OF CHEEKWOOD STUDIOS.

Matt Buttrey

Matt Buttrey went from a 7-year-old skater at Cape Girardeau's Plaza Galleria, to become Disney On Ice's youngest-ever Performance Director. Matt tells the story:

> During the summer of 1984, I remember sitting at the Grecian Steakhouse by the newly constructed Plaza Galleria, which housed an ice rink. I looked out the window and asked my mom the question that started it all, "Can I go skating?" I don't remember too much about those young days; they are a bit of a blur. But I do remember, I didn't fall in my first attempt on the ice.

Matt's mother said he was always a self-starter. "When Matt made up his mind, he persisted," she recalled. "He took to the ice like a duck takes to water." In September, the rink conducted its first recital. "Even though I was cast as a bumblebee," Matt remembered, "the performing bug hit me. I was in almost every show through 1997."

He progressed through those years, taking private lessons and entering competitions. "Those were hectic years," Matt's mother recalled.

> His dad worked all the overtime hours he could at the post office, and I did the same as a train master's secretary and at the Drury Hotel Call Center in order to generate money for Matt's coaches. We had to travel to get ice. His coach, Debbie Dodge Howe of St. Louis, would travel with us to meet other teachers from Chicago in Springfield, Illinois for lessons. I always believed Matt would have competed in the Olympics, if we could have afforded the additional training that was necessary.

Matt and his partner Sara did amazingly well:

- 1991 U.S. Figure Skating Championship—Intermediate Pair 2nd
- 1992 U.S. Figure Skating Championship—Novice Pair Alternate
- 1993 U.S. Figure Skating Championship—Novice Pair 6th
- 1994 U.S. Figure Skating Championship—Novice Pair 3rd
- 1994 U.S. Olympic Festival—Junior Pair 5th
- 1995 U.S. Figure Skating National Championship—Intermediate Pair 2nd

Matt continued on his own and gained:

- 7 Gold Freestyle
- 8 Gold Moves In The Field
- 9 Silver Pair
- 10–6th Figure
- 11 Silver Dance (Rocker Foxtrot)

Buttrey attended Notre Dame Regional High School in Cape Girardeau from 1991 to 1995. Even though he continued his regimens of practice and competitions, he found time to become active in their annual musical productions. "I've always been drawn to creating and performing. I loved working backstage providing the mood for the actors," he remembered.

> I guess it arose from my childhood when I played *Jesus Christ Superstar* over and over on my cassette player. I would assemble my little Playmobil toy people and arrange them in formations on a small wooden box lid that created a stage. I would fold pieces of construction paper to create backdrops and sets for the little figurines. I repositioned them for hours on end to the various songs of the musical, recreating the Broadway masterpiece in my dark bedroom.

Mentor and drama teacher Cynthia King said, "Even though Matt was nervous in the beginning, he was a good overall performer—acting, dancing, singing, and of course, skating." Upon graduation from high school, he entered Southeast Missouri State University in Cape Girardeau to study his real loves: interior and theatre design. However, he continued skating and competing in pairs throughout his high school and college years.

In January 1997, as a college sophomore, he auditioned for Feld Entertainment's Disney On Ice in St. Louis. He recalled, "I was scared to death." The casting director asked him, "Do you want to go to Japan?" Matt called his friend, teacher, and mentor Cynthia King and asked her what he should do. She replied, "Go for it! You can always get your degree."

Matt signed the contract and, in April, headed to Japan and Australia. He wanted only one year, but has stayed for over 10, touring the U.S., Canada, Europe, Central and South America, Mexico, Japan, and Australia.

Matt describes his first performance:

> I was very nervous. Everyone was from big cities; I was from Cape Girardeau. We went through two weeks of rehearsals before I actually hit the ice in the

real show. Everything was fast and furious. They threw everything at me at once. We reviewed, reviewed, reviewed. My brain was fried. But on the first night when the music started, I knew there was no turning back. This was what I had prepared for since I was seven-years-old.

In his ten years of performance, Matt skated in the ensemble for three years and in a principal pair for one. He continued to audition and understudy for other parts, and landed the principal role of Eric in *The Little Mermaid* for one year, *Prince Charming* in Cinderella for two, and back to Eric for three more years.

Matt's professional partner, Katy Griffitts, describes him as having "a spark about him that everyone loved. We skated together for seven years. Matt is an inspiration artistically, and it was an honor to be his partner throughout those years. I'm very lucky to have such a wonderful friend, and our relationship continues now that he has moved on to direct shows, and I, to coach figure skating."

The road is tough. The season generally runs from August to May. "We generally do 9 to 12 shows per week," Matt informed. "However, in Japan we skate in very small theatres, so we have done as many as 24 per week. In one $4\frac{1}{2}$ month tour, we did 186 shows; another time–239!"

Matt told of a day in Peoria, Illinois, when conditions were terrible.

The ice was soft and wet. There were puddles, and several cast members fell. We were all bummed out. Sometimes you forget where and what you are doing, and how lucky you are getting paid to do something you love and, under certain circumstances, would do for free. For the matinee, I was Peter Pan—all hooked up in a flying apparatus I never liked—40 feet in the air. As I swooped down towards the ice, I saw this little Down Syndrome girl with a pink bow in her hair, sitting in the front row. She grinned at me and with a slight slur, yelled, "Hi, Peter Pan," and boom, I've never felt sorry for myself since. I'm blessed.

My first principle role was in Florida in the spring of 2000, as Prince Eric, in *Under The Sea*. I called Mom and prayed a Hail Mary with tears in my eyes, as I thought of Dad and the many sacrifices he'd made for me. He had passed away a few months before. Mom saw me for the first time in that principal role in Memphis, Tennessee, in November of 2000.

She describes, "It was exciting. We filled a bus in Cape and headed for Memphis. My family, friends, and a group of young skaters and their families went along. It was a dream come true for all of us. When Matt came on the ice, I cried like a baby. Matt's dad wasn't there, but I knew he was looking down on us."

In the 10 years with Kenneth Feld Productions (they have 6 Disney On Ice shows worldwide), Matt has performed in 31 countries on 6 continents. Audience reaction varies. Matt explains, "In Japan, people are very reserved, respectful. European audiences are generally receptive. But in South America and other Spanish-speaking countries, the crowds are wild and enthusiastic. The kids jump up and down!"

Matt is now the youngest Performance Director in the history of Disney On Ice. He watches and evaluates every show. He's responsible for Quality Control/Technical Crew/Music/Lighting, everything. "My responsibility is to protect 100 years of Disney Magic," Matt proudly proclaims. "Initially, I wasn't prepared for the directing role. I was the boss of all my former skating peers, and the roles are very different. It was tough. I wanted to be everybody's friend. Instead, I had to enforce the rules. And most of all, I wanted to be creative. There wasn't and isn't time. I have to manage."

When I asked, "Matt, do you miss skating?" He answered, "No. I'm too involved in directing. I'm using a different part of my brain. I'm progressing back to the future to my first love in high school, and as a kid with my mobile figures—that of set design and artistic director."

On December 11, 2007, I had the opportunity to monitor Matt's presentations to Cynthia King's freshman drama class, and her senior stagecraft class at Notre Dame Regional High School. It was fascinating. There he stood, as a bright, 31-year-old executive-performer, with a two-day beard, spiked hair, tan cargo pants, striped French-cuffed shirt under an olive green, wool, crew-neck sweater. He dazzled everyone in the room (including me) with his wit, grace, charm, sense of humor, twinkle in his eye, and infectious smile. Matt is always smiling. During the class presentations, Matt used his laptop like a magic wand, moving around the room answering questions, laughing, throwing graphs and charts on the wall. He's quite the showman—even in the classroom.

Matt loves Paris, France. When I asked why, he answered, "Architecture. I love architecture. I take pictures of buildings and structures everywhere I go. I have thousands of pictures. In fact, I have over 30 gigabytes filled with pictures of my travels. I especially love Paris structures."

Looking back, Matt says he wouldn't do anything differently to this point. "I've tried to make the best of any situation. I don't fear the future. I'd like a house, but I can't. My life is a whirlwind really. So coming home to visit Mom and my family is a nice getaway. I appreciate home."

Matt's main goal in life is to sometime, somewhere, have a business that includes all his interests. "I don't know where I'll be or how I'll get there. I don't think I'll ever be finished. I'm on a *magical* journey."

Jim Uhls.

Jim Uhls

Jim Uhls is a writer, producer, and actor in Los Angeles. He arrived there as a result of a prophetic coin toss. After college, he couldn't decide if he wanted to be a screenwriter or playwright. Which would it be, L.A. or New York City? So he and his buddy Dan Irvine, flipped a coin and Los Angeles won.

Jim has been a dreamer all his life. As a young boy he was always making up adventures and casting himself as the lead character, with his friends in supporting roles:

> The narrative varied: espionage, war, science fiction, horror, fantasy and comedy—all suggested by movies and TV shows. We used multiple sets—my basement, backyard, frontyard, and various places in the woods and open fields. Bicycles were for scenes in motion: car chases, air raids, or goofy antics. I used toy figures and buildings to set up the larger view of the situation first, like wide shots, and we would move around the figures that were involved in the story. Then we would continue the action, playing the parts ourselves.

As Jim grew, performances became more structured. In junior high, he started acting in one-act plays on stage and comedy sketches for school assemblies.

> As a sophomore in high school I was cast in *Life With Father*. As a senior I played the lead part in the fall production *You Can't Take It With You* and the lead in the spring production of *The Impossible Years*. In between, I played Fagin in the musical *Oliver* for the community theatre accompanied by the Southeast Missouri State University orchestra.

After high school, Jim enrolled in Drake University as a theatre major. Fortunately, he was cast in leading or large supporting roles. Getting involved with the playwriting workshop rapidly got hold of him.

> I took the workshop every year. With no graduate school classes in theatre, I got to direct *American Buffalo* in the black box theatre. I was selected to go to the Eugene O'Neill Theater Center in Connecticut for a semester. Professionals from New York came to teach. Estelle Parsons was our acting teacher, and she was great.

After college came the coin flip. He enrolled in the UCLA Master of Fine Arts playwrighting/screenwriting program. The students, all writers, hung out at the "Pad

O' Guys" house. Four lived there and the rest just came over all the time. Some started getting work. Shane Black sold *Lethal Weapon*, and his agent took Jim as a client.

After several years Jim sold his script, *Dead Reckoning*, a science fiction action screenplay to producer Joel Silver. Silver got Ridley Scott to direct, but slowly, everything dissipated. Then Sylvester Stallone came aboard to play the lead, and they were back in business. Then Jim was replaced by another writer, and ultimately, the movie was never made.

Ten years later his screenplay *Fight Club* was made into a picture.

> At the release premiere, me, my wife, my mother, brother, sister, and brother-in-law walked the red carpet! I introduced them to Brad Pitt, Jennifer Aniston, Edward Norton, Salma Hayek, and Helena Bonham Carter. At the after-party, my brother and I spent some time with the director, David Fincher. Fincher had been one of the guys that hung out at "Pad O' Guys." We loved the film he made, set practically inside the mind of someone going insane.

Jim became friends with the writer of the novel, Chuck Palahniuk. "We would interrogate him for answers to our questions as we prepared the dialogue for the film. At times he would jokingly pretend that Fincher or my solutions would be 'yes, that's what I meant.' I was having an experience of a lifetime."

Jim stays active writing and producing in Los Angeles. He says scripts seem to gain a life of their own sometimes. "You never know," he reminds. He's working on a couple of feature film scripts and a pilot for television. He says the idea of creating characters that continually move through stories is appealing. He is also founder and director of "Writers & Actors Lab," a workshop teaching people how to write original screenplays.

Jim's screen credits include:

Fight Club	1999
Sweet Talk	2004
Jumper	2008
Rex Mundi	2009
Isobar	2009

Jacalyn and Candice Robert. CYPRESS GARDENS.

Jacalyn & Candice Robert

Jacalyn and Candice Robert have the distinction of being the most unique entertainers in this book. They both starred as skiers at fabled Cypress Gardens, the first Florida theme park. Cypress Gardens, located midway between Orlando and Tampa at Winter Haven, Florida, was established in 1936, and flourished for almost 70 years. A string of Esther William's movies and TV specials in the '50s and '60s glamorized the Ski Show Spectaculars, as beautiful young women in antebellum attire welcomed visitors from all over the country.

The Roberts started skiing at an early age at Lake Wappapello near Puxico, Missouri. Their mother Flo remembers, "Vernon and I took them camping at Wappapello every weekend during the summers. They were naturals. They took to the water immediately and even learned to ski barefoot early on."

The girls were three years apart, Jackie being the oldest. Flo explains, "They were regular girls growing up, but very competitive. Candice was energetic and outgoing. Jackie was more reserved, good hearted, and always for the underdog," Candice graduated from Cape Central and Jackie from Cape Girardeau Notre Dame Regional High School. They both attended Southeast Missouri State University.

Jackie got a job skiing professionally at Lake of the Ozarks, and one day she decided to go Cypress Gardens, where she was hired on her second try. Candice followed a year later. They performed there for five years, and Candy later performed at Sea World. Candice recalls:

> The 4-Tier Pyramid was the most demanding accomplishment in the show. The worst moments were when we skied in 35-degree temperatures and played the clown when you knew you were going to be in the water. However, it was a wonderful experience, especially at that time, because there wasn't a lot of opportunity to participate in any girl's sports growing up in Missouri. It was just a very good feeling having the opportunity to experience being really good at something and appreciated for it.

Flo says, "Vernon and I were so thrilled the first time we saw them perform. They were so beautiful, and their choreography with music was spectacular. Their sister-act was especially thrilling. We would go down for a week at a time, and many of our friends would go with us again and again. It was great fun."

The girl's favorite times were when their parents came to watch. They also loved when Cape residents attended, and they got to show them around and make them feel special.

Jackie remembers barefoot skiing as the hardest, but she placed second in the national finals one year. "We got to travel and perform in places like Las Vegas and Rio de Janeiro. It was great fun. There was nothing greater than skiing for a living. We made life-lasting friends, and Cypress Gardens opened many doors for both of us in later years. It helped me get my first real job teaching at Kansas State."

Jackie is married to Robert McComb and is a full professor at Texas Tech in Lubbock, Texas. She received her B.S. at Florida Southern, her Master's at Southeast, and her Ph.D. in Exercise Physiology at Ole Miss in 1989. Since then, she's been on the faculty at Texas Tech University, teaching and conducting research in Exercise Physiology.

Candice spent several years in medical equipment sales before becoming a tour director for Windstar Sail Cruises—sailing the Tahitian islands, smaller Caribbean islands, and crossing the Atlantic to the French Rivera and Yugoslavia. She now lives in Newport Beach, California, with her husband of 20 years, has two daughters, and is an executive with a laser sales company. As Candice states, "Life is good."

Ali Turner. Courtesy of Cheekwood Studios.

Ali Turner

Model Ali Turner is as comfortable walking the runway in 4-inch stilettos as she is in boots and jeans. Cowgirl barrel-racing Turner, a 25-year-old pre-school teacher in Cape Girardeau, began her remarkable modeling career with the prestigious Ford Agency with an assignment in Paris, France, at the age of 15.

It all started with a phone call from Cheekwood Studios in Cape Girardeau after a junior high school photo shoot. When her mother went to pick up the pictures, the people at Cheekwood said her daughter was extremely photogenic and had definite modeling possibilities. She exclaimed, "No way, not in a million years!" But after the shock, she asked Ali, and Ali answered, "Why not."

So they sent the photos to modeling agencies, and the Ford Agency called from Chicago saying they wanted them to come "as soon as possible." Ali and her mother traveled to Chicago, and Ford signed Ali on the spot. Ali says, "I was a huge tomboy/ country girl. I had no interest in hair and makeup or fancy clothes. I loved my trucks and horses. I was completely shocked. But I gave it my best shot."

At 5'11", Ali inherited her father's metabolism. "Weight gain is a neverending battle with models. Fashion is all about how young and skinny you are. My dad is tall and skinny, and eats whatever he wants," she exclaimed.

Modeling isn't always glamorous, as many people might suspect. It's a tough, grueling, exhausting, competitive business. Ali said account of her first experience:

> The Ford Agency sent my mother and me to Paris, France, when I was only 15. My age was a distinct disadvantage. We lived in a room where the carpet was full of holes, twin mattresses were on the floor, and paint was peeling off the ceiling. We quickly moved into another apartment, this time in the Red Light District across the street from the Moulin Rouge. We couldn't go out at night, because if we did, we would be thought to be a part of the scene (street-walkers). All the while, we went to casting calls, casting calls, casting calls, to no avail. Bills mounted: taxis, subways, meals, rent, etc. We got lost on several occasions, going to and fro, and Mom even got harassed by a street person. We were ready to go home.

Back from Paris, she finished high school in 2005, and spent three years doing shows for Tommy Hilfiger and other household fashion names. She was on the cover of *Women Wear Daily* in 2004. Ali has appeared in advertisements for Dillard's, Gb Jeans, Macy's, Marie Claire, and Tommy Jeans. She's worn clothes in ready-to-wear fashion shows for Catherine Malandrino, ChanPaul, Douglas Hannant, Gen Art, James Coviello, Palmer Jones, Wink, Kenneth Cole, Venexiana, Vivienne Tam, David

Rodriguez, Diane von Furstenberg, Mackage, Matthew Earnest, Richard Tyler, Twinkle, and Ya Ya.

Her best experience was at Roatan, a tiny island off the coast of Honduras. "I got to do what I do best, ride horses! Alban Christ was the photographer, and I got to ride horses on the beach all day long. Christ did an amazing job. The pictures turned out absolutely beautiful," she remembers. "One of my favorite stories is when Mom and my sister were about to enter a tent during the New York Fashion week. Many celebrities show up for the shows, and Britney Spears' main bodyguard knocked Mom to the ground as she pushed in an attempt to take Spears' picture among the throng that had gathered."

Turner finished in the Top 5 of Victoria's Secret's model search competition in December 2009. "It was a great experience. There were over 15,000 girls in the first walk-through. I never dreamed I would make the final cut, let alone end up in the Top 10 or Top 5. I got to stay in a $3 million penthouse in New York, work with great photographers, met wonderful supermodels, and held many interviews. It was a blast."

Ali's mother Patty says Ali was never happy or comfortable with the fame and glamour in New York that accompanies the industry. "She couldn't wait to come home after the shows. She missed the country and only modeled so she could buy a truck, horse-trailer, more horses, and land to put them on."

Turner currently keeps a hectic schedule. She signed with Centro Models in St. Louis, where she does runway shows; commercial work; appears in ads for Macy's, Dillard's, and others several times a month; works at Edible Arrangements; and has several other local job offers.

On Sunday morning, February 27, 2011, the last day of final updates to this manuscript, I sat down at our kitchen table for a cup of coffee. I opened the *St. Louis Post Dispatch*, and to my amazement, there was Ali, in the top-left corner in a large Dillard's display ad wearing a Calvin Klein outfit.

In a recent trip to New York, an agency wanted her to lose 20 pounds, again! "At this point, I'm not willing to do that anymore," Ali says. "So, life in the fast lane is fading. I'd rather be healthy and happy with the people I love than go back to that whole lifestyle. I'm 25, have been highly rewarded financially for my work, saved my money, building a house in Millersville, living with the love of my life, and ready to settle down, be a normal person, and have a family. I rodeoed professionally for a few years, and that's pretty much the direction I'd rather go. I love that lifestyle more than anything."

It sounds as if Turner is hanging up her stilettos and trading them in for a pair of spurs in the near future.

Buck McNeely.

Buck McNeely

Buck McNeely parlayed a college TV project into the largest television adventure series on television, *The Outdoorsman*. He premiered his adventure series on our local KBSI–TV station in June of 1985, and it now airs on over 600 TV stations and cable networks nationwide. His show has aired on networks such as ESPN, USA Network, Fox Sports Net, and the Outdoor Channel.

Buck was a Mass Communications major at Southeast Missouri State University here in Cape Girardeau. In the last semester of his senior year, he produced four episodes of his outdoor theme on the university cable access station. Viewer response was so positive, Buck decided to take a gamble and produce it commercially.

That first season, Buck honed his production technique shooting episodes locally: catfishing in the Mississippi River, goose hunting in Southern Illinois, hog hunting in the Ozarks, and frog gigging in the Diversion Channel south of Cape. He built a world-wide distribution base one station at a time by entertaining viewers with world-class locations, celebrity guests, and conservation issues in a family-oriented format.

The series has been shot all over the world in places like Siberia, New Zealand, Iceland, Brazil, four African countries, Argentina, Costa Rica, and of course, throughout North America. His celebrity guests from the world of sports, entertainment, and politics have included General Chuck Yaeger, Ollie North, Jesse Ventura, Kurt Warner, Daryle Lamonica, Reggie Theus, Joe Penny, John Ratzenberger, George Pataki, Frank Stallone, Dan Haggerty, Charles Napier, Roy Clark, Barbara Mandrell, and many more.

One can imagine many hazardous instances where things didn't go as planned while exploring the planet hunting, fishing, and trying to film animals and nature, as these next several stories attest.

Buck's son Max (9 at the time) hooked Kurt Warner while fishing on a farm lake near Ste. Genevieve, just as Warner had returned from his Super Bowl MVP victory. "I had to remind Max to be more careful because that was the St. Louis Ram's 'golden arm' he was messing with," Buck recalls.

Buck spent a week with General Chuck Yeager in New Zealand hunting and fishing. They hunted in the Southern Alps Mountains and fished the Tasmanian Sea for sharks. "On the New Zealand trip, I was taking some extra time shooting artsy camera angles, surrounded by the spectacular scenery, when Yeagar got bored and stated, 'Screw it, we're done,' and headed down the mountain. I gathered my gear and followed in the General's wake. What was I to do? Tell him to get his ass back up there? I don't think so!"

Even in the Ozarks, he had to unload a .357 Magnum into a wild Russian boar as it charged him. And he almost got sucked into a mud hole on a duck hunt in California when the mud encased his waders up to his waist. Only the quick thinking of unclipping the suspenders on those waders, snaking his way out of them, and crawling out of the marsh saved him!

One of the most harrowing experiences was when all hell broke loose as Buck and his companions found themselves being charged by 40 Cape buffalo in Botswana, Africa. One bull emerged, head down in full charge right at them. They emptied their guns on him, but the 2,000 pounder kept charging. He finally went down in a cloud of dust about 10 yards in front of them. As Buck recalled, "That night, there were more than a few drinks poured around the campfire."

My connection with Buck goes back to my youth. His mom and dad, Bob and Sharon Weiser McNeely, were in my class from elementary school through high school. I lived next door to the Weisers for over 10 years. Buck's grandfather Red Weiser was a city commissioner when my dad was mayor, and most importantly for me, he was a good dance band drummer performing with The Herb Suedekum Orchestra at the Purple Crackle Club in East Cape Girardeau, Illinois, on Saturday nights. As you've seen in this book, it's not unusual for creative genes to be transmitted from generation to generation, and Buck certainly inherited them.

Sharon remembers young Buck as "always strong-willed and aggressive, with a mind of his own." She's especially proud that Buck was always a good son and is a good husband and father.

Buck and his wife LaDonna have two sons, Max and Rex. Being around the TV show all their lives, they both are avid outdoorsmen. They have appeared on many episodes since they were youngsters. Max is a Mass Communications major in college and has done extensive production work on the series. Rex also plans a career in media. He loves to sing, act, and perform on camera. As Buck proudly proclaims, "The acorns didn't fall far from the tree."

Spending so much time in nature, Buck is passionate about conservation and environmental issues. Here, in his own words, are his views on our current situation:

> Hunters are a vital element in this nation's game management and conservation programs. Revenue generated from licenses and taxes on sporting goods fund our country's game conservation programs. I remember my grandfather, Lloyd McNeely, telling me that back in the 1920s when he was growing up, he rarely saw a deer or turkey in the woods. Sustenance hunters had harvested them out for food. After WWII, new game management programs, restocking, and strict hunting seasons have allowed the game population to increase to current abundant levels. It's estimated there are more deer in North America now than when Christopher Columbus discovered America. Today's farmers

provide ample food for these animals. Corn, soybeans, milo, and more are staple crops for man and beast alike.

Buck continues his passion for the outdoors and producing his show. Maybe it's because his love of nature is boundless. In January 2011, he was in Las Vegas for a Hollywood Celebrity Shoot, the jungles of Brazil fishing for peacock bass, Zimbawe hunting spiral horned antelope, Mexico wing shooting for ducks and snow geese, and Key West, Florida, fishing for dolphin and amberjack.

In a recent conversation, he reflected, "Sitting on a mountaintop overlooking a slice of God's creation is my favorite cathedral. These places are truly God's greatest churches."

You can find Buck on his website www.outdoorsmanint.com.

Photo by Bill Headrick.

Bill Headrick

Classmate Bill Headrick, an outstanding trombonist, retired from teaching art at the Cape Girardeau Seventh Grade Center, and for more than 25 years has become what many reviewers have proclaimed, and most people here in Cape Girardeau have never known, "the finest gun photographer in the world!" Headrick laughs, "I've worked with about every mainstream hunting, shooting, and sporting magazine in the country, and several abroad. My name is probably more well known in England, Germany, and Spain than it is right here in River City." Bill began his love of wildlife as a youngster. "Pop and his cronies had me afield and at streamside as soon as I could load my own shotgun and bait my own hook. Upon reflection a few years later, I realized they let me tag along because I could tote a sack of decoys, paddle a jonboat, and handle one end of a minnow seine."

Those early experiences spawned several decades chronicling sporting in the great outdoors. He began taking snapshots with a 35mm camera in junior high school and didn't get much more involved until the early '80s. He was asked by a chum to help in a magazine project he'd landed. The editor asked, "Who took those photos?" "I began working for that first editor and other editors saw my work, and it just sorta blossomed from there," Headrick recalls.

Bill also grew up shaping wood in the family business, Headrick Brothers Cabinets, started by his dad and uncle. Jerry McClanahan, owner of Jerry's Custom Cabinets, told me, "Bill knows all about glue." "Glue?" I asked, and he responded, "Yes, glue." Bill remembers, "I started working in my Pop's and Uncle's woodshop and millwork facility soon as I was big enough to wield a broom and dust pan to gather and burn saw-dust after school and weekends . . . that is, when Pop and I weren't camping, fishing, and hunting."

Bill built a lot of furniture, bank fixtures, school cabinetry, and church altars. His favorite, however, was the circular 390-degree staircase at the home of Charles N. Harris. He explains: "The architect only provided a circle drawn to scale, a few steps, an arrow indicating 'up,' and a note reading 'circular stairway.' We had to start from there. With my dad's help, we designed, engineered and built it, and yes, I did learn a lot about glue."

Headrick had trouble when he first enrolled in college due to enormous flights of migrating waterfowl. Bill claims those geese caused him to still hold the record for the lowest GPA in Southeast Missouri State University's history! Upon returning, Bill earned double majors in fine art and industrial technology, and three masters degrees in fine art, industrial technology, and secondary school administration. Those advanced degrees gave him additional training in composition and palette, which he put to good use.

Bill has always dabbled in augmenting his hunting experiences. He's spent a lot of time training and trialing retrievers and flying racing pigeons. For years he had a pigeon loft in his backyard. He exercised them each morning by freeing them for flight and tracking them to observe their return. "Racing homing pigeons is a real rush. On a good day, a homer can travel 700 miles. They are one of the toughest, most athletic critters on the planet," Headrick said. When asked if he missed tinkering with his birds, first looking a bit forlorn, he immediately smiled and replied, "Nah, it was fun, but now I'd rather shoot pigeons than race 'em!"

Rave reviews of Bill's work are not uncommon; for example, Steve Bodio's 2009 description of Bill's work is in the new book release *Gamefield Classics*, which has been described as a true celebration of the world's greatest sporting guns:

> The book features the stunning gun photography of Bill Headrick. Most of the major British shotgun makers and all of the major American makers are covered, plus various high-quality doubles from Spain and Italy and some classic rifles. The photography, as to be expected from Headrick, is superb, with the guns presented in "environments" of shells, decoys, feathers, and other objects; their composition is an art in itself.

On other occasions, Headrick has been called "the preeminent gun photographer in the country, if not the world" and "renowned sporting firearms photographer," along with "his artful images have proved influential in modern firearms photography," and "his photos display his mastery of lighting, as well as the former art teacher's skillful composition of accoutrements and props," "talented, multifaceted firearms photographer par excellence," and "Headrick stands alone at the pinnacle of firearms photography." With those kind of accolades, it's no wonder that he has been labeled "The Wizard of Light and Lens."

His works can be found in publications like *Double Gun Journal*, *Sporting Classics*, *Shooting Sportsman*, *Outdoor Life*, *American Rifleman*, *Ducks Unlimited*, *Single Shot News*, *Precision Shooting*, *Tactical Shooter*, *The Accurate Rifle*, *Grouse Point Almanac*, *Game Country*, *Insights*, and more. Headrick smiles, "I'm flattered that any number of authorities credit me and my style as having greatly influenced firearm photography all over the world. . . . I'd like to think for the better, of course."

His wife of 46 years, the former Donna Lemmon, is known throughout the world as "The High Priestess of Tolerance and Patience." She's been at Bill's side all these years rounding up accessories, props, and all manner of natural materials, and serving as his tried and true photo assistant. She's developed quite the eye for line, form, color, and texture. Donna says, "Bill's not easy to work with when it comes to things he's passionate about. It's been a lot of hard but satisfying work. We've handled some of the finest guns and rifles in the world, many quite historical in nature. And we've met some of the finest, brightest, and most gracious people in all the world."

Headrick is also a renowned wordsmith. His photographs are generally accompanied by his prose. As he developed a market for his photography, he found that adding his acumen with words to describe his knowledge and experiences along with the photos was a comfortable fit. In most circles, he's appreciated for his writing as much as for his photographs. As a result, he's in demand by book publishers like Down East, Country Sport Press, Voyager Press, Safari Press, and Live Oak Press, just to name a few.

Over the years, his articles have been generally in the 10-12 page length, regarding pricey double-barreled shotguns and double-barreled safari rifles. From the mid-90s until around 2007 and 2008, Bill also reached back to his younger years with some true but lighter fare that was met with substantial success.

In leisure time, many wrap themselves around a good book. When I'm lucky enough to have leisure time, I play my trumpet. So I'm not a good resource for reviewing books and articles of any kind. However, after a bit, I find myself mesmerized by the flow of Bill's words. It's as if I'm sitting on the bank of Ole Man River up at Honker's Boat Dock on a quiet, early misty morning, yearning for the sound of calliopes of the great paddlewheelers that have faded away.

In retirement, Headrick has slowed a bit due to a series of surgeries over the past two years. He's still columnist for *Precision Shooting*, writer/photographer with *Double Gun Journal*, and Senior Editor with *Sporting Classics*. He sees a few gigs on the horizon using existing photos and stories emanating from his beloved Coot Isle Gun Club. "Most members drink fine bourbon, smoke good cigars, shoot reasonably high-dollar double guns, and enjoy a fine telling of some tale from afield. One could look to having a more terrible future in the offing . . . huh?"

It's fitting that this is the final chapter of the book. Bill and I have come full-circle from our junior high days when we spent countless hours in Bill's home listening and learning from the jazz greats as we spun our 33 $\frac{1}{3}$ vinyl records. Since the trombone was his instrument of choice, J.J. Johnson, Kai Winding, Urbie Green, Bill Watrous, Jack Teagarten, Bob Brookmeyer, and others were generally on the menu. I figured if I'd ever write about Bill, it would be in the jazz idiom, because even at that early age, he was an accomplished "jazzer." But as life progressed and we went our separate ways, a sporting rifle, jigsaw, paint brush, camera, and typewriter intervened.

Precision Shooting magazine commissioned Bill to provide photos and text for their 2001 annual calendar, "A Dozen Guns to Remember." They asked the late Michael McIntosh, the world's foremost sporting gun authority, to write a few lines about Bill.

What can you say about someone who's been a treasured friend for almost 20 years; who's been a shooting partner, a colleague, a resource kind enough to share his vast knowledge of firearms any time I've asked; who's illustrated my books and magazine articles; and whose eloquence comes through the typewriter as readily as it does from behind the camera? Well, a couple of things come to mind: Bill Headrick is the finest gun photographer ever, the best who's ever pointed a lens at a subject that's both difficult to light and hard to compose into a photo as richly structured as a painting. And he can make you see them in words, too. Believe your eyes. It doesn't get any better than this.

Bill Headrick.

Coda

So there you have it. Dreamers who weren't afraid to follow their dreams. Let's also raise a glass to those who dared and didn't quite make it, and those who are still chasing their dreams. There are many in the Cape Girardeau area. Their stories have yet to be written. Their quest elevates us all.

Imagine with me:

> You're 14 years old, still just a kid. You can't drive a car, vote, drink alcohol, serve in the military; yet you've been asked to play in a dance orchestra for the first time because the band leader is in a bind for a trumpet player. You put on black slacks, a white shirt your mother has starched, black bowtie, a tuxedo coat that's way too big, and ride to the nightclub with adult members of the band, hoping they don't see you shivering under the large tux jacket. When you arrive, you apprehensively take your place on the bandstand. The house is one-third to half-full. The lights have dimmed, and the table candles are flickering. You shuffle the music and apprehensively place the unfamiliar first tune in front of you. The leader counts off the tempo. The ensemble begins with older, respected, seasoned musicians and you with a trumpet you've been playing for a scant three years. After several numbers, as people listen and begin to dance, it hits you. You can do it! The years of practice have paid off. You're surrounded by gorgeous sounds produced by others—and yourself. It's all come together. It's magic. And after over 50 years, it still is.